PRIVACY AS TRUST

It seems like there is no such thing as privacy anymore. But the truth is that privacy is in danger only because we think about it in narrow, limited, and outdated ways. In this transformative work, Ari Ezra Waldman, leveraging the notion that we share information with others in contexts of trust, offers a roadmap for data privacy that will better protect our information in a digitized world. With case studies involving websites, online harassment, intellectual property, and social robots, Waldman shows how "privacy as trust" can be applied in the most challenging real-world contexts to make privacy work for all of us. This book should be read by anyone concerned with reshaping the theory and practice of privacy in the modern world.

Ari Ezra Waldman is Associate Professor of Law and Director of the Innovation Center for Law and Technology at New York Law School. He is a widely published and internationally sought-after scholar of data privacy, online social life, and cyberharassment. He founded the first and to-date only law school clinic that provides free counsel to victims of cyberharassment. His scholarship on privacy and trust won the Otto L. Walter Distinguished Writing Award in 2016. Waldman also won the Best Paper Award, sponsored by the International Association of Privacy Professionals, at the 2017 Privacy Law Scholars Conference. He earned an AB, *magna cum laude*, from Harvard College; a JD from Harvard Law School; and a PhD in sociology from Columbia University.

Privacy as Trust

INFORMATION PRIVACY FOR AN INFORMATION AGE

ARI EZRA WALDMAN
New York Law School

CAMBRIDGE
UNIVERSITY PRESS

University Printing House, Cambridge CB2 8BS, United Kingdom

One Liberty Plaza, 20th Floor, New York, NY 10006, USA

477 Williamstown Road, Port Melbourne, VIC 3207, Australia

314–321, 3rd Floor, Plot 3, Splendor Forum, Jasola District Centre, New Delhi – 110025, India

79 Anson Road, #06–04/06, Singapore 079906

Cambridge University Press is part of the University of Cambridge.

It furthers the University's mission by disseminating knowledge in the pursuit of education, learning, and research at the highest international levels of excellence.

www.cambridge.org
Information on this title: www.cambridge.org/9781107186002
DOI: 10.1017/9781316888667

© Ari Ezra Waldman 2018

First published 2018

Printed in the United States of America by Sheridan Books, Inc.

A catalogue record for this publication is available from the British Library.

Library of Congress Cataloging-in-Publication Data
NAMES: Waldman, Ari Ezra, 1980–, author.
TITLE: Privacy as trust : information privacy for an information age / Ari Ezra Waldman.
DESCRIPTION: New York : Cambridge University Press, 2018. | Includes bibliographical references and index.
IDENTIFIERS: LCCN 2017061447 | ISBN 9781107186002 (hardback)
SUBJECTS: LCSH: Data protection – Law and legislation. | Privacy, Right of. | Confidential communications. | Personality (Law).
CLASSIFICATION: LCC K3264.C65 W35 2018 | DDC 323.44/8–dc23
LC record available at https://lccn.loc.gov/2017061447

ISBN 978-1-107-18600-2 Hardback
ISBN 978-1-316-63694-7 Paperback

For my family: always loving, always there.

Contents

Preface and Acknowledgments   *page* ix

Introduction: What's at Stake?   1

       PART I WHAT DO WE MEAN BY "PRIVACY"?   11

1   Privacy as Freedom *From*   13

2   Privacy as Freedom *For*   26

3   Social Theories of Privacy   34

       PART II PRIVACY, SHARING, AND TRUST   47

4   Trust and Sharing   49

5   What Does Trust Mean for Privacy?   61

       PART III A TRUST-BASED APPROACH TO PRIVACY
               AND INFORMATION LAW   77

6   The Responsibilities of Data Collectors   79

7   Previously Disclosed Information   93

8   Trust and Cyberharassment   108

9   Information Flow in Intellectual Property   122

10 Trust and Robots   134

    Conclusion: The Future of Privacy and Trust   148

Notes   151
Index   205

Preface and Acknowledgments

Studying privacy is an ongoing, evolutionary process, just like the development of this book. What began as a proposal on cyberharassment of LGBTQ persons grew into a doctoral dissertation on information privacy, generally. That, in turn, grew into several law review articles analyzing a broad range of topics, from sharing intimate photos to information flow in intellectual property. Throughout this time, my thinking on privacy evolved. It evolved after law school, then again after online and face-to-face harassment took national attention in 2010, and then again after reading the works of Emile Durkheim, Erving Goffman, Julie Cohen, Daniel Solove, Helen Nissenbaum, and others. This book is the result, but it is by no means a final word. It is a step along the way meant to contribute to a dynamic and important discussion about why privacy is important and what privacy means in a digital world. I hope that this book's theories and proposals will be approached critically, tested and tried out, and, yes, challenged.

This book is based on my doctoral dissertation in the Department of Sociology at Columbia University's Graduate School of Arts and Sciences. It is also the product of countless workshops, conferences, talks, discussions, and one-on-one "geek out" sessions with colleagues, friends, and inspiring mentors. Some of those who helped me think through these issues are, in alphabetical order, Alan Appel, Alessandro Acquisti, Derek Bambauer, Jane Bambauer, Ann Bartow, Jacqueline Beauchere, Barton Beebe, Tamara Belinfanti, Gaia Bernstein, Robert Blecker, Kiel Brennan-Marquez, Ryan Calo, Danielle Keats Citron, Richard Chused, Julie Cohen, Anthony Crowell, Rochelle Dreyfuss, Gregory Eirich, Gil Eyal, Joshua A. T. Fairfield, Jonathan Frankle, Mary Anne Franks, Brett Frischmann, Jeanne Fromer, Sue Glueck, Jeffrey Goldfarb, Eric Goldman, Woodrow Hartzog, Mike Hintze, Chris Hoofnagle, Leslie John, Ian Kerr, Bill LaPiana, Art Leonard, Amanda

Levendowski, David Levine, Gregory Mandel, Bill McGeveran, Jim Mourey, Frank Munger, Helen Nissenbaum Paul Ohm, Frank Pasquale, Mark Patterson, Ed Purcell, Joel Reidenberg, Neil Richards, Sadiq Reza, Andrew Selbst, Jacob Sherkow, Richard Sherwin, Jessica Silbey, Scott Skinner-Thompson, Daniel Solove, Ruti Teitel, Ann Thomas, Rebecca Tushnet, and Diane Vaughan. I would like to give special thanks to my research assistants during this time, Jeffrey Saavedra and Dawn Neagle, and to Rodger Quigley, who reviewed the manuscript and made important substantive suggestions and assisted with citations. They, along with the hundreds of New York Law School students I have had the honor of teaching these last four years, remind me every day that it is a privilege to do what I do. Thanks also to Bill Mills, my go-to for all obscure research and primary source materials. This project also benefited from important feedback at quite a few conferences and workshops, including, but not limited to, the 2015 and 2016 Privacy Law Scholars Conferences; the 2014, 2015, and 2016 Internet Law Works-in-Progress Conferences; the 2015 Works-in-Progress Intellectual Property Conference; the 2015 Intellectual Property Scholars Conference; and the 2016 Tri-State Regional Intellectual Property Workshop at New York University School of Law. These ideas were also discussed at invited talks at law schools throughout the country and at various law review–sponsored talks and symposia. Thank you to all the organizers, participants, speakers, and students who made those opportunities possible.

A final note of thanks. This book, and my career as a legal academic, could not have happened without the support of the Department of Sociology at Columbia University; my dissertation adviser, Gil Eyal; and Dean Anthony Crowell and the distinguished faculty of the New York Law School. These institutions and colleagues took a chance on me. I hope I have earned their respect.

Portions of this book were adapted from several articles, but the ideas expressed in this book represent significant developments and evolutions in my thinking. These articles include: *Privacy As Trust: Sharing Personal Information in a Networked World*, 69 University of Miami Law Review 559 (2015); *Privacy, Sharing, and Trust: The Facebook Study*, 67 Case Western Reserve Law Review 193 (2016); *Trust: A Model for Disclosure in Patent Law*, 92 Indiana Law Journal 557 (2017); *A Breach of Trust: Fighting "Revenge Porn"*, 102 Iowa Law Review 709 (2017).

Introduction
What's at Stake?

In May 2016, several Danish researchers released data on 70,000 users of the dating website OKCupid. Those of us who have tried online dating know that profiles on OKCupid (or Match, JDate, or eHarmony) are rich in sensitive personal information. The researchers published much of it: usernames, age, gender, and location, as well as sexual orientation, fetishes, religious views, and more. Given the breadth of that information, it wouldn't take much to figure out the identities of those involved. And the researchers neither obtained consent nor anonymized the data.[1]

This data dump posed a privacy puzzle. OKCupid users voluntarily answer hundreds of questions about themselves so the website can use an algorithm to connect them with supposedly compatible matches. The answers are available to all OKCupid members, with some basic information available to nonmembers via a Google search of a person's name. For these reasons, while they may have violated OKCupid's terms of use and ethical canons for research in the social sciences, the researchers felt they were on solid privacy grounds. They did not need to anonymize the data set, they said, because users had provided the information in the first place and other people had already seen it. By any traditional metric, they thought, this information was not private.[2]

Notably, this wasn't an isolated incident. Researchers have mined personal data before.[3] Retailers do it all the time, gathering everything from our browsing histories to Facebook "likes" to target us with advertisements they think we want to see. Google tailors its search results based on what it learns from our behavior across platforms, sometimes discriminating against us in the process.[4] Data brokers amass vast collections of information about us gleaned from across the Web and sell it to the highest bidder. Facebook is steaming ahead with frighteningly accurate facial recognition technology based on the millions of photos we upload for our friends.[5] Retailers analyze our purchasing histories to predict what we will buy next even before we know it ourselves.[6] And marketers are using our buying patterns and GPS technology to send sale notifications directly to our phones when we pass a brick-and-mortar store.[7]

We have a choice. Our society is at a crossroads. We can live in a world where these activities go on unabated, where stepping outside our homes and using technology are information-sharing events, where the law cannot protect us, and where the only things that are truly private are the things we keep secret. In this world, anyone, whether they are overeager researchers or online advertisers, can use our data because, as a matter of law and social practice, the information is already public. We share our data the moment we sign up for an account, or browse the Internet, or buy a book online.[8] In this world, privacy is dead.

Or, we could live in a world where privacy still matters. In this less totalitarian, more agreeable world, lawyers, judges, policymakers, teachers, students, parents, and technology companies take privacy seriously. Here, privacy has a fighting chance against other values and norms, and information can be shared with others without the entire world looking on.

Today, we seem closer to privacy's death than to its renaissance. Indeed, talking heads have been writing privacy's obituary for years.[9] That is in part because, like the Danish researchers who took a cavalier approach to their subjects' privacy, we have been thinking about privacy too narrowly. Strengthening privacy won't be easy, but getting to a better world starts with changing the way we think about privacy, how we integrate and manage it in our daily lives, and how the law is used to protect it. And that is what this book is about: I want to change the way we think about privacy so we can better leverage law to protect it in a modern world.

We are accustomed to conceptualizing privacy in certain ways. We often think that privacy is about separating from the prying eyes of others or keeping things secret; that's why we draw blinds when we don't want people looking in. Sometimes we associate privacy with certain spaces or property boundaries; what we do "in the privacy of our own homes" or "behind closed doors" or in our bedrooms and bathrooms, for example, is our business. Sometimes we think privacy is bound up with intimacy; that's what makes topics like sex, money, and medical care inherently personal. But I argue that limiting our understanding of privacy to these concepts alone is what allows our data to be mined and used with impunity. These ways of understanding privacy are, at best, incomplete and, at worst, hurtling us toward a dystopian future designed without privacy in mind.

For example, thinking that privacy is synonymous with secrecy could help us when someone hacks our personal network and publishes previously encrypted files, but it doesn't offer much consolation for users of OKCupid or for a victim of nonconsensual pornography who shared images with a now-ex-boyfriend only to have him upload those pictures to Pornhub. Once we share something, it's no longer secret, and we lose control of it.[10] Similarly, it may be sufficient for a homeowner who notices a drone-mounted camera by her window to think about privacy as bound up with enclosed spaces or property lines, but it would be radically insufficient the moment she stepped outside. And although some of these victims could fall back on the inherent intimacy of the information revealed to explain their feeling that their privacy was invaded, privacy-as-intimacy cannot, on its own, respond to the transfer of personal data among websites, behaviorally targeted advertisements, and "big data" predictive analytics that mine seemingly innocuous and nonintimate information from across the Internet to determine what we see, what we buy, and what we learn.

We need to change our perspective on privacy.

It may sound strange, but privacy is an inherently social concept. The very idea of privacy presumes that we exist in both formal and informal relationships with others: privacy only matters after we share within those relationships. When making sharing decisions, we rely on and develop expectations about what should happen to our information based on the contexts in which we share, thus integrating privacy into our lives relative to other people.[11] As the law professor Robert Post describes, privacy norms "rest[] not upon a perceived opposition between persons and social life, but rather upon their interdependence."[12] Privacy, then, is socially situated. It is not a way to withdraw or to limit our connection to others. It is, at its core, about the social relationships governing disclosure between and among individuals and between users and the platforms that collect, analyze, and manipulate their information for some purpose.[13]

For example, when we share the fact that we are HIV-positive with the 100 members of an HIV support community, we may expect a far greater degree of confidentiality and discretion from them than from two acquaintances at work. When we whisper secrets to a good friend, we expect confidentiality even without a written agreement. We share our bank account numbers with Bank of America's website and expect that it won't be shared with online marketers. And although we may recognize that using the Internet or joining a discount loyalty program requires some disclosure, we share our information with the expectation that it will be used for the specific purpose for which we shared it. What we share, with whom we share it, and how we share it matter. In other words, something about the social context of disclosure is the key to determining what is private and what is not.[14]

That key is trust. Trust is a resource of social capital between or among two or more parties concerning the expectation that others will behave according to accepted norms. It mitigates the vulnerability and power imbalance inherent in disclosure, allowing sharing to occur in the first place. Put another way, disclosures happen in contexts of trust, and trust is what's broken when data collection and use go too far. An information age demands an understanding of information privacy that recognizes that we share a substantial amount of personal data with friends, public and private institutions, websites, and online advertisers. More generally, a doctrine of information privacy must navigate the public/private divide in context, recognizing, among other things, that what we share, when we share, why we share, and with whom we share matter for determining whether disclosed information is still legally protectable as private.[15] And it must not only explain what we consider private, but also why certain things fall into the private sphere and why other things do not.[16] This theory must also reflect how information privacy is implemented on the ground, including how we determine when and what to share, how platforms manipulate us into disclosing more than we might otherwise have wanted, and how, if at all, technology companies embed privacy norms in the data-hungry products they create. And the theory must be administrable, capable of being applied by lawyers and judges in real cases to answer real information privacy questions. Finally, the way we think about privacy has to set us on a better path, one that not only helps privacy thrive in a modern world, but also has positive effects on society as a whole.

Because we share when we trust, I argue that we should start talking about, thinking through, and operationalizing information privacy as a social norm based on trust. In the context of information sharing, trust gives us the ability to live with and minimize the vulnerability inherent in sharing by relying on expectations of confidentiality and discretion. Indeed, all disclosures create vulnerability and imbalances of power. Elsewhere, as in doctor-patient or attorney-client relationships, where significant disclosures create similar power imbalances, we manage those risks with strong trust norms and powerful legal tools that protect and repair disclosure relationships. Reinvigorating information privacy requires similar norms and legal weapons, as well. So, when we share information with others in contexts of trust, that information should be protected as private. I call this argument *privacy-as-trust*, and, like other trust doctrines in the law, it allows disclosure to occur in safe environments buttressed by concurrent norms of confidentiality and discretion.

By the end of this book, my hope is that we will start considering trust as an important part of our notion of information privacy. More specifically, my goal is to argue that we should conceptualize information privacy in terms of relationships of trust and leverage law to protect those relationships. This, however, does not mean that all other visions of privacy are useless. Important rights-based concepts of privacy are not wrong; they are just incomplete. On their own, they have difficulty answering some modern privacy questions posed by new technologies like predictive analytics, social robots, and ongoing and pervasive data collection. Privacy-as-trust can help get us on the path to a better world where privacy not only exists, but thrives, and where society benefits from a rejuvenation and strengthening of trust norms among individuals and between individuals and data collectors.

It is also important to note what this book is not about. Privacy takes on many forms, in different contexts, with a variety of bogeymen ready to break or erode it. This project is about *information* privacy, generally, and privacy in times of disclosure, specifically. It is primarily about the ways in which we interact and share information with, and are vulnerable to, other private actors – other individuals and technology companies, for example – rather than government agents. That is not to say that conceptualizing privacy as based on relationships of trust is necessarily silent or unhelpful in a variety of contexts. But those extrapolations and extensions are for another book.

I construct my argument in three stages. Part I is about where we have been; it develops and then critiques the many theories of privacy that dominate current privacy scholarship, showing how each of them is a variant on the same theme and has helped bring us to where we are today. Part II is about the theory of privacy-as-trust itself; it teases out the definition of trust, provides empirical evidence in support of the relationship between trust and disclosure, and shows how privacy-as-trust is already being operationalized on the ground. It argues that trust must be part of our understanding of privacy, as a result. Part III is about the better world with trust in it. I apply privacy-as-trust to several vexing questions of privacy and information law, and show the contrast between conventional and trust-based approaches. In all cases, understanding privacy as bound up with the concept of trust brings about a better, more just world where privacy is a strong social value.

PART I: WHAT DO WE MEAN BY "PRIVACY"?

For many, privacy is about choice, autonomy, and individual freedom. It encompasses the individual's right to determine what she will keep hidden and what, how, when, and to whom she will disclose personal information. Privacy is her respite from the prying, conformist eyes of the rest of the world and her expectation that things about herself she wants to keep private will remain so. I will call these ideas the *rights conceptions of privacy* to evoke their

Lockean and Kantian foundations. And they can be divided into two categories. In Chapter 1, I discuss the definitions of privacy that are based on negative rights, or those that see the private sphere as a place of freedom *from* something. These notions of privacy include elements of seclusion and private spaces, as well as conceptions based on the sanctity of private things, like discrediting secrets or intimate information. Common to these ways of thinking about privacy is an element of separation, suggesting that they provide freedom from the public eye. Chapter 2 discusses the second category of rights-based definitions of privacy. These conceptualizations retain the assumption of separation, but use it for a different purpose – namely, for the opportunity to grow, develop, and realize our full potential as free persons. It conceives of privacy as affirmatively *for* the full realization of the liberal, autonomous self.[17]

The rights conceptions of privacy pervade privacy rhetoric, scholarship, and judicial decisions. They are the dominant ways we approach privacy problems today. They are, however, incomplete. They miss the fact that information privacy norms are triggered by disclosure. And disclosure is an essentially social behavior: once we share, we trade control of our information for reliance on powerful social norms, or background social rules that feed into our expectations of what should happen with our personal data. Privacy centered solely on the individual ignores those social norms even though they are not only essential to sharing but have positive effects on social solidarity. Without them, we risk narrowing privacy into oblivion.

Like the work of Robert Merton,[18] Michel Foucault,[19] Helen Nissenbaum,[20] and others, privacy-as-trust approaches information privacy and disclosure from a social perspective. Privacy-as-trust recognizes that information privacy is not about excluding others, but rather about regulating the flow of information to some, restricting it from some, and opening it up to others. This essential understanding about privacy's social role is not new, and Chapter 3 focuses on describing the development of social theories of privacy over the last 50 years. In that chapter, I argue that social theories of privacy to date may have recognized that privacy is what manages information flow in context, but they inadequately respond to the power dynamics at play in disclosure. That is the role of trust.

PART II: TRUST AND PRIVACY

Disclosure and privacy govern our relationships with others (persons as well as technology platforms); as such, they are social phenomena. Trust is the link between them. And strong trust norms are what allow sharing and social interaction to occur.[21]

Particular social trust is the "favourable expectation regarding other people's actions and intentions," or the belief that others will behave in a predictable manner.[22] It "begins where knowledge ends"[23] and is the mutual "faithfulness" on which all social interaction depends.[24] For example, when an individual speaks with relative strangers in a support group like Alcoholics Anonymous, she trusts that they will not divulge her secrets. Trust, therefore, includes a willingness to accept some risk and vulnerability toward others and steps in to grease the wheels of social activity.[25] I cannot know for certain that my fellow support group members will keep my confidences, so trust allows me to interact with them, disclose information, and rely on discretion with confidence. And I earn all sorts of positive rewards as a result.[26]

It makes sense, then, to turn to trust when thinking about what motivates us to share personal information online and what governs the related privacy norms in social interaction: Alice shares information with Brady because Alice trusts Brady with that information; the applicable norms – confidentiality and discretion – give Alice the confidence and comfort to share with Brady, mitigating the vulnerability inherent in someone else having access to her home. The same mechanism is at play when we share information with lawyers, doctors, and financial planners: strong trust norms, backed by tradition, professional standards, and the law, give us the confidence and comfort to share. Despite the intuitive appeal of that mechanism, particular social trust has been, at best, a silent undercurrent in a growing literature on our propensity to disclose personal information. Part II of this book teases out this privacy, sharing, and trust relationship.

The theory of privacy-as-trust is the subject of Chapters 4 and 5. Privacy-as-trust posits that information disclosed in contexts defined by trust should be legally protected as private. It is not an attempt at a unitary, a priori definition of privacy that applies to all situations.[27] But privacy-as-trust does give us a way of understanding how private disclosure contexts vary from context to context and why certain uses of data strike us as invasive and unfair. Thinking about information privacy as based on relationships of trust means several things. It means seeing privacy as something that can foster disclosure by mitigating the risks inherent in disclosure and rebalancing power between sharers and audiences. It means looking at the context of disclosure to determine the difference between public and private information. It means considering both norms at the time of disclosure and any background that has an impact on future expectations. And it means asking how the law can be used to strengthen relationships of trust between parties and equalizing the power imbalances that come with sharing. Doing this will have significant value to society.

Chapter 4 also offers some evidence that privacy-as-trust reflects how we operationalize privacy and disclosure decisions in practice. An empirical study of Facebook users, summarized here, suggests that trust is a key factor in users' decisions to share personal information on the platform. And, as scholars have shown, many companies with strong privacy leaders at the top think about their privacy obligations as protecting and fostering trust between the company and its customers.[28] Therefore, if trust is defining our understanding of privacy on the ground, perhaps the law and privacy theory can catch up.

PART III: PRIVACY-AS-TRUST IN ACTION

The balance of the book considers what information privacy law would look like if we applied privacy-as-trust to several ongoing privacy and information law controversies. There are five chapters in this section, each of which uses case studies to show how a privacy law regime based on trust would look different than the status quo. In each case, some amount of disclosure causes risk, vulnerability, and a loss of power; privacy-as-trust restores the trust norms that protect those disclosures in the first place.

Chapter 6 starts at the macro level, considering Internet platforms' obligations and responsibilities. The current regime, which requires data collectors do little more than provide us with notice of what information data they collect and what they do with it after collection, is based on the idea, discussed in Chapter 2, that privacy is about the freedom to choose when and how to disclose personal information. As many scholars have argued, however, this "notice-and-choice" approach is hopelessly flawed and inadequate. It gives users little to no help when making disclosure decisions, and it offers even less protection when Internet companies use our data in unexpected and invasive ways. This is especially problematic where web platforms use artificial intelligence (AI) or complex algorithms to learn about us, predict the things we want to see, and mediate our online experiences. A reorientation of privacy law around principles of trust would address these gaps, providing the necessary theoretical justification for holding data collectors to certain fiduciary responsibilities of loyalty. As the legal scholars Jack Balkin, Jonathan Zittrain, and others have argued, this would protect us from Internet platforms that are already inducing our trust, taking our data, and harming us for their own profit.

Chapter 7 goes from macro to micro, applying privacy-as-trust to several cases about the wide dissemination of information previously disclosed under limited circumstances. These cases apply the current privacy torts, including intrusion upon seclusion and public disclosure of private facts, which require judges to determine the difference between public and private information. But when judges, as many do today, define privacy as synonymous with secrecy, victims of privacy invasions are left out in the cold. Privacy-as-trust, like other social theories of privacy, recognizes that privacy exists post-disclosure and provides judges with clear, easy-to-apply questions to make more nuanced decisions.

Chapter 8 argues that privacy-as-trust forces us to think differently about privacy harms. Currently, most scholars and judges see invasions of privacy as attacks on the individual. Privacy-as-trust recognizes that because trust is what facilitates and regulates information flows, injuries to information privacy are injuries to the norms of social interaction. This opens up a new avenue for protecting personal privacy: a robust tort of breach of confidentiality. Traditionally marginalized in American law, the tort is perfectly suited to protecting the privacy of previously disclosed information. This chapter looks at one type of cyberharassment – nonconsensual pornography or so-called revenge porn – as an illustrative case study.

Chapter 9 steps outside the confines of privacy to show that privacy-as-trust can be used as a more general theory of information flows. Using a case study of patent law's public use bar, which prevents inventors from securing a patent if they have shared their invention with the public more than one year prior to application, this chapter makes several arguments. Judges today apply some of the same rights-based principles discussed in Chapters 1 and 2 to define "public" in the public use bar. This has the perverse effect of privileging wealthy corporate inventors because it ignores the unique social determinants of information flows among solo entrepreneurs. Privacy-as-trust not only addresses that imbalance but also provides a clear, administrable, and fair way to distinguish public from private inventions.

Finally, Chapter 10 discusses social robots. Social robots – like Sony's Aibo dog or Kaspar, a machine with humanlike qualities designed by the University of Hertfordshire to help children with autism learn how to respond to others – are machines that interact with humans on a social level. They pose special legal challenges that traditional understandings of privacy cannot compre-hend. Social robots are both wonderful and insidious, and their dangers are directly related to their benefits: while helping us meet foundational human needs of companionship, friendship, and emotional connectedness, they distract us as they sweep in troves of personal data. Plus, as machines with human*ish* tendencies, they elicit more emotional responses than rational ones. This makes us vulnerable, especially in a conventional privacy world where mere use of a technology product is considered consent to ongoing data collection. Privacy-as-trust explains the dangers of social robots – we are primed to trust them and, as result, eager to share – and suggests ways to protect ourselves in the process.

I conclude by summarizing my argument and suggesting avenues for future research. Privacy-as-trust is not about keeping more information private or making more information public. Thinking about privacy as a social norm based on trust can help individuals protect themselves against invasions of privacy. It can also foster disclosure where needed. It fosters productive relationships, both commercial and social. And it fosters powerful trust norms that could bring us closer to each other and to technology companies who act responsibly with our data. If we know that the websites we use respect our trust-based disclosure expectations, we may feel comfortable sharing more information to enhance our online experiences. We just need a new way of thinking about privacy that works for us, not just for data collectors. This book offers that opportunity.

PART I

WHAT DO WE MEAN BY "PRIVACY"?

Disclosures, whether to each other or Internet companies, create power imbalances. Sharers become vulnerable to their audiences when they disclose. A doctrine of information privacy must mitigate that vulnerability. If it doesn't, sharing stops. And a society of secret keepers is no society at all.

Developing that doctrine starts with determining what we mean by the word "private." This is an essential task. The way we think about privacy, in general, helps determine when we can leverage law to protect it. Scholars have been trying to conceptualize and frame a legal right to privacy since at least 1890, when Samuel Warren and future Supreme Court Justice Louis Brandeis wrote a now-famous article in the *Harvard Law Review*. It is hard to overstate the impact of their work. Now the most cited law review article of all time, it spawned a dynamic and still ongoing debate among lawyers, social scientists, and policymakers about what privacy means and how the law can protect it.

Privacy scholarship may be teeming with different conceptions of privacy, but the differences among them mask widespread agreement about their rights-based assumptions. And these assumptions are putting privacy at risk in the modern world because they inadequately respond to the power dynamics inherent in disclosure. My goal for Chapters 1 and 2, then, is twofold. First, I will tease out some of the traditional definitions of privacy and show that many of them are just different expressions of the same theme: privacy and society are in tension, the argument goes, because privacy is about privileging the individual and individual rights over society. And, second, I will show that, as reflections of that rights-based theme, these conceptualizations of privacy are not well equipped to answer a number of modern privacy questions. They are leading us down a path to a world where privacy no longer exists.

Chapter 3 looks at several attempts to take a different route, where privacy is understood socially rather than as a right or privilege of the individual. These are steps forward, and will set up our discussion of privacy-as-trust in the next section.

1

Privacy as Freedom *From*

When looking for a definition of privacy, there is an intuitive appeal to thinking about the private world as a place distinct or separate from other people. Private spheres presume the existence of public spheres, but only as things from which to detach. Diaries and bathrooms are paradigmatic examples: we think of them as private spaces because others are kept out, denied access, and excluded. Privacy, then, gets defined by walls, property lines,[1] or the "loss of shared experience."[2] The assumption that privacy is defined in opposition to others underlies many traditional theories of privacy, all of which see privacy as an individual right against the world. And it is for this reason that so many of them inadequately address modern privacy problems. Under these theories, once information is shared with anyone, it is no longer private.

Such an approach to privacy is draconian. It also highlights the troubling endpoint of a radically individualistic privacy agenda. In many ways, an individual right to privacy is liberating; some argue it is necessary to realize other important rights and freedoms. But there is a danger in going too far. Thinking about privacy only as a shield against others – us versus them or me versus the world – sells privacy short. And it collapses too easily in the face of ongoing disclosure. In a social world increasingly mediated by sharing platforms like Facebook, Instagram, and Amazon, such a vision of privacy collapses in on itself, keeping sharers vulnerable and eroding the very liberty it was meant to protect.

PRIVACY AS AN INDIVIDUAL RIGHT

Protecting individual rights seems like second nature to us. But it wasn't always that way. The notion that societies and governments should be structured around the individual is a product of the Enlightenment, a review of which is beyond the scope of this book. That said, I would like to talk briefly about two philosophers – John Locke and Immanuel Kant – who have had an outsized influence on many of the traditional conceptions of privacy and on the Western legal tradition, in general. Because we will see their fingerprints in the ideas discussed in the next two chapters, it is worth spending a moment on them and their work.

John Locke, an English philosopher and physician, developed a theory of property in the *Second Treatise of Government* that is particularly relevant for understanding traditional theories of privacy.[3] For Locke, humans start out in a state of perfect freedom.[4] We are free to go about our lives as long as we don't interfere with or violate the rights of others. Along with that freedom, God gave us the power of reason, the ability to make use of the land, and a limited ownership right in ourselves, our hands, and in the fruits of our labor.[5] So although we may start in a state of perfect equality and although land may start as a common good, anyone who works the land, changes it in some way, or, as Locke puts it, "mixe[s] his Labour with, and [joins] to it something that is his own," comes to own that land.[6] We then have the right to enclose it and keep others out.

This labor theory of property has direct implications for a right to privacy. If, as Locke argues, we own ourselves and the fruits of our labor, giving us the right to own land and exclude others, it stands to reason that we should also own our personal information and have the right to control its dissemination and exclude other people from it. We will see this theme repeated in several theories of privacy discussed below.

Locke isn't the only rights theorist that has influenced traditional privacy scholarship. The German philosopher Immanuel Kant offers another strong rights-based approach to privacy. Kant was a major figure of the Enlightenment; his *Groundwork of the Metaphysics of Morals* was published almost 100 years after Locke's *Second Treatise*, and it is at the foundation of Western liberal democracy.[7]

In *Groundwork*, Kant makes an argument about freedom that underlies how many scholars, lawyers, and policymakers think about the right to privacy. Every person is worthy of respect, Kant says, because we have the capacity to be rational and autonomous beings. This capacity to reason can be distinguished from our more basic and natural instincts (Kant calls them "inclinations") to avoid pain and seek happiness or pleasure. To be free means to be autonomous of these instincts, and to be autonomous is to act according to reason, not according to nature's or society's pressures. This may seem like an unusual way of thinking about freedom. To many of us, freedom consists of doing what we want, whenever we want. But doing what we want in this world is subject to explicit and implicit constraints upon our choices, making us subject to forces outside of ourselves. Only when we step beyond these forces, divorcing ourselves from the practical limitations on our reason, can we act rationally, morally, and freely.[8]

One of the implications of this vision of freedom has had a direct effect on privacy scholarship. For Kant, man's power to choose the rational and moral way forward is central to who he is. As the Kant scholar Christine Korsgaard has argued, "when Kant says rational nature . . ., it is the power of rational choice that he is referring to, and in particular, the power to set an end and pursue it by rational means."[9] What defines us, then, is our capacity to choose to do the rational thing. In Michael Sandel's words, the Kantian (and neo-Kantian) self is "a sovereign agent of [rational] choice."[10] The primacy of individual autonomy and choice will repeat again and again in traditional understandings of the right to privacy.

Despite the differences between Lockean and Kantian theory, they are both powerful justifications for structuring society around protecting individual rights. And given the pervasiveness of both philosophies in the American legal tradition, it is no surprise that privacy has traditionally been understood along Lockean and Kantian lines. These traditional approaches to privacy can be divided into two categories. Some see privacy as a negative right, or freedom *from* something, whether it is freedom from others, from conformity, from publicity, or from surveillance, for example. Other theories see privacy as a positive right, or the freedom *for* something, as in the freedom to make choices, to formulate ideas beyond the prying eyes of others, or to realize our potential as persons.[11] The individual is at the center of all of them. But because they fail to account for the social and power dynamics at play during disclosure, none of them help mitigate the vulnerabilities that are putting privacy at risk in the modern world.

SEPARATION, SEQUESTRATION, AND EXCLUSION

Privacy is often understood as a state of seclusion, separation from the public eye, and the exclusion of others from certain aspects of personal life. Although these conceptions align closely with Locke's theory of property and individual rights, they inadequately protect privacy today.

Samuel Warren and Louis Brandeis thought that separation was at least part of the "right to be let alone" when they argued that modern technology had made "solitude" and "retreat from the world" more necessary than ever.[12] This perspective makes sense given the context in which they thought and wrote about privacy.

In the late 1890s, the American media was experiencing exponential growth and change. Between 1850 and 1900, the number of newspapers exploded from 100 to 950, and readership grew from almost 800,000 to more than 8 million.[13] Although never a tame sector, it was becoming more sensational and aggressive, especially given the freedom offered by Eastman Kodak's new snap, or instantaneous, camera.[14] With this tool, the media engaged in a pattern of intrusive behavior to satiate the appetites of a growing and diverse readership increasingly interested in and frustrated with the upper class. If not precisely the late nineteenth century's versions of the Kardashians, the Warrens (and the Cabots, Lodges, Elliots, and any number of other storied New England clans) were at least their generation's Kennedys, Rockefellers, or Roosevelts. And to meet popular interest in elite culture, periodicals like the *Saturday Evening Gazette*, which "specialized in 'blue blood' items," became notorious for reporting on Warren's parties in lurid detail.[15] At the time, publishers felt that any right to privacy conflicted with their democratic imperative to reveal the truth, whether in the form of muckraking or detailing the excesses of the rich.[16] Therefore, when Warren and Brandeis wrote about a "right to be let alone," they may have been reacting to popular press intrusions into their and others' lives.[17] This suggests that a right to be left alone was always meant as a right to separate from the prying eyes of the public.

The legal scholar Anita Allen concedes the centrality of separation in privacy, as well. She explains part of her vision of privacy by listing examples that involved seclusion: "4,000-square-foot homes nestled among mature trees in bucolic suburbs," "vacation[ing] at remote resorts," and "spend[ing] an hour alone with a book behind closed doors."[18] She is suggesting that privacy had to include some measure of aloneness or separation because, otherwise, the public had access to us all the time. David O'Brien, a political scientist focusing on the intersection of law and politics, echoes the privacy-as-separation theme when he calls privacy "the existential condition of limited access" brought on by being alone.[19] And the philosophers Howard White and Sissela Bok similarly describe privacy, respectively, as a "right against the world"[20] and "the condition of being protected from unwanted access by others."[21] It seems, then, that separation from others is at least part of some of the legal, political, and philosophical conceptions of privacy.

Sociologists have also adopted the sequestration rhetoric. Edward Shils, an influential social theorist, has said that privacy is about living a "secluded life, a life separated from the compelling burdens" of society and the state.[22] Like Shils, the sociologist Donald Ball defines privacy as the "ability to engage in activities without being observed" by others.[23] Robert Laufer and Maxine

Wolfe, who studied notions of privacy among youth, understood it to be the process of separation of an individual from his environment.[24] That separation could be physical – literally hiding away in a space – or psychological – denying warmth, whispering, showing emotional distance. But in each case, a personal zone is created. Raymond Williams, a cultural critic and historian, understood privacy to be "the ultimate generalized privilege ... of seclusion and protection from others."[25] Notions of seclusion and protection necessarily take on a me-against-the-world bias, privileging the individual as the locus of private rights.

This vision of privacy also has distinct spatial overtones, using the rhetoric of walls and spaces to analogize privacy to separation.[26] For example, the historian Joseph Rykwert has shown that the ancient Greeks and Romans did this literally: women's rooms in the home were considered private; men's rooms were considered public.[27] In his work on secret organizations, Georg Simmel analogizes the secret to a wall of separation: "Their secret encircles them like a boundary, beyond which there is nothing but the ... antithetic."[28] And when the sociologist Robert Maxwell wanted to study sexual intimacy in preindustrial societies, he chose to study wall construction and material permeability, ultimately arguing that stricter intimacy norms in society were associated with increased privacy self-help (building secret compartments, for example).[29] Other scholars have followed suit. Jeffrey Rosen talks about privacy as a "shield" from public scrutiny.[30] The legal scholar Milton Konvitz argues that privacy is a "sphere of space" that the public cannot enter or control."[31] And others thought privacy requires "boundaries" and a "territory" of one's own that "insulated" individuals from the rest of the world.[32]

Even the sociologist Erving Goffman uses a spatial analogy to seemingly endorse a privacy-as-separation idea. Goffman defines private places as "soundproof regions where only members or invitees gather."[33] Private regions were physically bounded by walls or doors that offered physical separation between people and between different types of social interaction.[34] In *The Presentation of Self in Everyday Life*, Goffman uses an extended theatrical conceit to show that individuals present different parts of their personae in different contexts. He separates the front stage, where the performance of social interaction occurs, and the back stage, where individuals can drop the façade of performance and be themselves in private. The back stage was a place of hiding, used when one needed to use the telephone or the restroom in private. It was also cut off from social interaction by some barrier: a partition, passageway, or curtain. The back stage, therefore, provided the social actor with a private space – a home, a green room, or a bathroom – to engage in activities beyond the public eye.[35] As discussed more in depth in

Chapter 3, this interpretation of Goffman misses the mark, but it is worth noting here how spatial analogies of all sorts have come to pervade our thinking of privacy.

The legal implication of a theory of privacy based on space and separation is the attendant right to exclude others from that space and to determine who should gain entry. This is Locke's labor theory of property applied to privacy.[36] Many scholars have come to the same conclusion. Ruth Gavison calls privacy a limited right of access by others to our private spaces.[37] Alan P. Bates defines it as "a person's feeling that others should be excluded from something."[38] Larry Lessig advocates using the rhetoric of property rights, and the right to exclude, in particular, to advance the cause of privacy in the courts and in the court of public opinion.[39] The same principle animated Jeffrey Reiman's view that privacy "confer[s] title to our existence" and allows us to claim ownership over our thoughts and actions.[40] Even Warren and Brandeis recognize the correlation between privacy-as-separation and the right to exclude. They rely on Locke's ideas of personal ownership to argue that our "inviolate personality"[41] – the dignity owed us as fully formed, autonomous individuals[42] – meant that we had a right to exclude others from our "thoughts, sentiments, and emotions."[43]

Although faithful to the Lockean vision of individual rights, principles of separation, ownership, and exclusion harm privacy more than they help. As Daniel Solove has argued, conceiving of personal information as a property right devalues privacy to "the combined monetary value of particular pieces of personal information."[44] Under this vision, privacy is merely the value we can derive for our information on the market. And, as several courts have explained, that value is virtually nil. In *In re Jet Blue Airways Corporation Privacy Litigation*, for example, a federal court rejected a breach of contract claim against Jet Blue for this very reason. The airline had shared some of its consumers' information with a third party, prompting objections that the company had breached the obligations it set out in its privacy policy. The court said that even assuming a privacy policy could be interpreted as a contract, plaintiffs could not identify damages: there was "no support for the proposition that the personal information of an individual JetBlue passenger had any value."[45] Legal protection, therefore, was unavailable.

In addition, the spatial analogy used to justify and explain this property-based conception of privacy has become both pervasive and constraining in law. Indeed, it used to be the case that violations of the Fourth Amendment, which guarantees freedom from unreasonable government searches and seizures, depended upon a physical invasion of a private place. In *Olmstead* v. *United States*, for example, the Supreme Court rejected a Fourth

Amendment challenge to a warrantless wiretap because the tap, by virtue of the fact that it was installed on the outdoor phone line and did not require entry into the suspect's home, could not constitute a search: "[t]here was no searching. There was no seizure. The evidence was secured by the use of the sense of hearing and that only. There was no entry of the houses of offices of the defendants."[46] Although *Olmstead* has been overturned, the legal scholar Orin Kerr has shown that the private spaces and property theories that animated the *Olmstead* decision still pervade Fourth Amendment jurisprudence.[47]

The problem is even more pronounced online. The Internet has been subject to spatial analogies for decades. Julie Cohen shows how many of the attempts to consider cyber*space* as a separate space fail because of the phenomenological connection between our physical and online experiences.[48] But the law still has a tendency to treat the virtual world as a space different, separate, and apart from our physical space. As Mary Anne Franks has found, many judges, juries, and policymakers minimize hate and harassment online because they find online offenses less real and less worthy of legal protection than that they would for similar behaviors in the physical world.[49] Under this view, online attacks are either just words or easily silenced by closing a Twitter account or shutting down a computer. Cyberstalking, therefore, cannot be as serious as *real* stalking, and cyberharassment cannot be as serious as *real* harassment because they cannot cause real, physical harm. This, of course, is wrong, but the effect remains. Spatial analogies threaten to have the same minimizing effects on online privacy. A vision of privacy based on spaces, and the sanctity of those spaces, makes no sense in a world that lawyers and judges consider spaceless or, at least, a space not governed by the laws of our physical experience.[50]

More broadly, conceiving of privacy as detachment or separation from physical space has logical limitations. It would make privacy in public places impossible. What's more, it tells us little more than the mere fact that there are private places and public places and, therefore, cannot describe what makes public spaces public and private places private. That is, of course, what we really need to know.

INTIMACY, SECRECY, AND DEVIANCE

Some privacy scholars avoid the limitations of a theory of privacy based on separation, exclusion, and property by looking to *what* things are private, not *where* they are kept. Private things, like secrets, can go anywhere and retain their private nature. Conceiving of privacy this way also makes some intuitive sense: we tend to reflexively think that information about certain subjects, like our sexuality, medical conditions, and financial health, are private because of their subject matter. But although privacy-as-intimacy and privacy-as-secrecy theories retain the Lockean presumption of individual rights and are reflected in case law, it too narrowly circumscribes privacy and is often burdened by normative judgments about the underlying information. As such, privacy-as-intimacy does not help us protect previously disclosed information.

Many privacy theories implicitly include a conception of intimacy even when they overlap with theories of separation and exclusion. For example, to explain the difference between public and private, Howard White offered examples of privacy intrusions to which he expected we could all relate: a military officer asking a cadet if he or she is gay, an acquaintance asking why a friend only had one child, and anyone other than a romantic partner asking about sex.[51] Robert Gerstein and Jeffrey Rosen both argue that intimate relationships need privacy to function and flourish.[52] And despite the fact that they both concluded that privacy is really about controlling personal information, Jean Cohen and Julie Inness tie their idea to intimacy. To Cohen, privacy may be about choice, but the choice is about "whether, when, and with whom one will discuss *intimate* matters."[53] For Inness, privacy is the "state of . . . having control over [the] realm of intimacy, which contains her decisions about intimate access to herself . . . and her decisions about her own intimate actions."[54] Under these visions, intimacy, or anything that derives from an individual's sense of love and caring,[55] is the common denominator of privacy.[56]

Other scholars have gone further. Scott Skinner-Thompson, who focuses his work on privacy and the LGBTQ community, has identified the protection of intimate information – core identifying characteristics like sexual orientation, gender identity, and HIV status, for example – as one of information privacy's "concrete values."[57] In a world in which individuals can be fired simply for being gay, privacy, Skinner-Thompson argues, must protect sexual minorities from discrimination caused by the publication of intimate personal details. Framing privacy this way gives weight and concreteness to an otherwise ambiguous constitutional right to information privacy, thus avoiding the very pitfall that has made judges reluctant to identify such a right in the first place.[58]

Another advantage of privacy-as-intimacy is, as Daniel Solove has argued, that the concept is already reflected in federal privacy statutes and decades of Supreme Court jurisprudence. For example, the Family Educational Rights and Privacy Act protects information about students,[59] the Right to Financial Privacy Act protects financial holdings,[60] the Video Protection Privacy Act guards our video rental history,[61] and the Health Insurance Portability and Accountability Act secures some of our health data.[62] Data about minors, finances, and health are commonly understood as deeply personal because of the subject matter. Furthermore, Supreme Court cases like *Griswold v. Connecticut, Roe v. Wade, Lawrence v. Texas*, and, more recently, *Obergefell v. Hodges* reflect the Court's concern for the protection of intimate information.[63] Concluding his opinion in *Griswold*, which guaranteed a married woman's access to contraception, Justice Douglas explicitly connected the intimacy of the marital union to the right to privacy:

> We deal with a right of privacy [in marriage] . . . Marriage is a coming together for better or for worse, hopefully enduring, and intimate to the degree of being sacred. It is an association that promotes a way of life, not causes; a harmony in living, not political faiths; a bilateral loyalty, not commercial or social projects. Yet it is an association for as noble a purpose as any involved in our prior decisions.[64]

In *Roe*, the Court based its decision on similar grounds: a woman's decision to terminate a pregnancy is a fundamentally personal decision, involving an interest of great "significance and personal intimacy."[65] In *Lawrence*, Justice Kennedy struck down a discriminatory anti-sodomy law on the ground that gay persons, like all others, should be free to make their own intimate decisions free of government intervention: "[w]hen sexuality finds overt expression in intimate conduct with another person, the conduct can be but one element in a personal bond that is more enduring. The . . . Constitution allows homosexual persons the right to make this choice."[66] And in *Obergefell*, which guaranteed the right of gay persons to marry nationwide, Justice Kennedy returned to this theme, noting that "[l]ike choices concerning contraception, family relationships, procreation, and childrearing, all of which are protected by the Constitution, decisions concerning marriage are among the most intimate that an individual can make."[67] In all of these cases, the intimate and personal nature of the act in question – contraception, family planning, birth, pregnancy, sex, and marriage – was at the center of the Court's rhetoric and decision.

But it is not clear what limits the term intimacy. For the Court, intimate conduct was something personal, perhaps sexual or familial. Julie Inness felt that intimacy included a heartfelt emotional component.[68] To Tom Gerety, intimacy is a state of "consciousness" about the self.[69] Lots of things can be intimate, and what is intimate to one person may not be intimate to another. Therefore, limiting privacy to intimacy, variously defined, is not that helpful.

Many social scientists connect privacy, intimacy, and secret keeping. For example, Diane Vaughan, in her work on couples who separate, argues that "[w]e are all secret-keepers in our intimate relationships." Secrets can both enhance relationships, by smoothing over differences or by creating the intimacy of co-conspirators, and contribute to their collapse, by allowing one partner to have a life without open inspection, consent, or participation from the other partner.[70] Erving Goffman would agree that this type of secrecy is an important element of privacy. If we want to maintain a public persona, Goffman writes, "then [we] will have to forgo or conceal action[s] which are inconsistent" with that public narrative. In this view, privacy is the ability to conceal things that contradict the public persona performed on the front stage. And this is what the back stage is really for. It is not, as a spatial theory of privacy would suggest, a room or a stall or a secluded place; rather, it is the locus of private, intimate, and secretive behavior that we do not want others to see.[71] For example, in the back stage, servants use first names, workers laugh and take breaks, and employees may eat together and converse informally. In some cases, this culture is associated with a space (as in the PBS Masterpiece Classic show *Downton Abbey*); but it is what we do in the back stage, the secrets we hide there, that defines it.

There are, however, three fundamental problems with understanding privacy as a means of keeping secrets or hiding intimate details. First, sharing the secret, even with one other person, can extinguish its attendant privacy interest. Kim Lane Scheppele recognizes this in her study of the law's approach to privacy tort cases: "[w]hat is not secret cannot be considered private."[72] Daniel Solove has called this the "secrecy paradigm," or the tendency of judges to equate privacy with strict secrecy and refusing to recognize that anyone can have an expectation of privacy in any information that has ever been shared.[73]

The secrecy paradigm pervades the civil law of privacy. Among many other cases, conflating privacy and secrecy allowed the *San Francisco Chronicle* to disclose to the world that Oliver Sipple, the man who saved Gerald Ford from an assassination attempt, was gay because Sipple had shared that information with others.[74] But this ignored the fact that Sipple had gone to great lengths to only tell others in his close-knit community and keep his sexuality, a stigmatizing fact even today, from his family back home. The "secrecy paradigm" also allowed General Motors to gather personal information about Ralph Nader as part of the company's plot to discredit and harass him after he published his groundbreaking muckraking book, *Unsafe at Any Speed*, calling out the American auto industry for its willful disregard for consumer safety.[75] And judges are still conflating privacy with secrecy, tossing out a multitude of privacy claims at the first hint of previous disclosure. For example, in 2011, a judge dismissed a privacy lawsuit against a website that posted nude photographs of a young woman without her consent because the photos were previously shared with her (now former) boyfriend.[76] And a journalist was not held liable for publishing information about a police officer's mental health in a widely circulated Cleveland newspaper because, four years earlier, the officer's mental health was discussed for a few minutes at a Civil Service Commission hearing.[77] Limiting privacy to secrecy was problematic enough decades ago, but it is even more dangerous today, where almost every commercial, professional, and social interaction online requires us to reveal personal information to third parties.

A second problem with limiting privacy to intimate secrets is our tendency to conceive of secrets as discrediting, embarrassing, or, to use the sociologist's term, deviant. Deviant behaviors are those that violate the norms of some group.[78] When we burden others' secrets with perceptions of deviance, we place a severe limitation on any correlative legal right to privacy: if our secrets are so discrediting, society would rarely, if ever, see a need to protect them.

Much of the sociological literature on secrecy and intimacy devolves into just this kind of normative moral judgment. Despite professing to make no such judgments, Goffman's view of secret, hidden behaviors is negative; the back stage is, after all, littered with "dirty work" and "inappropriate" conduct. People "lapse" in the back stage, drifting toward indecorous behavior. They laugh at their audience, engage in mock roleplaying, and poke fun through "uncomplimentary terms of reference." They derogate others and brazenly lie and keep "'dark' secrets." Behind involvement shields, individuals do "sanctionable" or "unprofessional" things, like nurses smoking in a tunnel or adolescent horseplay outside of the view of others.[79] Goffman also points to the little transgressions that we engage in outside the public view:

> *While doing housework*: You can keep your face creamed, your hair in pin curls; . . . when you're sitting at the kitchen counter peeling potatoes you can do your ankle exercises and foot strengtheners, and also practice good sitting posture . . . *While reading or watching TV*: You can brush your hair; massage your gums; do your ankle and hand exercises and foot strengtheners; do some bust and back exercises; massage your scalp; use the abrasive treatment for removing superfluous hair.[80]

And he calls these activities "fugitive involvements," no less. In fact, Goffman echoes Emile Durkheim's famous distinction between the sacred and profane when he uses the word "profane" seven times in *The Presentation of Self in Everyday Life* to describe activities in the private sphere.[81] Privacy then becomes about concealing bad things, not just concealment in general. Under this view, the anonymity provided by privacy does not merely allow someone to do something different; rather, it allows him to "misbehave," to "falsely present[]" himself, or to do the "unattractive" things inappropriate in the public sphere.[82]

One of Goffman's major works, *Stigma*, is entirely concerned with negative or inappropriate behavior. That may sound like an uninspired conclusion given the title, but what is most telling is not the mere recitation of stigmatizing activities and things, but rather the implication that the private sphere is defined by stigma. Stigmas are "discrediting," "debasing," and "undesirable." They are "secret failings" that make us "blameworthy" and "shameful."[83] This moral judgment pervades the legal, philosophical, and social science literature as well. For Alan Bates, privacy does not simply protect against disclosures, but rather against "humiliating and damaging" ones about which others would "disapprove[]."[84] The sociologist David Diekema follows in a similar vein: privacy shields "improper" behaviors, "transgressions or nasty habits."[85] And Richard Posner argues that privacy protections grant people a right to conceal "legitimately discrediting or deceiving facts."[86]

It is hard to deny the moral burdens we tend to place on secrets and intimacy. For many scholars, the things we keep secret are stigmatizing, at worst, or dissonant with normal social interaction, at best. In either case, there is a normative judgment that burdens privacy with an attendant Durkheimian profanity. As such, if the private sphere is characterized by dark secrets or behaviors that society would not want to endorse, it is unclear how a right to privacy could ever exist.

The third problem with thinking about information privacy as protecting intimate information is that it only addresses a narrow portion of the power imbalances that are caused by sharing. Conceiving of privacy as a means of protecting individuals from the negative, harmful, or discriminatory effects of the release of stigmatizing information ignores the very real privacy concerns bound up with widespread disclosures of non-intimate information. The data we disclose when we use Google Search, browse websites, or join retail loyalty programs are not particularly intimate – we're sharing mouse clicks, not our HIV status. Therefore, although privacy-as-intimacy offers some solace to those looking to keep stigmatizing secrets from mass consumption, it does not alter the power asymmetries caused by many of the information disclosures inherent in modern life.

FREEDOM *FROM* AND ITS CRITICS

Conceptualizing privacy as the freedom to separate, hide secrets, or exclude the public makes a lot of intuitive sense. Even the origin of the word privacy is suggestive. In English, *privacy* comes from two Latin words: *privatus*, which refers to the withdrawal from public life or the separation from others; and *privare*, or privation and deprivation.[87] Thinking about privacy this way also echoes individual rights-based political philosophies that underlie much of the Western democratic tradition. For all these reasons, privacy-as-separation, -exclusion, and -intimacy just feels right. But it offers little privacy protection. Strict adherence to spatial analogies erodes privacy in public places and makes online privacy difficult to justify. And limiting privacy to secrecy is sometimes too narrow and sometimes too broad.

Traditional privacy theory does not stop there. As Julie Cohen has argued, limiting our conception of privacy to notions of property and exclusion is unfair to both privacy and to freedom: it ignores the fact that privacy can enhance individual liberty and that liberty is about much more than just a fight against social control.[88] Similarly, Locke's and Kant's visions for liberal selves are not merely defined by their capacity to exercise freedom from others. They are also empowered with reason, with the ability to choose their version of the good life. Privacy can be defined in these terms, as well. And that is the subject of our next chapter.

2

Privacy as Freedom *For*

In the last chapter, we looked at privacy as a negative right, or as the freedom *from* the prying eyes of government and society. This way of looking at privacy saw it as a right to separate from and exclude others from accessing information; it also included the right to hide information and keep secrets. But privacy as freedom from others gets us no closer to mitigating the vulnerabilities inherent in disclosure and protecting against abuses of power. When understood as a right to separate and exclude, privacy vanishes the moment we let others in. That erases privacy in today's technology-driven world, where some amount of disclosure of data is inevitable and often mandatory. If there is any hope for privacy, it does not lie in negative rights.

Several other theories of privacy take up the same mantle of individual rights and look forward, viewing privacy as a necessary condition for living as full, independent, and autonomous beings. This vision of privacy reflects the dignity owed to free, autonomous beings, relying directly on Lockean and Kantian visions of freedom. It is also reflected in much Supreme Court jurisprudence on privacy. And yet, it offers us little help: this vision of privacy is either hopelessly broad or hopelessly narrow. It gets us no closer to our goal.

INDIVIDUALITY, INDEPENDENCE, AND PERSONHOOD

Like Kant, whose metaphysics demanded that individuals be treated with dignity rather than as subjects of others, some scholars argue that respecting privacy is a necessary element of valuing individuals as ends in themselves. Stanley Benn channels Kant when he argues that individuals resent being watched because it makes them feel like tools in someone else's hands and not as free individuals "with sensibilities, ends, and aspirations of their own, morally responsible for their own decisions, and capable, as mere specimens are not, of reciprocal relations" with others.[1] Bloustein adds that privacy invasions have effects far beyond any physical encroachment or injury: one who is subject to intrusions "is less of a man, [and] has less human dignity" precisely because his privacy, a manifestation of his free self, is at risk.[2] This view evokes both Kant's mandate to treat everyone as ends in themselves and Locke's notions of self-ownership and his explanation for creating government out of the state of nature: the lack of individual rights and protection for the person's life, liberty, and property endangers her sense of self and her entitlements as a free, autonomous person.

One of those entitlements is the protection of individuality and free thought, and many scholars argue that privacy plays an essential role in making such independence possible. Alan Bates, for example, believes that privacy allowed individuals to process information before speaking, and the philosophers Mark Alfino and Randolph Mayes argue that a person requires privacy in order to reason about his choices.[3] That intellectual space both defines the individual and would be damaged by any interference from the state or society. A close corollary of this conception of privacy is the notion that privacy provides us the breathing room necessary to craft and edit ideas before public consumption. Ruth Gavison notes that privacy gives us the opportunity to express unpopular ideas first to sympathetic audiences, and then, "[a]fter a period of germination, [we] may be more willing to declare [our] unpopular views in public."[4] This idea, what Julie Cohen and Neil Richards refer to as "intellectual privacy," combines interests in personal autonomy and the metaphor of private spaces. It offers us the freedom to "explore areas of intellectual interest" that we might not feel comfortable discussing around other people, including unpopular ideas, deviant ones, or, more importantly, incomplete ones. It is, therefore, an essential part of our rights of self-determination.[5]

The primary advantages of this theory of privacy and personhood are its rhetorical strength and its ability to move beyond the limited visions inspired by detachment and intimacy. If privacy is essential to who we are as free selves, then privacy plaintiffs need not wait for a physical intrusion into a private space. Nor would they have to prove a piece of information was both private and stigmatizing. It could, therefore, address the intangible invasiveness of continual surveillance and "black box" data tracking. Surveillance damages our privacy in two important ways, both of which would run afoul of a privacy-as-personhood theory. First, as the philosopher George Kateb has argued, simply being watched could constitute an injury because it demeans us as persons. When we are subjects of surveillance, we are stripped of our entitlement to freedom as self-aware, rational individuals in a free society; we are "oppress[ed]," "degrad[ed]," and made the subjects of others.[6] Stanley Benn explains that we begin to see ourselves in a new light, "as something seen through another's eyes," which "disrupt[s], distort[s], or frustrate[s]" our ability to think and act on our own.[7] If privacy is an individual right essential to realizing our full, independent selves, constant surveillance poses a direct threat to that right even without specific injury.

Second, surveillance and tracking discriminate. Jeffrey Rosen notes, "[p]rivacy protects us from being misdefined and judged out of context in a world ... in which information can easily be confused with knowledge."[8] This is a particular problem today. As Frank Pasquale argues, data collectors, online platforms, and technology companies use black box algorithms to analyze the data they collect from us. Their opacity means that we not only have no idea how they work, but also have no opportunity to inspect our data and correct errors. And these algorithms determine much about our personal, professional, and financial futures.[9] Sometimes this is relatively innocuous, like when Google awkwardly shows a banner advertisement for ChristianMingle.com to an atheist. In other cases, it can be devastating and discriminatory. We know that at least one health care company denied coverage to an individual applicant when it found antidepressants in her prescription history and assumed (incorrectly) that she had a severe neurological disorder.[10]

Black box algorithms also discriminate against marginalized groups. Google shows ads for higher paying, more prestigious jobs to men and not to women;[11] ads for arrest records show up more often when searching names associated with persons of color than other names;[12] image searches for "CEO" massively underrepresent women;[13] and search autocomplete features send discriminatory messages, as when completing the search "are transgender people" with "going to hell."[14] These are not challenges to privacy when privacy is limited to property, sequestration, and secrecy; they do violate our rights when we understand privacy as something owed all persons as free and equal selves.

What's more, this rich conception of personhood is already reflected in long-standing Supreme Court jurisprudence on privacy and liberty. As Daniel Solove argues, "[t]he Supreme Court has espoused a personhood theory of privacy in its substantive due process decisions."[15] Indeed, Solove notes that theory was evident as early as 1891, in *Union Pacific Railway Co. v. Botsford*. In that case, the Court held that a party in a civil case could not be compelled to submit to a medical examination because he has the right "to the possession and control of his own person, free from all restraint or interference."[16] Later, when the Court had occasion to rule on a woman's right to choose, it explained the importance of decisions like contraception, family planning, sex, and terminating a pregnancy: "[a]t the heart of liberty is the right to define one's own concept of existence, of meaning, of the universe, and of the mystery of human life. Beliefs about these matters could not define the attributes of personhood were they formed under compulsion of the State."[17] Granted, activities we normally consider intimate were at the center of these cases. But the freedom to make those decisions is about more than their sexual nature. Rather, the Court suggested that these decisions define what it means to be treated with dignity as an autonomous individual in a democratic society.

This dignity and personhood theory of privacy inspires the most lyricism and poetry from scholars and the courts, but it also appears completely boundless. No scholar who understands privacy as primarily a matter of treating free individuals with dignity ever defines "dignity" or "personhood" other than by references to amorphous metaphysical concepts. But Kant's conception of dignity, as an intrinsic quality that we all share, could be used to challenge almost any behavior that someone believes encroaches on freedom. As such, it lends itself to absolutism while making it impossible to administer in privacy cases in the courts.

AUTONOMY, CHOICE, AND CONTROL

Existing alongside all of these theories of privacy are the concepts of autonomy and choice: the choice to disseminate information and the correlative right to control what others know about us. Seen in this way, privacy is about the freely choosing self exercising liberty in a democratic society. But like other theories of privacy, privacy-as-choice or -control either threatens too broad a reach, providing judges with no adjudicative path and pushing scholars toward intellectual confusion, or actually injures personal privacy.

Autonomy and choice are central to both Locke and Kant, as both agree that the freedom to choose defines who we are. Locke sees the state as a servant of individual rights because we choose to join together in government to mitigate the risks of the state of nature. The government, therefore, is there to serve us.[18] For Kant, autonomy and choice are part of man's transcendental rational nature: true freedom is only possible in an intelligible realm detached from the things that hold us back as humans.[19] Neo-Kantian liberalism takes the freedom embodied by pure rationality in the intelligible realm and argues that freedom is the right to choose one's own ends free from state interference. As the philosopher John Rawls stated, a "moral person is a subject with ends he has chosen, and his fundamental preference is for conditions that enable him to frame a mode of life that expresses his nature as a free and equal rational being as fully as circumstances permit."[20]

The choosing self is evident in the conventional understanding of privacy as our right to choose what others will know about us. Jean Cohen argues that privacy is the right "to choose whether, when, and with whom" to share intimate information.[21] Evoking Goffman, Charles Fried suggests that different groups of friends exist because we actively choose to share more with intimate friends and less with acquaintances.[22] This free choice gives us the right to control public knowledge of our personal selves. Privacy, then, as Alan Westin argues, "is the claim of individuals, groups, or institutions to determine for themselves when, how, and to what extent information about them is communicated to others."[23] It is, to Julie Inness, the idea that an individual has "control over a realm of intimacy" and, to Jonathan Zittrain, control over our information in general.[24] For the philosopher Steve Matthews, exercising privacy is making the choice to "control" and "manage" the boundary between ourselves and others.[25] The common denominator in all these descriptions is free choice and control, both of which are central to the rights ideal.

In his compelling text, *The Digital Person*, Dan Solove argues that the salient problem with private intermediaries and governments amassing digital dossiers about citizens is the loss of individual control over personal information. Collecting data that are already available or required for doing business, Solove argues, does not injure personal privacy in the conventional sense; that is, there is no "discrete wrong" that occurs through the behavior of some "particular wrongdoer" who, say, discloses personal information to the media. Rather, the problem is structural. Data are collected without sufficient controls, so Solove recommends a new architecture of data collection that "affords people greater participation in the uses of their information," i.e., more control. He recommends starting at the Fair Information Practices Principles (FIPPs), a series of recommendations from the Department of Housing, Education, and Welfare (HEW) in 1973 that are predominantly focused on ensuring individuals have control over their personal data. The guidelines include no secret recordkeeping, a pathway for individuals to read their records, a way for individuals to prevent their information from being used in different ways, and a method of correction and amendment.[26] At their core, these recommendations aim to shift control over data from the collector (an intermediary or a government agency) back to the source of that information (the individual).

This notion of privacy as control has arguably had a more profound impact on privacy law than any other theory. It is, first and foremost, at the core of the notice-and-choice approach to data privacy in the United States and Europe. Notice-and-choice refers to data collectors' responsibility to tell us what information they collect, how and for what purpose they collect it, and with whom they share it (notice) so that we can have the power to consent or decline and choose another product or platform (choice).[27] And it is based entirely on the idea that the right to privacy is the right to control dissemination of our data. This was true from the very beginning, when the HEW Report recommended that users be informed of data use practices, have the opportunity to correct their data, and consent to any secondary uses of their information.[28] Several years later, the Organisation for Economic Co-operation and Development issued similar guidelines, requiring, for example, that data gatherers disclose the purpose and scope of data collection, any security protocols, and all user rights.[29] The Federal Trade Commission (FTC), the federal regulatory agency dedicated to protecting consumers from unfair and deceptive business practices, got in on the act in 2000, urging Congress to require commercial websites to disclose a similar what-when-how of user data.[30] In so doing, the FTC identified notice as the most important FIPP,[31] and notice-and-choice became enshrined as the basic legal relationship between us and collectors of our data.[32]

At its core, notice-and-choice is premised on the idea of the autonomous user. As a doctrine of informed consent,[33] notice-and-choice allows us to exercise control over our information by making rational disclosure decisions based on all the evidence. As we have seen, autonomy and choice animated the FIPPs. It was also central to President Bill Clinton's "Framework for Global Electronic Commerce," which stated that "[d]isclosure by data-gatherers is designed to simulate market resolution of privacy concerns by empowering individuals to obtain relevant knowledge [about data collection and practices]. Such disclosure will enable consumers to make better judgments about the levels of privacy available and their willingness to participate."[34] And the FTC has explained that notice was "essential to ensuring that consumers are properly informed before divulging personal information."[35] In other words, notice-and-choice was meant to give us the tools we needed to exercise control over our information.[36]

Despite its pervasiveness, privacy-as-control is problematic. First, this conception of privacy may undermine itself. Privacy-as-choice or -control over what others know transforms all revelation into a conscious volitional act. Courts have run with that presumption and have concluded that individuals assume the risk that any disclosures to third parties could result in wider disclosure to others or the government, thus extinguishing privacy interests in all previously revealed information. A telephone user, for example, "voluntarily convey[s] numerical information to the telephone company ... [and] assume[s] the risk" that the telephone company would subsequently reveal that information.[37] A bank depositor has no legitimate expectation of privacy in the financial information freely given to banks because "[t]he depositor takes the risk, in revealing his affairs to another, that the information will be

conveyed by that person to the Government."[38] And this doctrine has been
extended to the Internet. Some federal courts have held that because any
information conveyed to an online service provider in order to access the
Internet is "knowingly revealed," there could be no invasion of privacy when
an Internet service provider (ISP) gives that information to someone else.[39]

But not all disclosures are free and voluntary.[40] If we want to engage in
online life at all, we not only share information directly (credit card numbers
on e-commerce sites, personal behaviors and interests on social networks, and
financial information with online banking platforms), but we also share what
websites we visit, what search terms we use, where we move our cursor, our IP
addresses, and hardware details via ongoing behavioral tracking. Facebook, for
example, follows us wherever we go online. Many websites have an embedded
"Like" button that begs us to "Like Us on Facebook" with a simple click.
When we visit these pages, Facebook may be receiving a significant amount of
information, including the amount of time we spend on the page, what we
clicked on, and the browser and operating system we use, to name just a few.[41]
What's more, since 2012, Facebook has been collecting data about our Internet
behavior even from websites that do not have a "Like" button.[42] And Facebook
channels that information into user-targeted advertisements.[43] Other than by
living a life without the Internet, we have little control over these disclosures.
But in a world where privacy is understood as the free choice to disclose
information to others, we bear the burden of responsibility for them, erasing
any privacy interest in previously shared information. Therefore, although the
ideals of autonomy and free choice appear to empower the individual with all
powers of disclosure, it logically leads to an evisceration of personal privacy
rights.

Second, it is not at all clear that greater individual control over personal
information would do much good. Even Solove, whose recommendations are,
in part, dedicated to giving individuals greater control over their information,
concedes the point: "people routinely give out their personal information for
shopping discount cards, for access to websites, and even for free."[44] Citing
Julie Cohen, Solove notes that individuals are incapable of exercising adequate control over each individual piece of information because they cannot
comprehend the enormity of the value of the sum of those pieces.[45] What's
more, scholars have shown that we do not make rational disclosure decisions
when given the opportunity to exercise control. Rather, as Alessandro Acquisti,
Leslie John, and George Loewenstein have found, disclosure behavior is based
on comparative judgments: if we perceive that others are willing to disclose,
we are more likely to disclose.[46] And other scholars have found that disclosure
can be emotionally manipulated: positive emotional feelings about a website,

inspired by website design, the type of information requested, and the presence of a privacy policy, correlate with a higher willingness to disclose.[47] Privacy-as-control ignores such contextual factors: it treats all disclosures as fungible and ruinous to privacy rights. Therefore, privacy-as-control is of little practical help.

FREEDOM *FOR* AND ITS CRITICS

Understanding privacy as the liberty to realize one's true self and choose the good life in a liberal democracy has certain advantages. It enriches privacy beyond merely separating from others and recognizes that privacy can serve the cause of freedom, not impede it. But personhood and choice theories of privacy are either too broad or too narrow to do privacy justice. And some communities, particularly those still burdened by state-sanctioned discrimination, cannot always exercise the choice to keep personal information private.

Even though there is a significant difference between seeing privacy as a negative or positive right, both views fall back on the same assumption that privacy is an individual right against the world. This feedback loop might explain why scholars are all over the place when discussing privacy. They use the rhetoric of autonomy when arguing for privacy-as-separation;[48] they see privacy as controlling dissemination of information, but seem to think of the information being disclosed as necessarily intimate;[49] and they talk of personhood and choice when considering deviance and secrecy.[50] The end result is the same: privacy law has been predominantly focused on protecting an individual right to control dissemination of information and to be able to separate from the public.

That may sound liberating on its surface, but it's contributing to the death of privacy. When privacy is about separation or choice, disclosure is always anathematic to privacy. And because so much of modern life requires disclosure – from buying goods on Amazon to engaging with others on Facebook to even going outside – such a vision of privacy cannot exist in today's world. Furthermore, when privacy is about intimacy, wide swaths of shared information about us are on the outside looking in, even when the collection and use of such data results in real harm. Under this theory, privacy may continue to exist for a subset of admittedly important needs, but it shrinks from answering vanguard privacy problems posed by new and increasingly invasive technologies. No wonder we think privacy is dying. The way we have framed privacy to date is tipping the scales.[51]

3

Social Theories of Privacy

Traditional approaches to privacy see privacy and society in conflict. But privacy is actually essential to social interaction. In his seminal article, *The Sociology of Secrecy and of Secret Societies*, Georg Simmel concluded that privacy is a "universal sociological form" defined by hiding something in certain contexts. It is universal in that we do it all the time. It is social in that privacy helps define social relationships: we never share everything with everyone; our relationships with different people differ because we share certain information with some and not with others. So understood, privacy allows us to maintain relationships that would be impossible in a world of complete knowledge.[1] Erving Goffman came to a similar conclusion. Both the front and back stages allow different social interactions to occur on informational terms appropriate to those contexts. For example, casual, familiar conversations among waiters in the kitchen look different than the more formal interactions of the dining room. Neither could occur if waiters presented themselves in the same way to patrons and colleagues.[2]

Simmel and Goffman allude to the social role and social value of privacy. Rather than being preoccupied with separating the individual from others and stopping the flow of information between people, social theories of privacy recognize that privacy actually serves a social function. Privacy also allows social interaction to occur by mitigating the vulnerability inherent in disclosure. It enables information flow to some and restricts it to others. Under this perspective, privacy facilitates sharing. We can share our deepest sexual desires with our partners, husbands, and wives, but not with acquaintances, strangers, or our parents. We can interact with employers and our friends differently. We can save passwords on secure platforms but not share them with Nigerian princes. Privacy, therefore, functions as a foundational element of social structure.[3]

This book learns these lessons to develop a sociological approach to privacy. To speak of a social theory of privacy seems counterintuitive. Social things are "collective representations that express collective realities."[4] Whereas social life involves assembled groups and is a manifestation of collective thought, privacy law's traditional focus has been the individual. Yet, social theories of privacy are not new: Daniel Solove, Michel Foucault, Robert Merton, Erving Goffman, Lior Strahilevitz, Robert Post, and Helen Nissenbaum, among others, have all discussed ways to conceptualize privacy as an important part of relating to society, not detaching from it. But although each of them recognizes that privacy only makes sense in context and has social value beyond its benefits to the individual, these theories are only the beginning of a larger research agenda on privacy and society.

If thinking about privacy strictly in rights-based terms is helping us speed toward the erosion of privacy in the modern world, these social approaches are, at a minimum, tapping on the breaks. But most social theories of information privacy to date do not go far enough to rebalance the power asymmetries caused by disclosure. Plus, they remain too theoretical for practical applicability and profess little to no normative angle, which, I think, is a lost opportunity. Privacy-as-trust, which will be described in the next section, is an attempt to solve those problems. In this chapter, I discuss the social theories of privacy on which privacy-as-trust is based, showing that although they represent important steps forward in privacy scholarship, they inadequately respond to the unequal power dynamics at play in a modern world of widespread disclosures.

PRIVACY'S SOCIAL VALUE

Daniel Solove's work is an important transition between traditional privacy scholarship and social theories of privacy. Solove's *Understanding Privacy* describes the inadequacy of many of the theories discussed in Chapters 1 and 2, considers privacy in a radically new way, and posits a distinctly social value for privacy.

Solove criticizes traditional conceptualizations of privacy as incapable of dealing with any number of modern information problems,[5] including how to respond to ongoing government surveillance, the collection and analysis of our online behavior, and the use of that data for targeted behavioral advertising.[6] The problem is that traditional privacy scholarship has always tried to reduce privacy to a common denominator, or essence. This effort is doomed to fail: any single conception of privacy had to be general enough to be applicable to a multitude of situations, but such generality made it broad, vague, and unhelpful.[7] We saw this for ourselves in Chapters 1 and 2.

His solution is elegant. Relying on the works Ludwig Wittgenstein and pragmatists like William James and John Dewey, Solove understands privacy as an "umbrella term that refers to a wide and disparate group of related things," not a single idea. This avoided one of the generality problems – namely, trying to make a single concept broad enough to capture every privacy situation. Because privacy is not one single idea, but rather a series of different collections of interests, it can cover different situations. Solove also shows that this pragmatic approach reflects how we actually talk and think about privacy. We discussed this in Chapter 2, as well. Scholars are all over the map when talking about privacy – for example, concepts of intimacy are combined with control; notions of autonomy are tied to concepts of separation and exclusion.

Solove not only accepts this problem; he sees in it a better way of thinking about privacy. He embraces the notion that privacy will always be a series of overlapping ideas, with the particular ideas varying from context to context. As such, Solove asks us to use analogic reasoning to identify when particular situations fall under the privacy umbrella: "[w]e should classify something as involving 'privacy' when it bears resemblance to other things we classify in the same way."[8] If we conceptualize privacy from the bottom up – from real life situations – we avoid the generality problem of a priori theories and allow privacy to evolve with changing values, culture, and technology.[9]

This way of understanding privacy is in stark contrast to the theories discussed in Chapters 1 and 2. The latter theories started with an overarching definition that tried to explain privacy in every situation. Solove's vision of privacy starts on the ground and varies from context to context, keeping it contingent upon the social dimensions of any given situation. Solove also values privacy differently. Where many scholars see privacy's value as protecting individual autonomy from stifling social and government surveillance, Solove argues that society has a strong interest in the protection of personal privacy. Again relying on Dewey, who himself relied on centuries-old social theorists, Solove noted that "the individual is inextricably bound up in society," not in tension with it. Therefore, when privacy law protects individuals, it does so for the common good.[10] Solove then recommends that judges considering privacy cases should balance privacy against opposing interests in particular contexts and protect privacy when doing so would benefit society, not just the individual.[11]

Solove was right to argue that limiting privacy's value to the individual alone sells privacy short. When understood as a purely individual right, privacy loses out to more powerful competing demands, like preventing terrorism or catching criminals.[12] Society benefits when individuals' privacy is protected, too. We are all better off, for example, when police obtain a warrant based on probable cause and when national security surveillance is subject to public scrutiny because democratic institutions cannot survive when government can impose its will on its citizens on a whim.[13] Michel Foucault made a similar argument. As part of his famous discussion of the Panopticon, Foucault argued that total surveillance is such an effective disciplinary tool not merely because it invades individual rights, but also because it makes any unsanctioned social practices impossible. Replacing the social norms of group interaction with disciplinary mandates erodes social vitality, damaging society as a result.[14]

Recognizing the social value of privacy represents a giant step forward in our understanding of privacy. Solove also takes us from stifling a priori definitions of privacy to a more practical, contextual approach. But Solove replaces one generality problem with another. Privacy may differ from context to context, but a "family resemblances" approach does not offer judges, policymakers, or privacy professionals any guidelines for how to balance privacy with competing needs in those contexts. Nor does Solove step too far away from traditional definitions of privacy. For Solove, there is social value in privacy specifically because privacy protects individual autonomy and freedom. That also sells privacy short. As we will see, privacy is also an element of social structure that allows different kinds of social interaction to happen with different people.

PRIVACY AS A SOCIAL FORM

Sociologists were instrumental in recognizing that privacy constituted an element of the social context of interaction. Social theorists like Robert Merton and Erving Goffman argue that we play many different roles in society at once, and privacy is what allows us to share, behave, and interact in ways appropriate to those roles. This, in turn, allows others to develop expectations about our behavior and construct norms unique to particular social contexts, permitting social interaction to continue. For these theorists, privacy was not a way to separate from society. Nor was privacy merely an individual right that also had social value. Rather, privacy was what allowed diverse social interactions to occur.

Merton elaborates on privacy's social value, arguing that it functions as an element of social structure. Merton's account of social structure, or a society's organized set of social relationships, is based on the idea that each person occupies different roles in society, each of which requires different amounts of information sharing and different norms of interaction. For Merton, each person occupies a "status" (a position in a social system) and a "role" (the behavioral expectations associated with that status). But we also occupy multiple statuses and play multiple roles. Public school teachers, for example, are teachers of students, colleagues of other faculty members, employees of administrators and school boards, members of teachers' associations, partners with parents, and public advocates all at the same time.[15] Although he defines privacy in traditional, autonomy terms, as the "insulation of actions and thoughts from surveillance of others," he recognizes that privacy serves a distinctly social function. It allows a public school teacher to be three things to different audiences at once.[16]

Erving Goffman takes this one step further. The primary focus of Goffman's sociological work is the relationship between people in public, including how individuals present themselves to others,[17] the nonverbal cues that guide social interaction,[18] and the strategies that we use in repeated discourse.[19] But he did have a conception of privacy. In *Behavior in Public Places*, for example, Goffman uses the word "public," or iterations thereof, 100 times;[20] he refers to privacy 27 times.[21] And much of his work focused on the ways in which selective disclosure helps keep social interaction humming along.[22] He concludes that individuals are the "central point in a distribution of persons who either merely know about him or know him personally, all of whom may have somewhat different amounts of information concerning him."[23] That is, Goffman would say that we "present" different parts of ourselves to others in ways that reinforce social expectations: waiters behave professionally in front of patrons, but let their hair down – changing posture, accents, demeanor, and language – behind closed doors.[24] This allows the same person to conduct two very different social interactions with two very different audiences. But, as the legal scholar Julie Cohen notes, Goffman's account of privacy is not about hiding information from others or controlling what others know about us. Rather, image management is about establishing the parameters of social space in ways that make continued interaction possible.[25] This is the social role of privacy.

Those parameters are defined on both sides. At the same time that sharers engage in image management practices to interact with the front stage, bystanders and audience members have a "tactful tendency ... to act in a protective way in order to help" sharers maintain their persona.[26] Privacy imposes an obligation on them to give "tactful inattention" to neighboring conversations, guaranteeing the "effective privacy" of all those involved. This tact, something we might call discretion, is simply a way of understanding how privacy, as an element of social structure, protects the norms of social interaction. In this way, privacy is a character of social spaces because it is part of the background context in which all social interaction occurs, and, as a protector of social norms, has significant social value.

Robert Post fleshes out Goffman's idea in more detail with an analysis of the tort of intrusion upon seclusion.[27] The tort, which protects against any form of invasion of "solitude or seclusion," would seem, on its face, to reflect the common understanding of privacy as separation and exclusion. Post argues, however, that the tort is meant to "safeguard[] rules of civility that . . . rest[] not upon a perceived opposition between persons and social life, but rather upon their interdependence."[28]

This is exactly what happened in *Hamberger v. Eastman*, a case in which tenants sued their landlord after discovering he had installed an eavesdropping device in their bedroom. In holding that the device was an invasion of privacy, the court was less concerned with whether the plaintiffs were actually injured, humiliated, or harmed in any way. Rather, the court relied on the broader objective principle that the installation of the eavesdropping device was an intrusion "offensive to any person of ordinary sensibilities."[29] Or, to use the Restatement's language, "highly offensive to a reasonable person."[30] This makes the tort of intrusion rather unique among torts. Successfully litigating most tort claims usually requires plaintiffs to prove that the defendant's underlying action actually caused some particularized harm or damage.[31] Claims of negligence, for example, require showing that the defendant's negligence in driving a car or operating a crane caused some "demonstrable injury."[32] But, as Post notes, the tort of intrusion is different: the offense is the action per se, and the injury it causes is to the social norms of society. This turns the plaintiff from the victim of personal injury, in the case of most torts, to a representative of society victimized by a breach of a social norm that we impliedly owe one another.[33] Post says that norm is "civility." The tort of intrusion "focuses the law not on actual injury . . . but rather on the protection of [the individual as] constituted by full observance of the relevant rules of deference and demeanor," per Goffman.[34]

This richer conception of privacy gives us more to work with, both to understand how privacy functions in society and to justify privacy protection. And we are beginning to address the vulnerability and power asymmetries that come with disclosure. When those with whom we have shared our information further disseminate it to others, they violate those norms. But this is a little ambiguous. What norms are violated? How do we know when those norms are present in a given context? Put another way, now that we understand that privacy functions in context to foster social interaction, we need a way to determine more specifically what privacy is and what it is not, and why.

PRIVACY AND THE FLOW OF INFORMATION

One way to do that, what I will call a pure relationship model, determines privacy based on the relationship, or lack thereof, between an individual and her audience – something is public when it is known by those, like strangers, presumably, with whom we have no special relationship, but private when it is only known to intimates. The relationship model explains why information disclosed in certain defined relationships, including fiduciary and trustee, attorney and client, or doctor and patient, are still considered private. The philosopher James Rachels, who defined privacy as a right of control and access, was a proponent of this model. Echoing Merton and Goffman, Rachels argues that our ability to "maintain different sorts of social relationships with different people" was the central goal of privacy.[35] For Rachels, the nature of those relationships determined the difference between privately and publicly shared information. We share what is appropriate to the particular interpersonal relationship, and what is appropriate is determined by the social norms associated with the relationship itself.[36] It is entirely appropriate, Rachels says, for our employers to know our salaries, and for our doctors to know about our health. That information may not be appropriate for strangers or even acquaintances.[37]

This relationship model is distinctly social: its interpretive tool – the relationship between social actors – lies beyond the individual. In this way, it does not face the absolutist and normative critiques plaguing the autonomy and rights-based conceptualizations of privacy discussed in Chapters 1 and 2. It also may rescue us from the erosion of privacy wrought by what Daniel Solove calls the "secrecy paradigm,"[38] or the conflation of privacy and secrecy. Indeed, the relationship-oriented approach presupposes that information can be shared with others – family, friends, and intimates – and still be considered private. But it nevertheless fails as a governing understanding of information privacy for several reasons. First, by focusing exclusively on relationships, the model makes information irrelevant. That, however, cannot be the case. Individuals may not be inclined to share embarrassing or stigmatizing information with intimates and feel perfectly comfortable sharing it with strangers and yet still feel that this information is private in some sense. Second, the model falls back on the assumption, held by many of the rights-based theories discussed in Chapters 1 and 2, that information shared with strangers cannot ever be private. In this way, we have still not escaped the "secrecy paradigm" trap because anything shared with even one stranger is considered public under the pure relationship model.

Edward Tverdek's modified relationship model consciously picks up where Rachels left off. It offers an alternative approach.[39] Tverdek acknowledges that the public–private divide varies based on an individual's relationships with certain others, but also argues that not all information is fungible. For Tverdek, there are two types of personal information: that which creates "esteem-based interests" in how we are regarded by friends and intimates, and that which creates "an interest in preventing the practical harms" that could occur if strangers or the public knew it. Each interest arises when different types of interaction partners are involved: esteem-based interests are more likely raised among close relationships, and interests in preventing practical harms are more likely raised among strangers. This is why, Tverdek argues, that we may prefer to hide a stigmatized sexual fantasy from those closest to us, but have few qualms talking about it to a stranger online. Or why we may barely safeguard our Social Security numbers around our spouses, but worry what would happen if strangers got their hands on them.[40]

Tverdek's is an improved taxonomy, if only because it recognizes that not all information is fungible. But it cannot be an accurate conceptualization of information privacy for several reasons. First, his esteem versus practical distinction does not fit a continuum as neatly as he suggests. Many people might not be so cavalier about their Social Security numbers, and most would arguably guard it around their friends and acquaintances, if not their spouses. And esteem-based interests do not disappear as intimacy declines, as the son or daughter of a clergyman or local politician would understand. Second, there is no place for strangers in Tverdek's taxonomy, leaving us once again victimized by the secrecy paradigm. Third, both Tverdek's and Rachels' models are focused on individual pieces of information – an identification number, a stigmatizing illness, or a salary, for example. As the law professor Frank Pasquale has noted, privacy problems in a networked world extend far beyond our concern for the disclosure of discrete bits of data; rather, any theory of privacy must also address the aggregation, analysis, and categorization of terabytes of data about individuals.[41] More analog relationship models, then, leave us ill equipped to handle some of the most vexing questions of modern information privacy law.

Although these relationship models take a step toward an administrable sociological theory of privacy, they do so rather tentatively. They focus on relationships and social interaction, but ignore the lessons of Merton and Goffman that privacy is a social phenomenon not merely because other people exist, but because it establishes social circumstances in which information flows from one party to another. Rachels is correct to argue that relationships matter. Tverdek is right to argue that the nature of the information shared also matters. Privacy is also an information flow problem.

In an article in the *University of Chicago Law Review*, the law professor Lior Strahilevitz suggested that the flow of information within and among networks, or the likelihood that a given piece of information would work its way through a given group of persons and transfer to a wider audience, should determine when information is public or private. More specifically, the law should consider information public, and no longer the basis of an invasion of privacy claim, when both the nature of the information and with whom it is shared make it likely that the information will escape its original circle of recipients. Based on ongoing research in social network theory, Strahilevitz concludes that the more "interesting" or unusual, surprising, revealing, or novel a piece of information is, the more likely it will be disseminated through a network. Complex or aggregate information, the sum total of pieces of data about a person, is not likely to be known outside of close-knit groups and, therefore, highly likely to stay confidential. But when information is disclosed to a group that includes highly connected, socially active individuals who are situated in multiple social networks, the information is likely to be disseminated further beyond the initial group. Therefore, Strahilevitz argues that if everyone we know, plus several we do not, knows something about us, that information is likely to move through the network and into other networks. That piece of information would be public. By the same reasoning, if just our friends know a fact, "but not any strangers," then we can expect it to remain with its intended recipients. Social network theory can help a judge determine whether information originally disclosed was likely to have become public regardless of any subsequent disclosure. If it was, it cannot be the basis for an invasion of privacy claim.[42]

This is a dynamic and powerful idea. Privacy scholarship is richer for Strahilevitz's contribution. And it incorporates the Rachels and Tverdek arguments that the nature of relationships and the type of information disclosed play a role in determining the privacy or publicness of information. There are, however, three challenges to using social network theory alone to determine the difference between public and private information. First, applying the theory requires making several arbitrary choices that may not reflect the reality of a particular social network. What may be an unusual or rich secret to a judge may be rather mundane among a different group of people. The social network theory of privacy would invite a judge to impose his or her normative interpretations on someone else's potentially different social network. This has the unique potential to damage marginalized groups with stigmatized identities whose network peculiarities might be wildly foreign to a mainstream judiciary, a problem Strahilevitz does not discuss. Second, the role of strangers in the calculus is problematic. Under

Strahilevitz's social network theory, the mere fact that a recipient of information is a stranger – namely, someone with whom we do not have personal, face-to-face, offline experience – may exclude the possibility that we can retain a privacy interest what we shared. But, today, some strangers know a lot about us, whether those strangers come in the form of websites or Facebook "friends" we've never met offline. Third, social network theory may explain how information spreads, but it does not explain why we share information in the first place, which is an essential piece of the puzzle for justifying retaining privacy rights in previously shared information.

PRIVACY AND CONTEXT

So far, we have seen scholars argue that several factors matter for determining whether previously disclosed information is still private: the relationships between the sharer and her audience, the nature of the information shared, and the network of people that characterizes the social context of disclosure. Helen Nissenbaum, a scholar of privacy and society, sees these few factors as necessarily underinclusive. They were attempts to once again reduce the complex, multifaceted concept of privacy to its essence, and that was bound to fail. Her theory of privacy as contextual integrity tries to learn the lessons of other social theories of privacy without narrowing it down to a simple heuristic by connecting privacy and contextual norms of propriety. Like Post, Merton, and Goffman, Nissenbaum recognizes that privacy is embedded in daily social life. It forms part of the background social structure in which interaction occurs. Like Solove, Nissenbaum asks us to think about privacy from the ground up, considering the nature and effects of privacy invasions. Nissenbaum argues that when new social interactions or new technologies change traditional information flows, those changes can be considered invasions of privacy when they are inconsistent with the norms associated with that context.[43]

Under this theory, privacy is about "context-relative informational norms" that "govern the flow of personal information in distinct social contexts (e.g. education, health care, and politics)."[44] In other words, privacy is about what is appropriate for different groups to know about us given the nature of the information and the context in which it is shared. Following Merton, Nissenbaum argues that social actors occupy different roles and engage in activities in those roles. And following Goffman, Nissenbaum notes that social norms serve to prescribe appropriate behavior to those roles, and those behaviors are geared toward certain goals. This is why patients feel comfortable sharing intimate details with doctors (with the goal of a successful diagnosis) and disclosing their credit card information with office administrators (with the goal of paying their co-pay). An invasion of privacy, then, would occur if the doctor's office manager sat in the examination room, or if patients could read every other patients' file, or if someone put all medical records online for everyone to see. Privacy, therefore, is determined in context, as

> a function of several variables, including the nature of the situation, or context; the nature of the information in relation to that context; the roles of agents receiving information; their relationships to information subjects; on what terms the information is shared by the subject; and the terms of further dissemination.[45]

Unlike the a priori definitions of privacy discussed in Chapters 1 and 2, the contextual informational norms emanating from these factors are not static. They can evolve over time, particularly as new technologies change information flow practices. This makes the theory flexible and adaptive.

Privacy as contextual integrity also helps explain why certain disruptions to informational flow norms are or are not morally problematic. Information flow contexts have specific ends and values. And, as such, ideal norms are the ones that promote the ends and values of those contexts. A simple example can illustrate these points. We limit access to HIV test results for various reasons: embarrassment due to the stigma associated with HIV, job discrimination, personal freedom, and other values. But, for the purpose of good public health policy, society also wants to encourage individuals to get tested. Any change to the flow of HIV test results that challenges those goals will strike us as intrusive, immoral, and, for lack of a better word, creepy.[46]

As a governing theory of information privacy, contextual integrity adds much to the rights-based theories discussed in Chapters 1 and 2. It also learns the lessons of the social theories discussed above. Nissenbaum's work retains the core presumption of a social theory – that privacy must account for information exchange among social actors – and eschews any problematic reliance on relationship categories that could arbitrarily limit our privacy interests.

Although Nissenbaum's is the latest and most profound attempt to bring social theory to our understanding of privacy, the theory is ambiguous and far too complex for judges and privacy professionals on the ground. And in an attempt to rescue social theories of privacy from narrow approaches, privacy as contextual integrity tacks too far in the other direction. It lacks administrable heuristics that would allow judges to determine what kinds of contexts reflect appropriate and inappropriate information flow norms. As with Goffman's and Merton's work, that was not Nissenbaum's goal.

WHERE WE HAVE BEEN AND WHERE WE GO FROM HERE

It is, however, one of our goals. Privacy scholarship has learned a lot since Warren's and Brandeis's articulation of a right to be let alone.[47] We have learned that a priori, rights-based definitions have dominated privacy theory, but are either too general, too narrow, or otherwise sell privacy short. Social theorists have taught us that privacy is best understood as a part of everyday social practice that allows social interaction to occur in context. Therefore, our conception of privacy needs to be contextual, flexible, and adaptive because that is how we make disclosure decisions.

Privacy scholarship needs a way of understanding information disclosure contexts so we can develop administrable legal rules for deciding privacy cases. We also need a way of talking about and thinking through information privacy so privacy professionals on the ground can better understand their obligations, implement privacy protocols, and protect personal privacy. In a world where sharing information is a necessary part of modern life, we deserve an approach to privacy that reflects our actual social behavior and does not expose us to the erosion of privacy at one hint of sharing. And our vision of privacy must help mitigate the vulnerabilities and power imbalances that are caused by sharing information in the first place. This is the role of trust, and it is the subject of the remainder of this book.

PART II

PRIVACY, SHARING, AND TRUST

I argue that our embodied experience with information privacy is bound up with our concept of trust. We share in contexts of trust because trust norms are what mitigate the vulnerabilities and power imbalances inherent in sharing information with others. Therefore, the law of information privacy should be oriented toward buttressing those trust norms and repairing them when those with power (information holders) violate the trust of those without (information sharers). This section of the book constructs this argument in detail.

4

Trust and Sharing

Trust pervades the privacy landscape. When chief privacy officers (CPOs) talk about privacy, they talk about it in terms of gaining user trust.[1] "[T]he end objective," one CPO reported, "is always: what's the right thing to do to maintain the company's trusted relationship with our employees, with our clients, with any constituency in society that has a relationship to us."[2] In a recent article in the *Harvard Business Review*, furthermore, several technology company executives argued that the way to ensure that increasingly privacy savvy users will continue to share data is to gain user trust and confidence.[3] Apple knows this already. When trying to log on to iCloud on a new device or desktop, Apple asks us if we "Trust this browser?" and requires us to enter a 6-digit code before we can gain access. And iPhones using iOS 8 or higher also ask if we "Trust this computer?" before sharing any data across platforms. Facebook also understands that we think about our privacy in terms of trust. For example, in 2013, Facebook asked its users, "How trustworthy is Facebook overall?" A spokesperson explained that Facebook was just looking for feedback to improve service and enhance user experiences.[4] But there is likely much more to it. We know that Facebook is an inherently social tool designed to create, foster, and expand social interaction.[5] We also know that Facebook routinely tinkers with its user interface to inspire user trust and, in turn, sharing. Its committee of Trust Engineers, for example, plays with wording, multiple choice options, the order of questions, designs, and other tools to encourage users to honestly report what they do not like about posts they want taken down.[6] That may be an important goal, but it shows that Facebook is well aware that trust and sharing are linked.

Government agencies and nonprofit advocacy organizations, and some privacy scholars agree. For example, both the Federal Trade Commission (FTC) and the California Attorney General's office recommended that online platforms be transparent about their data practices so as to inspire consumer trust.[7] This way, consumers will feel more comfortable about sharing their personal information.[8] The Future of Privacy Forum, a nonprofit research organization advocating for responsible data use practices, recently published an entire pamphlet on how technology companies operating in the sharing economy (platforms like Uber, AirBnb, and others) can build trust by protecting user privacy.[9] And the business and management scholar Kirsten Martin argues that, all else being equal, a website's failure to meet the privacy expectations of users will negatively impact the trust those users have in the website, thus reducing sharing.[10]

So trust is everywhere in the privacy space. But it is not merely a tool that websites use to encourage us to share. Trust is broader: it is a social norm of interactional propriety based on the favorable expectations of others' behavior. And, as I will show, it is a singularly significant factor in our decision to share personal information with anyone. It facilitates disclosures that serve society well, including romantic, professional, and personal sharing. Trust is also what mitigates the vulnerabilities that come with sharing. Therefore, trust is at the core of our expectations of privacy.

Information privacy, I argue, is really a social construct based on trust between social sharers, between individuals and Internet intermediaries, between groups of people interacting online and offline, broadly understood. And because trust both encourages the sharing and openness we need in society and because breaches of privacy are experienced as breaches of trust, privacy law – the collective judicial decisions, legislative enactments, and supporting policy arguments regulating disclosures, searches and seizures, data aggregation, and other aspects of informational knowledge about us – should be focused on protecting and repairing relationships of trust. In short, the only way to re-establish the balance of power between sharers and data collectors is to leverage law to enforce disclosure's trust norms: one can be held liable for invasion of privacy if he further disseminates information that was originally shared in a context that manifests trust.

Building on the work of the privacy scholars discussed in Chapter 3, as well as extensive social science research on trust, this chapter teases out the definition of trust in more detail and describes the connection between privacy, trust, and sharing. Privacy-as-trust, which is really how we have been approaching privacy from the ground-up all along, is a simple way of looking at problems both old and new, and one adaptable and administrable enough to stand the test of the real world.

WHAT IS TRUST?

There are three types of trust in the social science literature: general, institutional, and particular. Briefly, general social trust is the belief that most people can be trusted. For example, the question – "Generally speaking, would you say that most people can be trusted or that you can't be too careful in dealing with people?" – has been asked in the General Social Survey since 1972.[11] Institutional trust is the trust we have in institutions, government agencies, or corporate entities. A subset of this form of trust, well known in the technology literature, is trust in automation, or the automatic faith we have that a machine will work better than a human.[12] Particular social trust is the trust we have in specific other people.[13] This last form of trust is the subject of this research and for simplicity, I will refer to particular social trust simply as trust.

For the purposes of this book, I define trust as a resource of social capital between or among two or more persons concerning the expectations that others will behave according to accepted norms.[14] Let's unpack that definition. Social capital is an asset that derives from social relations and networks. As the sociologist Robert Putnam describes it, social capital is a "feature[] of social life – networks, norms and trust – that facilitate cooperation and coordination for mutual benefit."[15] On a micro level, social capital constitutes the advantages and benefits that individuals realize owing to their connected social status, like coworkers working together and learning from one another to achieve a specific goal,[16] or location in a group, like a leader who brings diversity and new perspectives to her life by bringing different groups of friends together.[17] On a more macro level, scholars like Putnam and Francis Fukuyama have described social capital as an attribute of communities and nations, both of which can collectively derive benefit from cooperation, cultural exchange, and other forms of interaction.[18] On all levels, social capital refers to the good things that develop out of our connections to others.

Trust is one of those good things. It is the "favourable expectation regarding other people's actions and intentions,"[19] or the belief that others will behave in a predictable manner according to accepted contextual norms. For example, if Alice asks her friend Brady to hold her spare set of keys, she trusts Brady will not break in and steal from her; friends do not break in to friends' homes. When an individual speaks with relative strangers in a support group like Alcoholics Anonymous (AA), she trusts that they will not divulge her secrets; AA members are bound to keep confidences. Trust, therefore, includes a willingness to accept some risk and vulnerability toward others to grease the wheels of social activity.[20] And if we never had to trust, our social lives would be paralyzed. As Niklas Luhmann has stated, trust begins where knowledge ends.[21] It is the mutual faithfulness on which all social interaction depends. I cannot know for certain that my neighbor will not abuse her key privileges or that my fellow support group members will keep my confidences, but the norms of those contexts tell me that they will. Trust is the expectation that people will continue to behave according to those norms. Therefore, trust allows me to interact with and rely on others.

Trust, then, is a natural, almost designed-in aspect of social life. Think of it this way. Because we cannot predict the future, trust is necessary in order to act. Sometimes we can know something will happen: a soccer ball kicked in the air will come down; the sun will set in the west. Those are predictable events backed by science. But most of the time, uncertainty reigns, especially with respect to the actions of other people. So trust, like hope or confidence, is a social phenomenon that allows us to act despite uncertainty. As the sociologist Piotr Sztompka notes, hope and confidence are passive. "I hope to be rich one day" is a passive feeling based on nothing more than desire. Confidence is an informed hope: "[b]ased on the evidence the prosecution presented at trial, I am confident the defendant will be convicted." Trust, however, is an active strategy for dealing with uncertainty, a solution to a problem posed by a lack of information.[22]

HOW DOES TRUST DEVELOP?

Trust that individuals will behave according to norms of confidentiality and discretion could arise in a variety of contexts. The four principal ways that trust develops are through repeated interaction, explicit or implicit cues, reciprocity, and transference from known trustworthy parties to unknown strangers or acquaintances. Each of them makes sharing possible.

Traditionally, social scientists argued that trust developed rationally over time as part of an ongoing process of engagement with another. This is the narrative of Alice and Brady: if Alice interacts with Brady over time and Brady acts in a trustworthy manner during those interactions, Alice is in a better position to predict that Brady will act trustworthily the next time they interact.[23] The more previous interactions, the more data points Alice has on which to base his trust, and the more likely she is to share with him in the future.[24]

Another obvious source of trust is when the disclosure context includes explicit cues, like a confidentiality clause or prefacing a conversation with a warning ("This is to be kept between us"). Subtler indications of expectations of confidentiality are just as strong: two people sharing a secret at a party might physically turn their bodies away from the crowd, huddle down, and whisper.[25]

Furthermore, a friend in need may ask another friend for advice regarding a particularly sensitive, intimate, or personal problem; trust and confidentiality are implied in context. Trust may be implied from certain professional contexts, like between doctors and their patients and between fiduciaries and their beneficiaries.[26] These explicit and implicit indicia of information security allow the disclosing party to trust that the recipient of her information will continue to respect prevailing norms of confidentiality, thus encouraging sharing by mitigating the risks of disclosure.

Strangers and acquaintances, even without the benefit of repeated interaction or explicit cues, trust each other, as well. First, trust emerges through norms of reciprocity. This is illustrated by the classic "trust game" from Joyce Berg, John Dickhaut, and Kevin McCabe's famous article, "Trust, Reciprocity, and Social History." In this game, two people – the sender and the responder – are each given $10. The sender can send some, all, or none of her money to her anonymous responder. The responder gets three times whatever the sender sends. She then chooses how much to send back. Any money the responder does not return is hers to keep. In sending money, our sender exhibits trust; in returning money, our responder exhibits reciprocity. In a game where norms of reciprocity are strong, that is, where the sender knows that there will be significant pressure on the responder to send money back, the sender is more likely to share (i.e., trust).[27] This mechanism has been shown to work on online social networks, as well: sharing increases when users can expect greater reciprocity (favorable responses, or "likes," and additional sharing among friends and followers).[28]

My own research suggests that norms of reciprocity build trust and encourage sharing of intimate information on geolocation dating apps like Tinder and Grindr. Grindr, which is geared toward gay and bisexual men, presents users with a grid of photos and uses GPS to present those closer to a user's location higher up on the grid. Tapping and swiping up on a photo reveals a short profile, which may include a screen name, age, a short personal description, physical characteristics, interests, and HIV status, among other information. Over the last two years, I have interviewed or surveyed more than 500 gay and bisexual men who use Grindr, almost all of whom have shared intimate, revealing, or naked pictures of themselves with others on the platform. As many users indicated in their interviews, they do so based on norms of reciprocity and trust. For example, Steven P., a 24-year-old gay man who lives and works in Boston, has been using Grindr for "a little over a year to meet new people." He has met several men his age, some of whom, he says, "have become my closest friends in this town. I moved here not knowing anybody." One man "seemed nice enough" and "very friendly and cool, so I sent him a few pictures. I remember one was naked, the other, from the waist up, both included my face." In our discussion, he volunteered the view that the norms of the platform make such sharing possible: "if you don't share photos, you can't really participate. I think we all do it expecting that the guy on the other end can be trusted to be discreet." Steven also noted that he only sent his pictures after the other man sent his, noting explicitly that "that was how it worked." He went on: "I think the tit-for-tat exchange makes people trust the other person: it's not one of you being vulnerable to the other; it's both."[29] Semi-structured interviews with approximately 50 other Grindr users and open-ended responses on more than 500 anonymous surveys revealed similar views: Grindr operates with sophisticated reciprocal disclosure norms that make users vulnerable and open to each other, thus building trust and encouraging the sharing that makes interaction possible.

Trust emerges among strangers in yet another way. We transfer the trust we have in those we know to strangers, or from people we know to those we do not. For example, we may trust experts and other professionals based on their degrees, transferring the trust we have in a school's reputation, which we know, to one of its graduates, whom we do not.[30] There is some evidence that we trust lawyers and doctors based on firm or hospital affiliations, respectively,[31] and even office location in prime real estate[32] and office design.[33] The transference process does not end there. Many of us do not choose doctors based solely on their degrees. Rather, we rely on the recommendations of others and, in particular, those that we respect.[34] In all of these cases, trust in experts makes us more comfortable sharing important information with them.

Transference also operates in the lay context, with the same effects on sharing. Mark Granovetter has shown that economic actors are more likely to do business with people they don't know based on how embedded they are in a familiar and trusted social network.[35] Recommendations from close colleagues, referrals from friends, and personal recommendations transfer the trust necessary for interaction. And several studies have shown that social actors tend to trust strangers if they share the same important, perhaps stigmatizing, in-group identity.[36]

THE CONNECTION BETWEEN TRUST AND SHARING

It makes sense, then, to turn to trust when thinking about what motivates us to share personal information, whether online or offline: Alice shares information with Brady because Alice trusts Brady with that information; the applicable norms – perhaps confidentiality and discretion – give Alice the confidence and comfort to share, mitigating the risk inherent in disclosure.[37] Despite the intuitive appeal of that mechanism, particular social trust has been, at best, a silent undercurrent in a growing literature on our propensity to disclose personal information.

Our impression is that privacy and sharing decision-making is haphazard. In the course of researching this book, I have spoken formally and informally with hundreds of individuals who use online social networks and e-commerce platforms. Almost all of us do. Nearly every non-expert Internet user I interviewed assumed that we share information indiscriminately, without reason or limitation, in order to engage socially or buy products. These are just some of the most common sentiments: "No one ever cares about their information. We just type in whatever they ask so we can buy stuff." "There is no *why* we share personal information. We hand it over all the time, even to get $1 off a coffee." "I don't make decisions about my privacy. I just assume everyone knows everything already, so why even bother." "I think most of us share without thinking." "I know that I'm being watched online, but I don't really know how to factor that into what I do. I mean, it's not like I can decide not to enter in my credit card information if I need to buy something on Amazon."[38]

These concerns have been reflected in scholarship on sharing and privacy decision-making. We tend to give up personal information for small rewards and generally would not opt to protect our privacy if it meant giving up certain small benefits.[39] Teenagers tend to share a significant amount of information with strangers.[40] And in a relatively early study, the information and technology scholars Alessandro Acquisti and Jens Grossklags show that we do not make these online sharing decisions with perfect rationality.[41] There are, after all, many factors that influence our actions, including psychological, social, and cultural factors.[42]

But later studies showed there is method to our behavior. Acquisti, Leslie John, and George Loewenstein have found that disclosure behavior is based on comparative judgments: if we perceive that others are willing to disclose, we are more likely to disclose. Acquisti and his colleagues asked individuals to respond to a series of ethics questions, some of which required them to admit to stigmatizing behavior. The study participants were more likely to respond that they had engaged in bad behaviors when told that previous respondents made similar admissions.[43] Based on research that established a link between how professional a website looks and its security,[44] Leslie John also finds that individuals are, perhaps counterintuitively, more willing to admit to bad behavior on unprofessional-looking websites. In other words, contextual cues within an unprofessional website interface caused people to suppress privacy concerns and increase disclosure.[45] Other scholars have found that disclosure can be emotionally manipulated: positive emotional feelings about a website, inspired by website design, the type of information requested, and the presence of a privacy policy correlate with a higher will-ingness to disclose.[46] Still others have found that knowledge of a website's data use practices can influence disclosure behavior.[47]

This literature teaches us, among other things, that our propensity to share is contextual. And that context is at least partly influenced by the other individuals around us. That could mean that our propensity to disclose is subject to a herding effect: when we are around others who disclose, we disclose.[48] Another possible explanation is that knowledge that others have shared inspires particular social trust: the disclosures create vulnerability and expec-tations of reciprocity that link even strangers together and establish a basis for social norms.

This is particularly true for social sharing on the Internet. James Grimmelmann, a law professor and technologist, has shown how social con-texts are essential to our decisions to share information on online social networks. He says that we "have *social* reasons to participate on *social* network sites," and identifies several heuristics we use to determine whether to share on Facebook.[49] All of them are proxies for trust,[50] and they can be summarized under two umbrella concepts.

First, *bigness*. Facebook's pride in being the largest social network on the planet is not rooted in a simple obsession with size. Rather, having lots of other people sharing is essential to encouraging us to share with them. As Grimmelmann notes, millions of people can't be wrong. Our "Facebook-trusting friends" must know that the platform is safe. And bigness shields us from the risk of being singled out for a privacy invasion.[51] In both of these ways, size is one way to identify a context of trust: more than one billion users actively sharing information on Facebook is like Alice safeguarding Brady's spare keys one billion times. Facebook's size and growth make it more predictable as a safe place for sharing. We see massive crowds posting infor-mation, and rarely, if ever, hear about anything going wrong. And Facebook is designed to emphasize its bigness. Step one after signing up lets us use our email contacts to see which of our friends are already members and which we can invite, thus making the community bigger. Whenever another member sends us a "friend request," or a request to be added to our network, Facebook lists her network size and the number of mutual friends we have in common. And it includes the number of people who have liked or commented on a post above and below the content on our News Feeds. And, of course, Facebook brags about its size all the time.[52] It does so because platforms that are big are more trustworthy.

Second, *community*. Facebook's design makes us think that we're talking to specific other people in controlled spaces. We see others' faces and are taken to others' personal profile pages to interact with them. This creates perceptions of safety and familiarity.[53] The members of our social networks on Facebook also tend to be like us in some ways, so we assume they are like us in a lot of ways.[54] The more familiar someone else appears to us, as Max Weber and Talcott Parsons note, the more we are likely to bring her into our confidences.[55] Facebook also breeds a sense of familiarity in two additional ways. First, because our closest friend and that guy we met at yoga are all defaulted as "friends," Facebook makes all our friends seem fungible. This makes us think we can share similar information with all of them. Second, almost every interaction on Facebook occurs in public, for everyone to see. Our friends' posts are listed on our News Feeds, the running narrative we see when we log in to Facebook. And every item includes some indication as to how our friends interacted with it, including whether they "liked" or "commented" on another's post. Mutual surveillance, Grimmelman reminds us, creates trust because "we'll see if [others] betray us"[56] and because it helps us make the comparative judgments Acquista, John, and Loewenstein found were so powerful determinants of our propensity to disclose.

Empirical evidence bears this out. Studies of interpersonal exchange suggest that trust is a precondition for self-disclosure precisely because trust mitigates the risks involved in sharing. As early as 1971, Sidney Marshall Jourard, the Canadian psychologist and pioneer in self-disclosure research, observed that "a person will permit himself to be known when he believes his audience is a man of goodwill. Self-disclosure follows an attitude of love and trust."[57] More recently, Mary Culnan and Pamela Armstrong have found that even Internet users that report significant interest in protecting their privacy are willing to disclose personal information to a website and have that information used to create consumer profiles if the website has fair and transparent procedures in place to protect privacy. These procedures, the authors note, act as "as an intermediary to build trust" given the power imbalance between users and commercial websites.[58]

To build on this research, I designed a study to test the link between trust and sharing on social networks, asking: What effect, if any, does particular social trust have on Internet users' willingness to share personal information online?[59] This study included survey questions to identify what information respondents shared on Facebook (a General Sharing metric), why they share it, and for what reasons, if at all, they would share information with strangers. The survey also asked about sharing different kinds of disclosure. For example, a willingness to share intimate photos or deeply personal stories of loss paints a richer picture of users' disclosure behavior than just asking if they would repost a news article or a cute picture of dog. Because the type of information shared varied, I could measure both a respondent's willingness to share, generally, and her willingness to share intimate information (an Intimate Sharing metric). And the results suggest that trust is a singularly important factor in our decision to share personal information with others.[60]

Although several pieces of data included in the survey could correlate with a willingness to share information on Facebook – age, gender, education, sexual orientation, race or ethnicity, networked level, time spent online, general social trust, trust that Facebook will protect user privacy, how many friends one has on Facebook, and how many close friends use Facebook – only those factors speaking to trust were found to have any statistically significant association.[61]

With respect to sharing, generally, and sharing personal information, a greater propensity to share on Facebook is positively associated with the number of Facebook friends one has,[62] the number of close friends that use Facebook,[63] and the extent to which one trusts Facebook to protect user privacy.[64] This means that having more friends, more close friends who use Facebook, and greater institutional trust in Facebook are all associated with greater sharing of personal information. When controlling for the other variables, these associations remained significant.

Regression analysis confirms a relationship.[65] Proxies for trust – trust that Facebook will protect our privacy, the number of "Facebook friends" we have, and the number of close friends we have on the platform – are the only statistically significant predictors of a willingness to share, generally. More specifically, for every two notches up on the trust scale ("Trust in Facebook," where "1" refers to "no trust" and 10 refers to "complete trust") users are likely to share an additional piece of personal information. Similarly, respondents with more than 1,000 "Facebook friends" share, on average, one more piece of information on the platform than those with 501–1000 friends. And those with "many" close friends on the website share, on average, two more pieces of information than those with "some" close friends on the platform. Although these factors may only account for just under 20 percent of sharing behavior, factors related to trust must be included in the conversation about our propensity to disclose information.[66] What's more, the effect of trust is also strong when we focus on sharing particularly intimate or personal information: those with "many" close friends on Facebook share more personal information than those with fewer close friends on the platform.

Other data that can also speak to the relationship between particular social trust and the decision to share are motivations for accepting Facebook friend requests from strangers. As discussed above, overlapping networks and sharing an important or in-group social identity have been found to be strong indicators of trustworthiness in strangers. The survey asked respondents several questions about whether a given piece of information about a stranger, defined as an individual they had never met offline in person before, would make it more or less likely that they would accept the stranger's friend request. They covered a wide range of possible reasons for accepting a friend request from a stranger, from "large number of mutual friends" and "the stranger is friends with your close friends" to "physical attractiveness" and "you will never see the stranger in real life." Answers to the first and second questions would speak to the strength of overlapping networks and the presence of particular social trust in that network. Respondents were also asked if they are more likely to accept a friend request from a stranger who shares their minority status. This last question was used as a proxy for determining the role of an important in-group identity in developing a connection with a stranger.

Many of the factors that received an overwhelming concentration of "more likely" and "much more likely" answers are proxies for particular social trust. For example, 85 percent of users would accept a friend request from a stranger if they shared a large number of mutual friends. More than 81 percent of respondents would accept a request if the stranger was friends with their close friends. And although only 18.3 percent would be more likely to accept a friend request from a stranger that shared their same sexual orientation, approximately half of those respondents also identified as members of the LGBT community. These are cues of trustworthiness based on strong overlapping networks and in-group identity: as discussed above, individuals routinely transfer the trust they have in known entities (friends and close friends) to unknown entities (strangers). The next most important factor was evidence of active participation on Facebook (63.3 percent), which is another social cue of trustworthiness: active participation suggests that the account is real, mitigating the risks associated with bringing a stranger inside a network. This is, of course, precisely the role of particular social trust.

Given the amount of information someone can learn about us if they are among our Facebook "friends," accepting friend requests from strangers based on transferring trust indicates the power of particular social trust in the propensity to share information. Attractiveness or sharing similar names, genders, hometowns, locations, or hobbies and interests were not considered important or, in only a few cases, made respondents less likely to accept the friend request. These factors are unrelated to particular social trust: none of them are strong indicators of predictable behavior according to accepted social norms. Notably, 27 percent of respondents stated that they were less likely to add a stranger to their network if they knew they would never meet the stranger in person, suggesting that, at least on Facebook, anonymity is not an invitation to share. But trust is.

5

What Does Trust Mean for Privacy?

Trust, whether developed from repeated interaction, explicit or implicit cues, reciprocity, or transference, is at the core of our contextual decisions to share personal information with others. We see it in real life, from trust games to online social networks, from familiar interaction among friends to limited exchanges among relative strangers online. Trust gives us the confidence and willingness to share because it mitigates the vulnerabilities inherent in disclosure.

So, if trust and sharing are linked, what does that mean for privacy and privacy law? When recognized to date, the relationship between privacy and trust is usually functional – namely, privacy builds trust, and trust yields disclosure. Such a view may make privacy good for business (which it is), but I'm interested in a different question. If we want privacy to thrive in a world that requires significant disclosures to participate in modern life, we need sharing, in some contexts, to be compatible with privacy. In other words, we need to reorient privacy law toward protecting disclosures that emanate from social relationships of trust.

PRIVACY BUILDS TRUST

Implicit in laws like the California Online Privacy Protection Act[1] and explicit in recommendations from the Federal Trade Commission[2] is the notion that protecting privacy builds trust. These policies require and encourage web platforms to both be honest about data uses and aggressively protect users' personally identifiable information. Scholars are taking note. Neil Richards and Woodrow Hartzog, for example, have argued that privacy should be conceptualized as a builder of trust rather than as a shield against invasions. Part rhetorical, part substantive, Richards and Hartzog's argument is that privacy laws should be the tools that build trust in information sharing relationships.[3] The legal scholar Jessica Litman makes a similar point: "[w]hy do we expect the merchants, banks, and insurance companies we deal with to respect our privacy? . . . [They] encourage it. It's profitable. Without that trust, we'd be reluctant to volunteer our credit card numbers; we'd think twice before making embarrassing purchases or watching certain pay-per-view movies."[4] Litman goes on to say that the use, aggregation, and sale of consumer data is a breach of trust, and it is, but not for the reason she describes.

Litman's and Richards and Hartzog's arguments are important first steps in reminding online platforms that privacy is good business. But if, as I have argued above, sharing occurs in contexts of particular social trust, it is not clear that these understandings of privacy are sufficient to adapt privacy to the digital age. In a world where so much of our data are in the hands of third parties and at risk of further disclosure to private as well as government actors, saying that privacy builds trust does not provide a clear doctrinal path for continued privacy protection for information known to some others. Merely requiring notice of data use practices under the governing notice-and-choice approach to privacy ignores the myriad ways in which web platforms can manipulate our propensity to share by leveraging, among other tools, website design and the information they collect about our social networks. And seeing trust as a by-product of a functioning privacy regime misses the fact that sharers tend to expect privacy protection where trust exists already.

INVASIONS OF PRIVACY AS BREACHES OF TRUST

Indeed, trust functions as a counterweight to the vulnerability and loss of power inherent in disclosure. It forms the background social structure that allows sharing to occur in the first place. And we experience invasions of privacy at the moment that those norms of trust are broken, not after. This is as true in interpersonal contexts as it is online.[5] As we have seen throughout this book, this way of understanding privacy is different from many traditional, rights-based approaches. The contrast is put in stark relief in the context of platform use of "big data" for behavioral targeting, predictive analytics, and automated decision-making.[6]

Online behavioral advertising, or the use of web browsing history and other data to target particular ads to those more likely interested in seeing them,[7] is the norm online. Google Ads are targeted, as are the recommendations we see on Amazon. The in-line advertisements we see on most of the websites we visit are also based on our online behavior over time. That is why we see ads for new televisions after searching "flat screen televisions" on Google or under Amazon's electronics marketplace.

The use of our data by web platforms does not stop there. In 2012, the *New York Times* reported on the story of a father who stormed into his local Target to object to the massive retailer sending coupons for baby clothes and cribs to his teenage daughter. The father thought that the coupons were a particularly craven way to both encourage her to get pregnant and then goad her into buying maternity clothes, baby formula, diapers, and onesies at Target. The real story was much creepier. The young woman *was* pregnant, but she had yet to tell anyone, including her father. The company's marketing team wanted to know which customers were pregnant *before* those customers made announcements on Facebook, Instagram, or elsewhere so they could preempt the inevitable barrage of baby-related advertisements from rivals. Therefore, at the behest of the marketing department, Target statisticians created a pregnancy-prediction model using "big data" and an algorithm. It input customer shopping habits, Facebook "likes", marital status, estimated salary, credit card usage, web browsing history, and much more, eventually resulting in specific names of customers.[8] The subsequent mailing not only took away a young woman's power over her body and her decisions, but it caused a family squabble over otherwise sensitive, personal, and private information.

Sometimes, data collection, aggregation, and analysis can be helpful – if I did a Google search for "flat screen televisions," I may actually want to see that a 55-inch Samsung is on sale at Best Buy for $450. Sometimes, it can be annoying, creepy, and invasive. At other times, it can be insidiously discriminatory. Kate Crawford has found that a smartphone app that allowed Boston drivers to automatically report potholes for repair was going to be biased toward those areas where residents are more likely to own smartphones, i.e. wealthier neighborhoods.[9] Furthermore, by giving landlords and employers the tools to use Facebook "likes" – which, studies show, can predict a user's gender, race, sexuality, and political views quite accurately[10] – to identify and advertise to the types of applicants they prefer, big data sets permit discriminatory targeting without having to advertise "Whites Only" or "Gays Need Not Apply."[11] Google returns advertisements related to arrest records when typing in names associated with persons of color at higher rates than it does for white-sounding names.[12] And law enforcement's use of big data sets to predict crime and allocate resources can lead to discriminatory tactics that, by overpolicing certain neighborhoods, biases crime data even further.[13]

Data analytics is, therefore, a privacy powder keg. Ad targeting, not to mention Target's behavior and algorithmic discrimination, strikes many as invasive.[14] In a recent study, several scholars at Carnegie Melon University found that many Internet users thought that deploying Internet-based tracking to target them with tailored advertisements was "creepy." Many participants expressed an aversion to being tracked. They not only worried that their personal information could be shared or that it might be incorrect; they also experienced the mere collection of their data as an intrusion. They were, at times, "freak[ed] out" or "scar[ed]" about the practice.[15]

But the theories of privacy discussed in Chapters 1 and 2 are ill equipped on their own to explain these reactions to the mere fact of data collection and its use for audience targeting and prediction. The information that web platforms use to develop behavioral profiles is not private under any traditional metric. We share it with websites and service providers as a matter of course. As such, the information is not secret. By using the Internet, we apparently make a choice to visit a free website in exchange for sharing data with that website.[16] Nor is the data particularly intimate. For example, it includes the fact that we visit www.nytimes.com four times per day, that we spent anywhere between one and seven minutes at the website each time, that we used the latest iOS, and that we bought a subscription to the crossword puzzle.

The same can be said in response to any unease toward Target. Customers had already disclosed every piece of information that Target funneled into its pregnancy-predictive algorithm. They all had Target IDs, which tracked their purchases; linked to those IDs were basic demographic data points, from income and credit cards, to location and how long it took them to drive from home to the store. Target also bought publicly available data on ethnicity, job history, reading habits, bankruptcies, divorces, college, consumer preferences, politics, charitable giving, and car ownership. Plus, that Target had or could have access to this information, and use it to "enhance" user experiences, was disclosed in its online privacy policy. All Target did was hire talented statisticians to process it all. As such, customers had notice, gave consent, and ostensibly handed over the information willingly.

These arguments miss the mark for several reasons. First, the "it's already public" justification from Target, online advertisers, and other data collectors presumes that Internet users relinquish or diminish their privacy rights the moment they go online. But, as we have discussed, that is only true if our conception of privacy remains limited to rights-based notions of separation, autonomy, choice, and control. Under these approaches, the inflexion point for determining the difference between private and public information is the fact of disclosure, not the context, eroding privacy down to secrets. It would make the mere act of using the Internet equivalent to handing unlimited power to use our data over to any and all third parties.

That is not how we approach our Internet use. Rather, we disclose information to websites or technology companies under narrow expectations of how our data will be used. As various scholars have shown, consumers trust websites to respect the "terms of use" around shared information. And when those terms are violated – namely, when data collectors break trust norms by going too far or sharing our data with third parties outside our expectations – we perceive our privacy invaded.[17] Therefore, beyond rights-based approaches to privacy, which have difficulty responding to the "it's already public" canard, we need an approach to privacy that matches our phenomenological experience with online data collection and recognizes that unbridled use of our data for advertising, predictive analytics, and automated decision-making can constitute invasions of privacy.

Second, even if the individual data points can be considered public and available for use, aggregated data is more than the sum of its parts, making the analysis and processing of "big data" a separate privacy concern. Any individual piece of information may not be particularly intimate or personal, but its sum total can paint a detailed picture. Reasonable minds on the Supreme Court have warned us about this for decades. For example, in his dissent in *Smith v. Maryland*, the case that made the it's-already-public rationale a matter of constitutional law, Justice Powell argued that law enforcement should not be able to access the telephone numbers we dial without a warrant because even though a single number may not reveal much about us, a list "could reveal the identities of persons and the places called, and thus reveal the most intimate details of a person's life."[18] And in *United States v. Jones*, a case about GPS tracking, five justices wrote or joined opinions arguing, at least in part, that one of the reasons GPS surveillance over an extended period of time constitutes a search is because the aggregation of observable behavior reveals much more than just observing snippets of that behavior.[19] Justice Sotomayor made this concern explicit, arguing that the mere fact that police used a GPS device to track a car on public roads did not necessarily make extended surveillance of that car without a warrant constitutionally permissible. She reasoned that "the unique attributes of GPS monitoring" – in particular, its allowance of nonstop and precise surveillance – implicates the Fourth Amendment's guarantee against unreasonable searches and seizure:

> I would take these attributes of GPS monitoring into account when considering the existence of a reasonable societal expectation of privacy in the sum of one's public movements. I would ask whether people reasonably expect that their movements will be recorded and aggregated in a manner that enables the Government to ascertain, more or less at will, their political and religious beliefs, sexual habits, and so on.[20]

Allowing mass aggregation and analysis of information in such profoundly invasive ways is, as Justice Sotomayor suggests, not what we think we are doing when we step outside our homes. We may expect some measure of publicity; that's why we wear clothes in public. But that expectation is not the same as universal acceptance of all types of uses of our data. Unlike rights-based conceptualizations of privacy, which struggle to distinguish among types of data manipulations, we need an approach to privacy that is constructed around separating trusted uses of data and those that break norms of trust embedded in social life.

Third, behavioral targeting, predictive analytics, and automated decision-making are exercises of power embedded in the structure of disclosures. But traditional, rights-based conceptions of privacy misunderstand the dynamics. If privacy is about inaccessibility or choice and control over information, going online and acknowledging that we have read a website's privacy policy make us accessible by choice. We have, the argument goes, given up control of our data in exchange for the convenience of Amazon remembering what we left in our cart. So understood, disclosure is an exercise of *our* power to choose: we let websites use our data pursuant to our express and implied permission. That is why the Federal Trade Commission focuses so much of its time and energy on ensuring websites provide adequate notice rather than minimum standards of information protection.[21] It is also why websites can manipulate our data as they see fit. Conceptualizations of privacy that presume we have given consent to data use at the moment of disclosure contribute directly to an "anything goes" mentality about user data.

But that, of course, is not what really happens. Much of our online life is necessary, not voluntary, and, as such, our related disclosures cannot be seen as the subject of free choice. In other words, we cannot assume the risk that our data will be used, shared, sold, and manipulated if we never had a choice to share the data in the first place.[22] And even if we could separate out purely voluntary online interactions, we often lack the tools to manage our disclosures. Websites make privacy policies inaccessible, inscrutable, and impossible to read.[23] They fail to keep their privacy promises.[24] And they mislead us about the power we have to manage our preferences.[25] They, therefore, make it difficult, if not impossible, to exercise whatever power we may have.

Instead, behavioral targeting and other data manipulations are exercises of the power websites have over us. Like the friend who holds our secrets, websites' considerable power derives from our disclosures. They aggregate, analyze, sell, and manipulate our data, quite simply, because they can. Indeed, for many platforms that depend on a steady stream of personal information from its users so they and their advertisers can target potential consumers, their business interests are orthogonal to privacy. Elsewhere, where disclosures cause significant power imbalances between sharers and audiences, trust norms and powerful legal weapons step in to protect the vulnerable from predation. In attorney–client and doctor–patient relationships, for example, where sharing is essential and socially beneficial, ethical norms ensure that attorneys and doctors will keep the confidences of those that trust them.[26] Fiduciaries, some of whom are actually called "trustees," owe duties of loyalty to those that rely on them. Those are trust norms. And if norms of practice collapse, those victimized by breaches of trust by the powerful can sue. The power dynamics at play in many online disclosures are similar.

TRUST AND PRIVACY LAW

Now we're ready to define privacy-as-trust. If trust is a benefit of social connectedness that mitigates risks inherent in disclosure and, therefore, creates the circumstances that facilitate sharing information with others, then information privacy is a social norm of information flow based on trust. The law of information privacy, then, gives effect to that norm by using both its coercive and expressive power to protect trust, repair it when it breaks down, and constrain the power of data holders. Under privacy-as-trust, lawsuits against those that invade our privacy, statutes that protect our information, legal rules the govern relationships between consumers and data collectors, and judicial opinions on vanguard privacy problems would focus on both expressing the value of relationships of trust and protecting them from harm by limiting the uses of our shared information in accordance with our social expectations.

Several principles should guide judges, policymakers, and regulators when implementing privacy-as-trust. The first principle is this:

Sharing is not only inevitable, it is necessary.

We are a society of sharers. Bernard Harcourt calls us "exposed."[27] We share information with others all the time, whether chatting with a friend or loved one over dinner or sharing personal stories inside a support group. Doing so satisfies innate psychological needs and realizes significant social, public, health, and political benefits. Privacy-as-trust not only accepts the inevitability and necessity of sharing and disclosure. It is constructed to foster, encourage, and protect it.

There is also very little that is truly free about much of our disclosures on the Internet. Although no one physically forces us to list our favorite movies or "like" our friends' posts on Facebook, we are, for the most part, involuntary online sharers. Buying anything on Amazon, using our bank's online platform, or paying for goods with a credit card involves significant online data disclosures. Even browsing the Internet is an information sharing event. Much of that sharing is impossible to avoid if we hope to participate in modern life. And because it is done out of necessity, it cannot truly be a matter of free choice.[28]

That much of our online sharing is constructively involuntary renders many of the "it's already public" arguments moot. We have seen those arguments through this book. For example, a husband and wife could not object when a newspaper published a picture of them kissing because they were doing so in full view of all the patrons at a farmers' market.[29] And anyone who used a telephone could not object when the phone company handed over to the government the numbers we dial because that information was already disclosed.[30] Similarly, cardholders were not allowed to object when American Express shared customer purchasing histories and other information because that data had been freely handed over whenever they used their cards.[31] And air travelers who bought their tickets online could not object when their airline shared customer information outside the company. Those customers, the airline argued successfully, chose to use the Internet to buy their tickets and key in various pieces of data.[32] But what's the alternative? We cannot be expected to spend our entire lives indoors, off the phone, and without the Internet. Some amount of disclosure is a by-product of modern life. Much privacy law today does not reflect that.

Our initial disclosures in these and other cases are not the results of perfectly free choice. Most of them are the result of living in a world where networked technology is, as Durkheim would say, a social fact of modern life and, thus, a constraint on our behavior.[33] In other words, engaging with others and with businesses online is a necessary fact of our existence. As is, therefore, the data sharing that comes with it. Our choices within that world are not free. Justice Marshall, in a particularly powerful privacy dissent, captured the legal implication of this idea: "[i]mplicit in the concept of assumption of risk," the common law doctrine at the heart of the erosion of privacy interests in previously shared information,

> is some notion of choice . . . [U]nless a person is prepared to forgo use of what for many has become a personal or professional necessity, he cannot help but accept the risk of surveillance. It is idle to speak of "assuming" risks in contexts where, as a practical matter, individuals have no realistic alternative.[34]

Marshall was talking about the telephone, but if he were writing today, his words could equally, if not more so, apply to the Internet. Privacy law, therefore, must adapt to the necessity of disclosure in modern social, commercial, and professional life.

If sharing is often necessary and inevitable, the second principle of privacy-as-trust is what protects us from the risks inherent in disclosure:

> *Rather than a shield separating individuals and society, privacy is an element of social structure that facilitates sharing and social interaction by constraining the power of information holders.*

Efforts to maintain privacy are not just inward looking or defensive. Nor are they only about separating us from others. Sometimes, they are outward-looking social behaviors that help shape expectations and social norms.[35] Scott Skinner-Thompson gives the example of wearing a hoodie in public: A hoodie's ability to hide someone is marginal at best, but it is a powerful statement against the pervasive surveillance of modern life. Disclosures in contexts of trust are similar.[36] Although we cannot know for sure that our disclosures will be used in accordance with our expectations, we share based on trust, following and cementing norms along the way. This has a significant effect on privacy law's focus and its underlying purposes and perspectives. Whereas privacy law has been traditionally designed to protect individual freedom, privacy and information law under privacy-as-trust would focus on protecting and repairing relationships of trust. This means leveraging law to, among other things, protect disclosure contexts rather than just injured individuals, hold data collectors responsible for the information we send them, and permit the flow of information rather than stop it.

The legal scholars Neil Richards and Woodrow Hartzog have made a similar point. Lamenting privacy law's "pessimism problem," Richards and Hartzog note that our approach to privacy has been primarily about righting wrongs.[37] Warren and Brandeis, for example, developed the notion of a "right to be let alone" because they were worried that "instantaneous photography" would allow unprincipled journalists to pry into the private lives of others.[38] And the Federal Trade Commission, which protects consumer privacy based on its authority to stamp out unfair and deceptive trade practices, finds data use practices are unfair when they are "likely to cause substantial injury to consumers which is not reasonably avoidable by consumers themselves and not outweighed by countervailing benefits to consumers or to competition."[39] This, Richards and Hartzog argue, orients privacy law toward harms, invasions, and injuries.[40] They are correct. Privacy-as-trust would emphasize a further point – namely, that the injuries that have traditionally drawn privacy law's focus have been injuries to individuals and to an individual right that was meant to give individuals respite and freedom from society. But invasions of privacy are also injuries to the background structure of society that allows sharing to occur in the first place. Privacy-as-trust would orient the levers of law toward those injuries, as well.

This has powerful effects. As Cass Sunstein and others have argued, law serves multiple functions: it curtails activity directly by punishing unlawful behavior, and it indirectly signals appropriate behavior by expressing collective ideas about social morality.[41] Privacy law's traditional focus on injuries to the individual has limited its coercive effect: it only works when a person can prove individualized, specific, and, often, pecuniary harm. That is, after all, what the Supreme Court recently held in *Spokeo v. Robins*.[42] In that case, a man tried to sue the website Spokeo, which is like a search engine for information about individuals. Anyone who visits the website can type in a person's name, phone number, or email address, and Spokeo will conduct a broad search for any information associated with that data. When Robins found out that Spokeo was reporting incorrect information about him, causing him to worry for his privacy and resulting in significant psychological harm, he sued.[43] The question of whether what happened to Robins was enough to start a lawsuit – what lawyers call "standing" – went all the way up to the Supreme Court. There, the Court threw cold water on Robins's lawsuit. The justices found that because Robins had only identified "intangible" harm caused by Spokeo's publication of inaccurate information, he hadn't suffered sufficiently "concrete" injury.[44] This is particularly problematic for victims of data privacy invasions, who often experience intangible, psychological, and hard-to-quantify injuries as a result of some privacy intrusion.[45] *Spokeo*, therefore, may cut off many victims of data breaches and misuses of information from ever bringing cases in the first place, frustrating our need to hold data collectors accountable for their actions.

Privacy's focus on the individual has also limited its expressive effect. Privacy law's narrative is both narrow and radically individualistic. Because it operates only against direct injuries to individuals who want to be left alone, it is maligned as both ineffectual and an antisocial tool. This is why many people, from technology company executives to ordinary Internet users, feel that we "have no privacy anyway" and should "get over it."[46]

It is also why some scholars have come to criticize privacy. Amitai Etzioni has argued that public health and public safety sometimes come into conflict with strong privacy protections, like when so-called Megan's Laws require sex offenders to register with local authorities.[47] And, in that case, privacy should lose. Our desire to protect our children overrides the privacy rights compromised when someone who has paid his debts to society has to bear the cross of his conviction for the rest of his life.

Criticizing privacy from a different angle, Judge Richard A. Posner, a pre-eminent law and economics scholar, has argued that privacy laws allow people to conceal information about themselves in order "to mislead those with whom [we] interact[]."[48] To Posner, this creates inefficiencies, transaction costs, and injury. "At some point," he writes, "nondisclosure becomes fraud."[49] In other words, why should the law rightly prevent sellers from lying about the quality of their goods yet allow individuals to lie about who they are? As Posner notes, "people 'sell' themselves as well as their goods. They profess high standards of behavior in order to induce others to engage in social or business dealings with them from which they derive an advantage."[50] And the pioneering feminist scholar Catherine MacKinnon criticizes privacy as a weapon against women's equality. In particular, the vision of privacy underlying cases like *State v. Rhodes*,[51] which used the concept of "domestic privacy," or the privacy inherent in marriage, to allow a husband to beat his wife, meant that privacy was a tool of the status quo, a trap that reinforced entrenched hierarchies and power rather than protected individuals in need.[52] For MacKinnon, privacy was a right for "men to be left alone to oppress women" beyond the reach of the state.[53]

But even these powerful critiques still presume that privacy is about the individual's right to hide, conceal, or separate from society. Etzioni worries about the risks to children if recidivist sex offenders could hide their identities. Posner sees economic harm coming from concealment of data points on which we base our social, commercial, and professional decisions. And MacKinnon rightly notes that men could hide behind the pretext of marriage to protect themselves from laws against assault and battery.

Privacy-as-trust challenges this assumption by reorienting privacy law toward protecting, fostering, and repairing trust among individuals and between individuals and technology companies. Its coercive power would ensure that those who possess personal information about us treat that information in accordance with the expectations under which it was disclosed in the first place, thus constraining the "anything goes" power over our data. And its expressive power would highlight the social solidarity that emerges from taking trust seriously in society.

There is a third principle of privacy-as-trust, and it is a practical one. Recognizing that many disclosures – especially those online – are not purely voluntary and understanding that privacy is an element of social structure based on trust that rebalances the power relationships in disclosure contexts, judges, lawyers, and policymakers can then translate

privacy-as-trust into an administrable doctrine by identifying those disclosure contexts that manifest trust.

> Judges can identify disclosure contexts that are characterized by trust by looking
> to the experience of the parties, explicit and implicit social cues, reciprocity,
> and transference from knowns to unknowns.

These heuristics reflect the best social science evidence we have about our
propensity to disclose personal information and lend themselves easily to
policymaking and evidence in court.

Traditional privacy law has looked to underinclusive bright line rules to
determine the difference between public and private. As Daniel Solove argued
in his 2005 book, *The Digital Person*, too many of our privacy law decisions are
based on what he called a "secrecy paradigm," or the idea that only secret
information can be private.[54] Common law property principles have also
governed privacy decisions on the conventional, rights-based idea that ownership, the ability to exclude, and property lines define the limits of our privacy
interests.[55] And federal privacy policymaking reflects the privacy-as-autonomy
principle when it limits corporate privacy obligations to posting notices about
data use practices.

Privacy-as-trust rescues privacy and information law from these narrow
approaches. Learning the lessons of social approaches to privacy, privacy-as-
trust suggests that the legal protection of previously shared information
depends on whether the information was shared in contexts of trust. Trust is
empirically observable; that is, we know the social forces that contribute to
trust in disclosure contexts. Lawyers just need to look for them, not be scared
by the sometimes-ambiguous nature of social interaction, and get creative
when proving trust.

But this raises an important question: if privacy-as-trust is a contextual,
social way of understanding sharing and privacy invasions, what, then, does
it add to the conversation? How is it different from the other social theories of
privacy we discussed in Chapter 3? Privacy-as-trust makes three important
contributions. It is built from the ground up, based on empirical evidence
about how we share and the power dynamics at play. It is administrable,
allowing judges, lawyers, juries, privacy professionals, and even the public to
conceptualize and apply privacy in real life. And, it reflects our social values;
we need a society that more frequently, more expressly, and more effectively
values trust.

Privacy-as-trust takes the advice that Daniel Solove offered in
Conceptualizing Privacy, where he called for a ground-up approach to understanding privacy. Indeed, privacy-as-trust starts on the ground, based as it is on

empirical evidence of our social behavior. Scholars have shown that our propensity to disclose information online is influenced by contextual cues, from the behavior of others to design.[56] Underlying much of that research is particular social trust. And in Chapter 4, I discussed the results of a survey of online social network users that indicated that trust in others and trust in platforms are statistically significant factors in our decisions to share online. This held true for relatively personal or intimate information, as well. Undoubtedly, this research must be replicated, expanded, and continued; this project is by no means the final word on the relationship between trust and sharing. But that it is based on data, that it reflects a growing understanding of how we actually make privacy and disclosure decisions on the ground, makes it more capable to being deployed to answer modern privacy problems in the information disclosure context.

The ground-up approach of privacy-as-trust should be familiar to most of us, especially to lawyers. Similar power dynamics are at play in many disclosure contexts, including doctor–patient relationships and fiduciary–beneficiary arrangements. In these situations, disclosure is necessary. Trust norms, developed over time through a mixture of canons of ethics and common law duties of loyalty, mitigate disclosure risks and allow information sharers to feel less vulnerable. Privacy-as-trust learns these lessons because they hold true for disclosure contexts, generally.

That privacy-as-trust is data driven and reflects our behavior on the ground also means it comes with clearly defined guidelines that make it an administrable standard in information privacy contexts. Undoubtedly, any standard that tries to answer legal questions by looking at context is necessarily going to be more complicated than bright line rules like the secrecy paradigm or privacy-as-intimacy.[57] The simplicity and coherence of those approaches are part of what make them so attractive. But that simplicity masks razor sharp edges. Such rules are underinclusive, even in the narrow confines of voluntary sharing of personal information. We've seen this play out in countless cases that turn on the it's-already-public dogma.[58]

Context matters, and contexts play out differently in different cases. Privacy-as-trust attempts to take an otherwise boundless conversation about the social context of disclosure and distills the factors most likely associated with our propensity to share. If disclosures in contexts of trust are to remain legally protectable as private – and we have evidence that trust develops through experience, explicit and implicit social cues, reciprocity, and a transference from knowns to unknowns – then judges, juries, and lawyers have guidelines for how to litigate and adjudicate information privacy cases. Lawyers know what kind of evidence to gather, and fact-finders know what kind of evidence to evaluate. That is, they need not stop at formal agreements, confidentiality clauses, or explicit cues. Privacy-as-trust is more dynamic. Although it may require judges and juries to dive into contexts rather than rely on easy bright line rules, case-by-case litigation is uniquely suited to the task.

Finally, and perhaps most importantly, privacy-as-trust reflects an important social value.[59] Trust is, for lack of a better expression, a good thing, and one that can and should be fostered by law's expressive power.

Trust helps us deal with uncertainty and complexity by allowing us to rely on the advice of others.[60] There may be a hundred yoga studios from which to choose, but only one or two come with the recommendation of a 15-year yoga veteran. Trust allows us to take risks,[61] cooperate with others,[62] make decisions despite complexity,[63] and create order in chaos,[64] among so many other everyday functions. Trust also encourages therapeutic sharing by giving all individuals, from alcoholics and those suffering from depression to close friends, the confidence they need to disclose personal and perhaps stigmatizing information.[65] In these situations, the norms that we expect others to follow – confidentiality and discretion – are essential for creating the circumstances necessary for sharing in the first place.

Trust also has positive effects on society. Trust has been shown to contribute to economic success and effective civic engagement because it fosters teamwork and cooperation.[66] Organizations with a high level of trust are also more efficient and tend to outperform competitors.[67] That should make sense to anyone who has ever worked on a team. When coworkers understand that they can expect each other to behave according to accepted corporate norms – including, confidentiality with respect to corporate secrets, dedication to the company mission, and respect for achievement, among others – individuals are more likely to share new ideas, work hard, and give credit where credit is due.[68] The capacity to trust others to maintain those norms makes teams more effective. Trust is also a necessary condition for the development of social and political trust,[69] both of which are overwhelmingly positive forces in society. Trust is essential in a modern, heterogeneous society where social, economic, and political actors do not know each other.[70] It is the "bedrock of cooperation" and fosters economic prosperity.[71] It makes democratic institutions run better, more efficiently, and less corruptly.[72] It helps connect us to people different from us and encourages sharing and greater, more meaningful interaction.[73]

Trust is also essential to law. It is, after all, at the core of the general notion of confidentiality and the more specific doctrines of privilege. As the legal scholars Neil Richards and Woodrow Hartzog have noted, "perhaps the most basic assumption people make when disclosing personal information," whether to doctors, lovers, or Internet service providers, "is that the recipient will be discreet." They note that we trust doctors "not to reveal information about our health and mental state" and trust lovers "not to kiss and tell."[74] Richards and Hartzog's formulation of discretion, therefore, is based on trust, or the expectation that individuals will continue to behave according to accepted social norms. We expect doctors to keep our medical confidences and our lovers to keep our sexual confidence because doing so conforms to presiding norms. And, as a result, we share intimate details with them. Trust and confidential norms also justify privilege doctrines, including attorney–client, doctor–patient, and spousal privileges,[75] because such norms encourage the kind of full and frank disclosure necessary for effective counsel,[76] supportive care, and love.[77]

And we need to be more forthright about these normative benefits. Privacy today is losing out to values we understand as having great benefit to society, like free speech, national security, and law and order. We want individuals to understand how privacy benefits them and we want corporations to see how privacy is good for business. Privacy-as-trust highlights these normative benefits because it binds privacy to trust, an essential element of the good life. In so doing, privacy-as-trust makes privacy a more powerful rallying point in civic discourse.

The next and last part of this book illustrates what it would look like if the law did in fact reflect privacy-as-trust. By studying contrasting approaches to five current privacy and information law debates – including determining the legal relationship between consumers and data collectors, applying the privacy torts, online harassment, intellectual property, and social robots – I will illustrate how applying privacy-as-trust will more effectively protect our privacy in a world of extensive disclosures.

PART III

A TRUST-BASED APPROACH TO PRIVACY AND INFORMATION LAW

Privacy law today is, for the most part, structured around concepts of autonomy, choice, and individual rights. We discussed this in Chapters 1 and 2. Judges deny recovery even when data collectors misuse our information because we supposedly made the free and voluntary choice to share our data in the first place. Therefore, we assumed the risk that our information could be further disseminated and shared. Previously disclosed information is, in this view, no longer private. And on the assumption that we make rational privacy and disclosure decisions, federal and state privacy laws focus much of their energy on requiring data collectors to draft and publish privacy policies that list, in tortuous detail, the companies' data use practices. Were it not for the Federal Trade Commission's robust privacy enforcement, data collectors would have few, if any other, responsibilities with respect to our data after disclosure.

Privacy-as-trust recognizes that these ways of thinking about privacy are either outdated or just incomplete. Using trust as a benchmark for privacy would reorient privacy law away from a narrow focus on individual choice to a broader focus on the relationships that give rise to disclosure. In this part of the book, we will look at exactly what that means. Privacy law is a multifaceted animal; it is, among others things, a collection of common law responsibilities, court decisions, federal and states statutes, and regulatory enforcement actions that manages the rights and responsibilities of citizens and data collectors alike. The next five chapters use five different case studies to tease out some of the effects of privacy-as-trust on various facets of privacy and information law. Although privacy-as-trust may not change the result of every case or change every regulation, the collective result of approaching privacy law as a protector of trusted relationships is to more effectively protect privacy in an information age where data sharing is inevitable, ongoing, and extensive.

Each chapter is structured to illustrate the contrast between traditional approaches to privacy and a current legal regime, on the one hand, with privacy-as-trust and its legal implications, on the other. Chapter 6 looks at the legal rules governing our relationships with companies that collect our data and use complex, opaque algorithms to control what we see online. This chapter argues that privacy-as-trust, contrary to traditional understandings of privacy, explains why predictive analytics based on "big data" are, at their core, privacy invasions. Based on the work of Jack Balkin and others, this chapter proposes treating some data collectors as fiduciaries of our information as a way to solve the privacy dangers of obscure, black box artificial intelligence. Chapter 7 moves from macro to micro, showing how privacy-as-trust would be able to protect as private some previously disclosed information. Chapter 8 considers the problem of cyberharassment, using the case study of nonconsensual pornography, also known as "revenge porn," to show how privacy-as-trust would empower the tort of breach of confidentiality help victims find redress. Chapter 9 steps outside the privacy context to information flow problems in intellectual property. This discussion suggests that as a doctrine of how data is shared, privacy-as-trust can better protect the rights of traditionally marginalized inventors and creators. Finally, Chapter 10 looks to the future. Here, I argue that privacy-as-trust is best suited to understand the privacy dangers inherent in social robots, or robots with humanlike qualities that are meant to trigger basic human needs for connection, socialization, and love.

6

The Responsibilities of Data Collectors

Companies that collect, aggregate, analyze, and share our information have considerable power over us. But, under current law, their responsibilities are minimal. That is because our relationship to data collectors is based on principles of privacy-as-autonomy. Although the rules vary to some extent by industry,[1] the general approach is the same: on the theory that we have the right to decide for ourselves how and when to disclose our information, data collectors are required to provide us with little more than a comprehensive list of their data use practices and the opportunity to consent to data collection or use another platform. This regime is called "notice-and-choice," and it is woefully inadequate.

Under privacy-as-trust, however, websites would have more significant obligations to their users. Notice-and-choice hinges data collection on notice. Privacy-as-trust hinges it on trust. There is precedent for this. Doctors, investment managers, and estate executors have control over our health, money, and futures much like websites have control over our information and digital lives. Therefore, just like the law of fiduciaries gives experts power over us only if they act with our best interests in mind, and holds their feet to the fire when they don't, privacy-as-trust would requires what Yale Law School Professor Jack Balkin has termed "information fiduciaries" like Google, Facebook, and other companies to do the same.[2]

In this chapter, I lay out the contrast between platform obligations that end with notice-and-choice and those more extensive duties of information fiduciaries as two very different ways of structuring our legal relationships with Internet and technology companies. The former, based on traditional privacy principles, is ill suited to protect our data in a world in which our online experiences are almost entirely determined and constrained by algorithmic design. The latter, based on privacy-as-trust, would account for the power asymmetries caused by disclosure and give us the confidence to engage with technology knowing our interests are protected.

NOTICE-AND-CHOICE

As a governing legal regime, notice-and-choice is self-explanatory. Companies that collect our data are supposed to tell us what information they collect, how and for what purpose they collect it, and with whom they share it. That's the notice part. We then have the opportunity to opt out.[3] That, or the option to use another platform, is the choice. Once we give our consent based on that notice, data collectors can use our data in accordance with their privacy policies.

Notice-and-choice comes from the Fair Information Practices Principles (FIPPs) that developed out of a 1973 report from the federal Department of Housing, Education, and Welfare (HEW).[4] The report recommended that any government agency collecting information from citizens should have to publicize its data use practices, give everyone the opportunity to correct their data, and seek individuals' consent for any secondary uses of their information.[5] The Federal Trade Commission (FTC) took these recommendations to heart and urged Congress to require commercial websites to disclose a similar what-when-how of user data.[6] In so doing, the FTC identified "notice" as the most important FIPP and elevated the privacy policy, a statement of a company's data use practices, into the operative legal document outlining the extent of a data collector's duties to its users.

Unlike in the European Union or Canada, there is no comprehensive nationwide privacy protection law in the United States.[7] Notice-and-choice was codified into American law through a series of federal and state data privacy laws.[8] Federal data privacy protection in the United States is "sectoral," or limited to specific types of information. For example, the Health Information Portability and Accountability Act (HIPAA) helps protect the privacy of some medical information,[9] and the Gramm-Leach-Bliley Act gives individuals notice and some control over information held by certain financial institutions.[10] HIPAA and Gramm-Leach-Bliley, along with the Children's Online Privacy Protection Act (COPPA)[11] and other statutes, are among the many federal laws that, like the FIPPs on which they are based,[12] pay most of their attention to requiring data collectors to provide us with notice and choice.[13]

COPPA, for example, which guards against unauthorized use, collection, and dissemination of information of children 13-years-old and younger,[14] requires certain child-oriented websites to disclose what data they collect, whether it is obtained actively or passively, how it will be used, whether it will be shared with others, and how to delete data or opt out of collection.[15] The Gramm-Leach-Bliley Act requires certain financial institutions to explain their data collection and use practices to their customers. They must state what information is collected, the names of affiliated and outside third parties with whom information is shared, which data is shared with them, and how to opt out.[16]

HIPAA is even more specific in its content requirements. All HIPAA notices must have the same introductory sentence, informing readers of the purposes of the policy. They must also disclose what information is collected and how it will be used, patients' rights with respect to their data, how the health-care company will protect their data, and whom to contact for further information.[17] As with COPPA and Gramm-Leach-Bliley, HIPAA's primary regulatory focus with respect to data collectors is to require them to provide us with notice of data use practices.

State laws also regulate online intermediaries, protect personal information, and require companies to inform users of their data use practices. State attorneys general have issued guidance documents, pressured Internet companies, and initiated privacy enforcement litigation to enhance user notice and choice, as well.[18] California's Online Privacy Protection Act (CalOPPA), for example, is a groundbreaking law that requires commercial websites and other online service operators that collect information about California residents to provide us with notice of data use practices and to comply with those notices.[19] Like COPPA, Gramm-Leach-Bliley, and HIPAA, CalOPPA requires companies to disclosure what information is collected, with whom it may be shared, how the data will be used, and how individuals will be notified about policy changes.[20] A similar focus can be found in the state's "Shine the Light" law. This law, passed shortly after CalOPPA, requires businesses that have disclosed personal information about California residents to third parties for marketing purposes within the last year to disclose their data use and information sharing practices.[21]

Other states have followed California's lead. In New York, the Internet Security and Privacy Act requires state agencies to create, adopt, and display a data use notice on their websites.[22] Once again, the statute requires a what-when-how of data use practices: the policy must disclose what and under what circumstances information is being collected, whether the information will be retained by the state, how the data is gathered (actively or passively), the voluntariness of collection, how users can go about gaining access to their information, and what steps the state is taking to secure the data.[23] Connecticut and Michigan have laws requiring similar disclosures of any person or entity that collects Social Security numbers in the course of business.[24] In Utah, the state's Government Internet Information Privacy Act mandates notice before any government agency can collect citizens' data.[25]

And Delaware's Online Privacy and Protection Act requires the same what-when-how disclosures of CalOPPA.[26]

Privacy policies are the primary manifestations of notice-and-choice. And the Federal Trade Commission enforces those privacy policies as setting out corporate data privacy obligations.[27] Although the FTC has since developed an expansive privacy jurisprudence that is effectively the "law of the land for businesses that deal in personal information,"[28] many of its enforcement actions focus on companies that fail to provide adequate notice of their data use practices. This is evident both in the FTC's complaints and its settlements. At both ends, the lion's share of the FTC's focus has been on enshrining notice as the law governing the relationship between users and data collectors.

For example, the FTC brings these "broken promises" actions when a company says one thing – "Personal information voluntarily submitted by visitors to our site ... is never shared with a third party"[29] – and does the opposite. In *Eli Lilly & Co.*, for example, the FTC alleged that the company violated its privacy policy when it sent out an email to nearly 700 people that disclosed personal information from customers who used the website Prozac.com.[30] The company's privacy policy had promised "security measures" that would protect consumers' confidential information.[31] Since no such security measures had been in place, the company had broken its promise. The FTC has also moved against companies that have promised yet failed to protect the confidentiality of their users' data,[32] to collect only certain types of data,[33] to put in place adequate security safeguards,[34] and to maintain user anonymity,[35] just to name a few examples. Broken promise litigation, which, by its very nature, is about ensuring adequate notice, remains a significant share of the FTC's overall privacy enforcement actions.[36]

The second way the FTC codified notice-and-choice was by requiring companies to make specific notice disclosures as part of its settlement orders. In its first privacy enforcement action, the FTC alleged that GeoCities sold its customers' personal information in express violation of its privacy policy.[37] As part of a settlement, the FTC ordered the company to comply with the notice-and-choice regime by disclosing the what-when-how of data use: what information it collected, why it did so, to whom the information would be sold, and how customers could access their information and opt out.[38] The FTC has continued this laser focus on notice in its more recent privacy enforcement actions as well. In *In re Frostwire, LLC*, for example, the FTC alleged that the company, which developed peer-to-peer file-sharing software, misled customers into thinking that certain files would not be publicly accessible on the peer-to-peer network. Frostwire also failed to adequately disclose how the software actually worked.[39] And in *In re Sony BMG Music*

Entertainment, the FTC alleged that Sony failed to inform customers that the software it installed on certain CDs would transmit music-listening data back to Sony.[40] The FTC settled both cases. In each settlement, the FTC ordered Frostwire and Sony to make specific what-when-how disclosures to its customers.[41] Each time, the FTC focused its regulatory muscle on effectuating notice-and-choice through detailed, comprehensive privacy policies.

As Daniel Solove and Woodrow Hartzog found, almost all FTC enforcement actions settle. And they settle with some common recurring elements, including, in particular, requirements that the company notify its customers of its wrongdoing, make substantive changes or additions to privacy policies, and establish a comprehensive privacy and data security program and inform users about it.[42] Once again, the legal obligations of companies that collect our information are often limited to providing notice of their data use practices.

Notice-and-choice makes sense as the limits of platform responsibility if we understand privacy through a lens of autonomy and choice. We discussed this in Chapter 2. Notice-and-choice is, at its core, a doctrine of informed consent premised on autonomous decision-making: provide us with all the information we need in a privacy policy and allow us the freedom to make our own informed decisions. If companies disclose the details of their data use practices, the argument goes, our consent to share our information will be a rational exercise of our power to control our information.[43]

CRITIQUES OF NOTICE-AND-CHOICE

But notice-and-choice doesn't work. Critiques of the sectoral and notice-and-choice approaches to data privacy focus on its underlying theory, substance, and effects in practice. As a theoretical matter, the notion of the autonomous user is a myth,[44] a relic of an earlier time when idealists and cyberlibertarians[45] like John Perry Barlow called the Internet "a world where anyone, anywhere may express his or her beliefs, no matter how singular, without fear of being coerced into silence or conformity."[46] The *New Yorker* expressed this point in one of its famous cartoons. A dog, sitting at a computer desk, looks down at his doggy friend on the floor and says, "On the Internet, nobody knows you're a dog."[47] That, of course, is just not true. Our entire online lives are not only mediated by the platforms through which we access information, but those platforms know quite a bit about us. Their artificial intelligence tools and algorithms determine much of our online experiences, from the search results we see to the advertisements and sales we're offered.

And, as we discussed in Chapter 5, we do not make perfectly rational disclosure decisions.[48] The law of notice-and-choice ignores our embodied experience and the contextual nature of privacy expectations.[49] What's more, notice-and-choice is meaningless in a world of ongoing data collection. As several chief privacy officers have said, concepts like "notice" and "consent" play "limited role[s]" in the ways their companies approach privacy questions because users cannot be expected to continuously evaluate their disclosure preferences over time.[50]

Notice-and-choice is also hopelessly underinclusive. It reflects an arbitrary and selective approach to the FIPPs, which also included limitations on data collection, security requirements, a rejection of black boxes, user rights to data, and robust accountability policies.[51] There are administrative critiques, as well: it is difficult for companies to comply with a patchwork of laws, including the innumerable state laws governing data privacy, that apply to some information in the hands of some entities some of the time.

Privacy policies are inadequate, as well. They are confusing,[52] inconspicuous,[53] and inscrutable.[54] They are also ineffective: no one reads privacy policies,[55] in part because they are long[56] and difficult to understand.[57] Even experts find them misleading.[58] Many of them are single-spaced, written in small font sizes, and hard-to-distinguish whites, grays, and blacks.[59] Lorrie Faith Cranor, a computer science, engineering, and public policy scholar at Carnegie Mellon University, estimates that it would take a user an average of 244 hours per year to read the privacy policy of every website she visited.[60] This translates to about 54 billion hours per year for every U.S. consumer to read all the privacy policies he or she encountered.[61]

And, as a practical matter, privacy policies provide little protection. They can be changed on a whim and at least one court has held that because most of us do not read privacy policies, they cannot represent a "meeting of the minds" and, therefore, are not valid, binding contracts that hold companies to specific obligations. Privacy policies are so unhelpful that some scholars argue that we should instead rely on visceral forms of notice[62] or a website's user-controlled privacy settings to set platform privacy obligations.[63]

Finally, notice-and-choice inadequately protects users against the privacy harms associated with big data, algorithmic targeting, and predictive analytics. This is true for two reasons. First, so-called big data algorithms are built to create their own personally identifiable information,[64] the collection and use of which cannot, by definition, be disclosed in a privacy policy. Consider the Target example. Target combined information directly provided by customers with data automatically generated from use of the Target website, social media information, and data available from third parties to generate information – in this case, pregnancy status – about some of its customers. But because that predicted information was generated through a math equation as opposed to gathered from some online source, it is not listed in Target's privacy notice.[65] Second, the algorithms companies use to tailor, mediate, and constrain our online experiences are opaque. We don't know how Target generated its list of pregnant customers. Nor do we know how Google ranks its search results, how Facebook orders its News Feed, or how credit bureaus determine our credit scores.[66] These algorithms are either jealously guarded[67] or protected by the law of trade secrets.[68] As such, adequate notice of the ways in which predictive analytics use our information is impossible.

A TRUST-BASED APPROACH

Proposals to improve notice – with clearer and simpler writing, more pleasing designs, and broader context beyond a privacy policy – operate within the current notice-and-choice framework. They thrust upon us all the responsibilities for maintaining our privacy, and they retain the autonomy-based idea that privacy means little more than the freedom to decide for ourselves when to disclose our personal information and that, once disclosed, information is no longer subject to privacy protection. Alone, these ideas fail to protect vulnerable users in the face of powerful data collectors. Privacy-as-trust goes further. Rather than limiting corporate responsibility to giving us a list of data use practices for rational privacy decision-making, privacy-as-trust recognizes that data collectors are being entrusted with our information. Therefore, they should be held to a higher standard than mere notice. They are, in fact, fiduciaries with respect to our data, and should be obligated to act in a trustworthy manner. This argument, developed most recently and comprehensively by Jack Balkin, follows directly from reorienting privacy law toward relationships of trust.

Fiduciary law is a common law construct, which means that judges developed it over time to respond to changing realities on the ground. Where contract law sets out the obligations of parties formally bound in voluntary agreements and where tort law establishes the background rules of social interaction, fiduciary law focuses on a few special relationships that are based on trust and confidence. In short, a fiduciary has special obligations of loyalty and trustworthiness. A client puts his trust in a fiduciary, and the fiduciary has an obligation not to betray that trust. She must act in her client's interests, not in a way that harms him.[69] Estate managers, investment advisers, lawyers, and doctors are classic examples of fiduciaries: they handle their clients' money, secrets, and livelihoods under duties of loyalty and care.[70]

As Balkin explains, fiduciary duties are "duties of trust." Even the word "fiduciary" comes from the Latin word for "trust." And, as I argued in Chapter 5, "trust and confidence are centrally concerned with the collection, analysis, use, and disclosure of information."[71] Therefore, those that handle our personal information, whether a doctor, lawyer, or an online social network, have "special duties with respect" to our information. These parties are "information fiduciaries."[72] Several other leading privacy law scholars agree. In *The Digital Person*, Daniel Solove argues that businesses that are collecting personal information from us should "stand in a fiduciary relationship with us."[73] The law professor Danielle Keats Citron also suggests that a fiduciary relationship between data brokers and users would help fight the massive power imbalance online.[74]

All fiduciary relationships have two overarching similarities – namely, asymmetry and vulnerability. Doctors, lawyers, and investment managers have special skills that their clients do not. As much as we might fear hospitals, we can neither diagnose nor perform surgery on ourselves. Instead, we rely on physicians to perform these tasks. We also lack the ability to effectively monitor or evaluate our doctors' job performances. Because of these asymmetries, we are in a position of vulnerability vis-à-vis our fiduciaries. We put our information, our money, our health, and our fate in their hands.[75]

Companies like Facebook, Google, Uber, and Match.com should be considered information fiduciaries for the same reasons that doctors, estate managers, and investment analysts are considered fiduciaries. First, our relationship to these companies "involve[s] significant vulnerability."[76] Traditional fiduciaries have special skills unavailable to their clients, just like many Internet and technology companies. They know everything about us; trade secrecy keeps their algorithms hidden from us. They monitor every step we take online; we know little about how they process our information. Second, we are absolutely dependent on these companies. We cannot engage in modern life without the Internet, and our movements online are tracked as a matter of course.[77] Third, many Internet companies market themselves as experts in what they do: Facebook is the best and largest social connector,[78] Match.com calls itself "#1 in dates, relationships, and marriages,"[79] and Google is the dominant search engine and primary avenue to the World Wide Web for most Internet users.[80] And, fourth, these companies hold themselves out as trustworthy. As Kenneth Bamberger and Deirdre Mulligan find in their groundbreaking research on privacy professionals, many leading chief privacy officers around the world feel that corporate privacy strategy is about maintaining user trust and being sufficiently flexible, adaptive, and forward looking to meet consumer expectations whatever they may be.[81] It is not about doing the least they could to prevent a lawsuit. Rather, they must engage in ongoing management of risk and keep up with consumers' changing expectations.[82] Several CPOs talked about their jobs in fiduciary terms: they were "steward[s]" of data and "responsibl[e]" to consumers.[83] In short, several privacy leads saw their primary objective as creating and maintaining "the company's trusted relationship" with customers, employees, and society.[84]

Given this asymmetrical relationship, posting an obscure, inscrutable, and vague privacy policy is not enough to meet the fiduciary duties of care and loyalty. On top of the duty to inform, Balkin and the cyberlaw scholar Jonathan Zittrain propose "to adapt old legal ideas to create a new kind of law – one that clearly states the kinds of duties that online firms owe their end users and customers." The most basic of those duties is to "look out for the interests of the people whose data businesses regularly harvest and profit from." In other words, information fiduciaries should never act like "con men," inducing trust and then actively working against their users' interests. Balkin and Zittrain give the perfect example: Google Maps should not hold itself out as providing the "best" or "fastest" route from Logan International Airport to the Westin Copley and then deliver a route that drives passes an IHOP simply because IHOP paid Google $20.[85] Even if it never explicitly promised to offer users the fastest route on Google Maps, Google and other information fiduciaries should be held accountable when they induce trust in any way and then break it.

Balkin and Zittrain add several other obligations on top of not acting like con men. Companies "would agree to a set of fair information practices, including security and privacy guarantees, and disclosure of breaches. They would promise not to leverage personal data to unfairly discriminate against or abuse the trust of end users." And here's the kicker: "[a]nd they would not sell or distribute consumer information except to those who agreed to similar rules."[86] Or, as Balkin writes, "[w]hat information fiduciaries may not do is use the data in unexpected ways to the disadvantage of people who use their services or in ways that violate some other important social norm." This is the essence of privacy-as-trust. As we discussed in Chapter 5, trust is a resource of social capital between two or more parties concerning the expectations that others will behave according to accepted norms.[87] We share information with others, including online data collectors, with the expectation that those companies will treat our data according to prevailing norms and promises. We experience the further sale or dissemination of our data to unknown third parties as violations of our privacy precisely because such dissemination breaches the trust that allowed us to share in the first place. We know nothing about those third parties, particularly their data use practices. Under the law of information fiduciaries, online data collectors would not be allowed to share the data they collect with third parties that do not comply with the same data privacy obligations.

APPLYING INFORMATION FIDUCIARY OBLIGATIONS IN PRACTICE

Changing the relationship between data collectors and users from the law of notice-and-choice to the law of information fiduciaries is a direct result of thinking and talking about privacy as protecting relationships of trust rather than as the liberty to separate and exclude others. Balkin and Zittrain propose a "grand bargain" whereby online data collectors would agree to take on the responsibilities of information fiduciaries in exchange for a federal statute that would preempt a wide range of state and federal privacy laws.[88] Such a proposal would have a significant effect on data privacy law in the United States, limiting what Internet companies could do with our data. It would also have a powerful expressive effect. If the law started treating data collectors as our trustees, as acting in our best interests rather than theirs, the prevailing norms under which we use the Internet and share information online would change. We would use our credit cards knowing that our purchasing histories would not be abused. We would share our personal sexual desires with dating websites in a safe space. We would state our opinions without fearing that a platform would tolerate harassment. And we would download mobile apps knowing they would not tap into our microphones and cameras to listen and watch us wherever we go.

There are other implications, as well. As Balkin and Zittrain argue, a primary result of treating some data collectors as information fiduciaries means that they cannot induce trust among us and then use it against our interests. But that is exactly what many online platforms do now. Snapchat is a perfect example.[89] Snapchat, the ephemeral messaging service, held itself out as a privacy-protective platform. It induced trust among its core base of millennial users by marketing the idea that any image or video, or "snap," sent across the platforms would automatically disappear after several seconds. Before sending a snap, users were shown a screen that required them to designate the amount of time the snap will survive before disappearing. Snaps could not be sent without selecting an option. But, in fact, there were several ways snaps sent, could be saved, downloaded, or copied. This gave users a false sense of trust, reinforced in the platform's product descriptions and Frequently Asked Questions, that they actually had control over what their recipients could do with their snaps.

Behind the user interface, furthermore, Snapchat's original design also compromised privacy. Until October 2013, it stored all videos in unprotected spaces on users' phones, which allowed recipients to simply search for and download a video they wanted to save. Snapchat also allowed any third party application to access its application programming interface and download or copy videos and images.[90] Not only were these vulnerabilities not conveyed to users, but the platform's design created contrary expectations. The FTC initiated an enforcement action against Snapchat based primarily on the contrast between Snapchat's promises and the reality of its design. But the Snapchat case is a perfect of example of what "no con men" litigation could look like under privacy-as-trust even without the misleading privacy statement.

The FTC would be emboldened by privacy-as-trust. As Solove and Hartzog have argued, the FTC has already developed a robust and diverse privacy jurisprudence.[91] Privacy-as-trust would give the agency a doctrinal foundation for including inducement of misplaced trust as a "deceptive business practice" under Section 5 of the FTC Act, allowing it to step in where platforms leverage their design to induce trust and then act against their members' interests. Indeed, the FTC already has a long track record of regulating deceptive practices that are similar to inducing trust. It has challenged deceptive product demonstrations that present products as better than they actually are,[92] the inducement of customer disclosures through pretextual or deceptive phone calls,[93] and the collection data via deceit,[94] among many other examples. Understanding privacy as protecting relationships of trust between consumers and the websites we use would allow the FTC to cement and grow this jurisprudence.

Here is another example. Facebook designs its platform to build its users' trust so we will share with each other, or as the law and technology scholar James Grimmelmann has argued, to "scratch its users' social itches."[95] If privacy-as-trust animates our privacy jurisprudence, then Facebook should not be allowed to build our trust and then use it against us. That, however, is exactly what Facebook does.

Facebook designs in several elements that induce trust and encourage sharing. It lets us craft and maintain public profiles, which allow us to articulate a particular message about who we are. It also lets us join affinity groups and causes and publicizes what we post on others' Timelines. Facebook deepens our connections to friends and helps establish new ones: we add people as contacts or "friends," send notes or messages or pictures of birthday cakes with our friends' names on them, and "tag" people in our own content.[96] And it does all of this publicly to encourage reciprocal sharing.

Facebook also helps us find community and establishes our value in that community. We add connections, make comments, and share our passions because doing so helps us find other, similarly situated potential friends and mates. And adding connections increases our social capital.[97]

Facebook also leverages trust, thereby encouraging us to share, by telling us what our friends are up to. When we join, it tells us who else has joined and lets us invite friendly faces along with us. When we seek to join affinity groups or causes, those pages immediately tell us who among our friends are also members of the community. When we log on, our friends' likes, viewpoints, and interests are on the home page, visible to us by a default organizational algorithm that privileges the social interactions of those closest to us. When we receive friend requests from another Facebook user, the number of friends we have in common appears immediately below the user's name. Hovering over the number tells us our mutual friends, or who sits in both networks. This information gives us clues as to the requester's trustworthiness, allowing us to transfer the trust we have in our friends to an unknown, which is particularly important for someone we have never met offline.[98]

In a series of updates from April 2015, through July 2016, Facebook stepped up its strategy of leveraging trust to encourage us to share. More specifically, the News Feed algorithm was tweaked to give greater preference to posts and interactions from friends and family, pushing them to the top.[99] Facebook sold this change as a way to realize the platform's founding "idea of connecting people with their friends and family" and to keep us "connected to the people, places and things [we] want to be connected to."[100] That may be true, but no Facebook design change can be understood independent of the platform's insatiable appetite for user data. Privileging the posts of friends and family over the posts of third-party publishers themselves may limit the reach of a naked post from Vocativ or Upworthy, but not when one of their videos is shared by a friend. That is ideal for Facebook for two reasons. First, users tend to dislike seeing posts from third parties; second, under the new design, most third-party content that users see will come through their trusted social networks of friends. This cues the trustworthiness of the post far better than any naked post from a publisher ever could.

Member posts from inside and outside our networks notify us if a friend has recently added a comment – "Lisa Simpson replied to a comment on this post" – or is simply mentioned in the post – "Charlie Brown and Peppermint Patty were mentioned in a post." Furthermore, rather than just listing the number of "likes" for a given post, Facebook tells us that "Abbi Jacobson, Ilana Glazer and 76 others like this." When none of our friends have liked a post, the note reads, "9 people like this." After an update to its design in July 2016,

Instagram does this, too. This design strategy, when applied to social posts, helps grease the wheels of social interaction by indicating that the post is real, engaging, and trustworthy.

When applied to native advertisements, or third-party links that are designed to look like social posts, however, this tactic violates privacy-as-trust's "no con men" principle. Facebook is inducing trust among its users and then manipulating us into clicking on a third party's post even when doing so makes us vulnerable to weaker or nonexistent privacy protections. Like social posts, these advertisements are often preceded by the names of our friends who have "liked" the advertiser's page. For example, a statement like "Clara Oswald, Sarah Jane Smith, Martha Jones and 7 others like JCrew," might appear at the top of a J.Crew advertisement about the new spring line. And "Alice, Barry, Catherine, and 22 others like Adidas" may appear above an advertisement for the newest Adidas running shoe. The information about our friends, not the advertisement, is the first thing we see. The only thing that distinguishes these advertisements from our friends' social posts is the word "Sponsored," written in light gray text under the name of the company and sandwiched between the advertisement's much larger graphic content and Facebook's bolded trust cue. And Facebook has a significant, financial interest in inducing us to put our trust in these third parties, even though that trust might be misplaced: the more clicks native advertisements earn from targeted users, the more Facebook can charge for News Feed real estate.

These tactics violate the responsibilities of information fiduciaries. If they are accurate portrayals of our friends' behavior, Facebook's notifications on social posts can cue trust and help us keep on top of social interaction. But when used to obscure the difference between social and commercial posts and between social interaction and endorsement, exploiting the trust-sharing link can be deceitful and coercive. Given that Facebook's interest in inducing us to click on its advertisers' posts potentially conflicts with prevailing privacy norms and the asymmetry of power between us and Facebook, Facebook is in a position to take advantage. It exploits the relationship between particular social trust and the propensity to share – just like we are more likely to accept a friend request from someone with whom we share mutual friends, we are more likely to click on a link that our friends, especially our close friends, have also clicked – to induce our trust in the name of profit.

The FTC's jurisprudence under privacy-as-trust could regulate this in any number ways. It could ban native advertisements, but that's heavy-handed, may have some unintended negative effects, and, in any event, is unlikely to happen. The FTC could also take Balkin's advice and find a compromise. Information fiduciaries must be able to collect and earn money from our data:

"[i]t cannot be the case that the basic business model of free or subsidized online services inherently violates fiduciary obligations." At the same time, we are entitled to online platforms that do not "abuse [our] ability to collect and use personal information for profit." This means that social networks should not manipulate us into voting for a particular candidate or GPS apps should not take us the long way around just to make a profit.[101]

With respect to Facebook's use of trust cues on social posts and native advertisements, the FTC could require a simple design change to make the News Feed more transparent about native advertising. It could restrict Facebook from using social trust cues on advertisements, thereby retaining Facebook's business model without manipulating trust. Or, the FTC could require more distinguishing designs. The word "sponsored," which is confusing to many users,[102] should be larger and more obvious, not obscured by a light-colored font and other, richer content. The Associated Press mobile application is a good model. Standard news articles on the interface are in white text on a black background. A picture associated with the article is on the right; the headline is on the left. Sponsored posts not only reverse the position of the picture and headline, they are also prefaced by a bright yellow bar that reads "Paid for by . . . ." The added transparency eliminates the misleading elements that could induce misplaced trust.

The FTC has already developed a robust privacy jurisprudence. As Daniel Solove and Woodrow Hartzog point out, the agency's unfair or deceptive practices litigation is broad, including, for example, inducing Internet users to share personal information.[103] Manipulating trust to induce sharing and then working against the interests of users would, therefore, fit neatly within the FTC's authority and expand privacy protections for users of data hungry platforms and products.

7

Previously Disclosed Information

In the last chapter, we saw how privacy-as-trust would create new responsibilities for companies that collect, analyze, and use our data. We share information with these companies in relationships of trust and confidence. They hold themselves out as trustworthy. They know a lot about us, but we know very little about them. We are vulnerable to their actions. And we lack the ability to monitor their behavior. Therefore, if we think about privacy through the lens of privacy-as-trust, we would consider these companies information fiduciaries, and they should be prohibited from acting against our interests. We also discussed how the fiduciary obligation to not induce and then abuse trust would fit well within the Federal Trade Commission's "unfair and deceptive" jurisprudence, allowing it to regulate companies that design their platforms to unscrupulously profit off our manipulated disclosures to advertisers.

At the heart of privacy-as-trust and information fiduciaries is the notion, discussed in Chapter 5, that information shared in contexts of trust can still be considered private. Chapter 6 showed how current federal and state laws governing our relationship to data collectors have made that impossible. Current privacy tort law, which helps regulate interactions between private parties, has the same problem. In his article, "A Social Networks Theory of Privacy," the legal scholar Lior Strahilevitz addressed this head on. He argued that analyzing questions of information flow through the lens of network theory could help maintain what he called "limited privacy," or privacy in previously disclosed information.[1] Jumping off Strahilevitz's work, this chapter shows how privacy-as-trust would change the way we determine the difference between public and private information for the purposes of tort law – from the secrecy paradigm to protecting relationships of trust.

THE FOUR PRIVACY TORTS

Before 1890, there were only 27 federal cases that even mentioned the word "privacy," and they ranged from libel (2), search and seizure (5), polygamy/sex (1), property (6), fraud and contracts (4), evidence and testimony (4), bankruptcy (1), intellectual property (1), drugs (1), and even boats (2).[2] Understandably, there were more cases out of the various state courts before 1890. Not only did most American law originate and get resolved at the state level before 1900, but the common law tort claims associated with privacy had always been the exclusive purview of the states. However, most of these state courts declined to recognize explicit claims about invasions of privacy. State courts recognized and issued 42 opinions in cases that raised claims about trespass and libel/slander before 1890, but dismissed every claim (7) for an explicit "invasion of privacy."[3]

Samuel Warren and Louis Brandeis changed that. In their groundbreaking article "The Right to Privacy," they argue that the common law of torts could be used to protect personal privacy. By "common law," Warren and Brandeis were referring to the ever-evolving judge-made law at the heart of the Anglo-American legal tradition. In particular, they argued that because the common law of torts had already evolved from providing only narrow protection against physical harm to redressing emotional and psychological injuries, tort law was the natural weapon to protect individuals from the intangible harms associated with invasions of privacy. The catalysts for their article were unscrupulous newspapers and nosy photographers publishing personal details about private individuals. They called this common law doctrine "a right to be let alone."[4]

Slowly, the common law did evolve to protect Warren and Brandeis's right to privacy. Two cases are illustrative. In 1902, New York's highest court was faced with the case of Abigail Roberson, a teenager who sued the Franklin Mills Flour company for "invasion of privacy" for using her likeness on thousands of advertising flyers without her consent. Roberson claimed that the use of her image caused her humiliation and injury, but the New York Court of Appeals could find no precedent for bringing a privacy action in Anglo-American common law.[5] The decision inspired unprecedented criticism: the *New York Times* published five pieces on the decision in the weeks that followed, including several critical letters to the editor, and the backlash was so sharp that one of the judges in the *Roberson* majority felt compelled to justify his decision in the pages of the *Columbia Law Review*.[6] One year later, the New York legislature became the first to create a tort for invasion of privacy when it passed Section 51 of the New York Civil Rights Law.[7]

In the similar case of *Pavesich v. New England Life Insurance Company*, the Georgia Supreme Court followed Warren's and Brandeis's advice and updated state common law to fashion a remedy for a victim of invasion of privacy. In *Pavesich*, an insurance company's newspaper advertisement included a photograph of the plaintiff that was used without consent. The plaintiff sued, alleging an invasion of privacy, a claim, the Georgia Supreme Court said, that "derived from natural law." The court held that, subject to certain limitations, "the body of a person cannot be put on exhibition at any time or at any place without his consent . . . It therefore follows . . . that a violation of the right of privacy is a direct invasion of a [long-standing] legal right of the individual."[8] That is exactly what Warren and Brandeis argued. Over the next 30 years, state common law slowly evolved to follow *Pavesich*. By 1939, § 867 of the First Restatement of Torts included an individual right to privacy: "[a] person who unreasonably and seriously interferes with another's interest in not having his affairs known to others . . . is liable to the other." By the next decade, 14 states and the District of Columbia recognized at least one privacy tort with similar language.[9]

Years later, the legal scholar William Prosser would survey the development of privacy tort law and identify four "privacy torts" that victims of invasions of privacy had been using since 1890 to obtain justice: intrusion upon seclusion (for when a photographer pushes his camera in your face or takes pictures through your window), public disclosure of private facts (for when he publishes a photo of you undressing), false light (for when the published photograph depicts you as depraved), and appropriation (for when he uses a photograph of you to advertise his photography services).

As the privacy law theorists Neil Richards and Daniel Solove have shown, Prosser's work puts American privacy law on a particular path that suited Prosser's – and Warren's and Brandeis's – governing theory that the right to privacy was a tool to keep others out.[10] Consider the torts themselves: three require particularized harm from the *public* dissemination of information; all require the taking of personal, closely held information. Prosser wanted it this way: as Richards and Solove argue, Prosser was skeptical of the privacy torts that had been developing in American common law because he found them too ambiguous and capable of impinging on other individual rights if they grew too broad.[11] As a result, his article narrowed the torts' reach by emphasizing that invasive conduct had to be "extreme and outrageous" or "highly offensive" and he excluded any mention of other common law torts that plaintiffs had also used to protect their privacy.[12] We will talk more about one of those torts – the tort of breach of confidentiality – in the next chapter.

Prosser's inclusion of the four privacy torts in his 1960 article and in the *Second Restatement of Torts*, for which he served as the lead contributor, had the effect of cementing these torts – and no others – as the framework for privacy law in the United States.[13] This happened for two reasons. First, Prosser was taking diverse and seemingly contradictory case law and harmonizing it in an ostensibly neutral way in line with the "consensus thinking" of mid-twentieth century academia.[14] Prosser's genius, scholars argue, "was to acknowledge and identify various interests to be balanced, while relentlessly asserting . . . that the results of the cases, on proper analysis, were . . . consistent examples of Prosser's own general rules."[15] Working at a time when such harmonization was highly valued in the legal academy, Prosser emerged as its paradigmatic and exemplary practitioner. As a result, the entire legal world paid attention to his four privacy torts. On a more practical level, Prosser's version of the privacy law narrative succeeded because it had no rival. As the legal scholar Sharon Sandeen has argued, privacy was unlike related areas of law – particularly trade secrecy, which protects confidential business information – in that it escaped the drive for comprehensive law reform: as chiefly concerned with personal information, haphazard common law development of privacy rules never caught the ire of business interests and their attorneys, the principal driving forces behind uniform model codes from the American Bar Association or the National Conference of Commissioners of Uniform State Laws.[16] As such, Prosser's particular narrative emerged as the only narrative shaping future developments in privacy law.

PRIVACY TORTS AND PREVIOUSLY DISCLOSED INFORMATION

Victims of invasions of privacy look to one or more of the four privacy torts when another private party – an individual acting in his personal capacity or a corporation, for example – violates their "right to be let alone." According to the Restatement §652D, a person is liable under the tort of public disclosure of private facts, for example, if he "gives publicity to a matter concerning the private life of another . . . if the matter publicized is of a kind that (a) would be highly offensive to a reasonable person, and (b) is not of legitimate concern to the public." There are four elements to this tort: (1) public dissemination of a (2) private matter that would be (3) highly offensive and (4) not newsworthy. The tort of intrusion upon seclusion (§652B) holds civilly liable anyone who "intentionally intrudes, physically or otherwise, upon the solitude or seclusion of another or his private affairs or concerns . . . if the intrusion would be highly offensive to a reasonable person." This tort has four elements, as well: (1) intentionally (2) intrudes on (3) seclusion or privacy (4) in a highly offensive way. Therefore, both torts require judges to determine whether something was private in the first place.

Lior Strahilevitz has argued that judges are not making that determination with any clear or coherent methodology, choosing instead an "I know it when I see it" approach.[17] As we have seen, traditional rights-based approaches to privacy would determine the difference between public and private by falling back on draconian bright line rules, like what Daniel Solove called the "secrecy paradigm." But a rule like that, which extinguishes privacy rights upon almost any revelation, erodes privacy rights to nothing.[18] Several cases, many of which formed the basis for Professor Strahilevitz's article, illustrate the current approach. I will use these and other cases to show the gaps in current approaches to cases involving the further dissemination of previously disclosed information.

Recall the case of Oliver Sipple. After Sipple saved then-President Gerald Ford from an assassination attempt, the *San Francisco Chronicle* published a story about Sipple's heroism. The article, and the many other pieces that cited it, disclosed that Sipple was gay and speculated that President Ford's failure to promptly thank Sipple was due to Sipple's sexuality. Although many in San Francisco's LGBTQ community knew Sipple was gay, Sipple had never come out to his family and kept his sexuality a secret outside the tight-knit gay community. And once his family found out, they disowned him. Sipple sued the newspaper, claiming an invasion of privacy. The court rejected the claim because information about Sipple's sexual orientation was not private.[19] In support of that conclusion, the court cited these facts:

> that prior to the assassination attempt[,] appellant spent a lot of time in "Tenderloin" and "Castro," the well-known gay sections of San Francisco; that he frequented gay bars ... ; that he marched in gay parades on several occasions; ... that his friendship with Harvey Milk, another prominent gay, was well-known and publicized in gay newspapers; and that his homosexual association and name had been reported in gay magazines (such as Data Boy, Pacific Coast Times, Male Express, etc.) several times before the publications in question. In fact, appellant quite candidly conceded that he did not make a secret of his being a homosexual and that if anyone would ask, he would frankly admit that he was gay.[20]

Some of these "facts" are more quaint stereotypes than facts. Spending time in the Castro is not evidence of sexual orientation. But, for the court at the time (1984), the evidence suggested that Sipple's sexual orientation was known, at least among gay San Franciscans. This publicity was enough to make an invasion of privacy claim impossible.

Another famous case, *Nader v. General Motors*, figured prominently in Strahilevitz's work. The case arose out of GM's attempt to discredit Ralph Nader, the consumer advocate, after the publication of his broadside against the auto industry, *Unsafe at Any Speed: The Designed-In Dangers of the American Automobile*. The book showed how car companies, including GM, knew of but ignored significant safety risks in their automobile designs in order to cut corners and reduce costs, thus putting their customers' lives at risk. GM responded by trying to discredit Nader in the eyes of the public. Among other tactics, agents of GM tried to unearth incriminating information about Nader by interviewing some of his friends and associates under false pretenses. When Nader objected, New York's highest court held that "[i]nformation about the plaintiff which was already known to others could hardly be regarded as private," ignoring that those "others" were some of Nader's close friends.[21]

A similar narrative played out in *Johnston v. Fuller*, in which apparently long-standing animosities between two men spilled over into a workplace investigation. Johnston alleged an investigation into threats made against his life turned into an invasion of his privacy; that is, instead of investigating the behavior of the employee who made the threat, the employer spoke to friends of Johnston and learned of details of Johnston's sexual behavior and past disruptive activities. Johnston claimed that these prying interviews intruded upon his seclusion, but the court rejected that argument for the same reason it rejected similar arguments in *Nader*. Whatever information had been learned was already known to others and, therefore, no longer private.[22]

Similarly, in an ironically well-publicized case, a Michigan court found that Consuelo Sanchez Duran, the Colombian judge that fled her country after indicting drug kingpin Pablo Escobar, had no privacy right in her relocated Detroit address. Because she used her real name when leasing an apartment and told several curious neighbors why she had security guards, the court found that she had made the choice to make her identity "open to the public eye."[23]

Sometimes, these cases are particularly tragic. In *Doe v. Methodist Hospital*, for example, a postal employee (Doe) was rushed to the hospital with an apparent heart attack. Although Doe had previously disclosed that he was HIV positive to a "small circle of close friends and coworkers," he had not revealed it "[to] his co-workers generally." He told the paramedics in the ambulance, who recorded the information in Doe's file. Because Doe's sexual orientation and HIV status had been the subjects of rumors for years, several coworkers started asking questions. One coworker called his wife, who worked at the hospital and had access to Doe's chart, and she learned that Doe was

HIV positive. The news spread. Coworkers asked one another for corroboration. Another postal worker, Cathy Duncan, was particularly active in spreading the information about Doe's HIV status, speaking to several coworkers and approaching one of Doe's closest friends at work, Ron Okes, to try to verify the rumor. Okes was one of the handful of people to whom Doe had shared that he was HIV-positive. Okes refused to confirm Duncan's gossip, but the latter shared it anyway. Doe sued Duncan for invasion of privacy, but the Supreme Court of Indiana rejected the claim for two reasons. First, "Doe had already disclosed to" Okes the information that Duncan was trying to spread. Because others already knew the information, Doe could not prove the "private matter" element of the public disclosure tort. And, second, Duncan had not spread her gossip to a sufficient number of people to meet the publicity requirement of the tort.[24]

I do not argue that all of these cases turned out wrong. But the courts arguably erred when they treated all disclosures the same. Mr. Sipple's sharing his sexual orientation with the San Francisco gay community, Mr. Nader's sharing information with his friends, Ms. Duran's mandatory disclosures on a lease and her explanations to a few neighbors, and Doe's narrow disclosures to a few friends were all fungible – they were all considered "public" disclosures for the purposes of the privacy torts – because, under many of the traditional theories of privacy we discussed in Chapters 1 and 2, any disclosure erodes privacy rights. They all made the choice to share personal information with others. Having done so, they assumed the risk that the information could be more widely disseminated.

But, of course, not all disclosures should be treated equally. Several courts have recognized this. In *Sanders v. American Broadcasting Company*, for example, the California Supreme Court found that an undercover news reporter violated the privacy rights of one of the employees of the company she was investigating. The reporter obtained employment at a "telepsychic" company, or a company that delivered psychic readings over the phone for a per-minute fee, so she could investigate accusations of fraud. She recorded conversations with various employees, including Sanders, using a small camera concealed in her hat and a small microphone hidden in her bra. When video of some of those conversations aired on television, Sanders sued, claiming his conversations with someone he thought was a coworker were private. ABC argued, however, that any privacy right was extinguished by the simple fact that Sanders's coworkers had been present and could overhear conversations. In other words, the conversations were already public. The court agreed with Sanders. Privacy, the court said, "is not a binary, all-or-nothing characteristic . . . 'The mere fact that a person can be seen by someone does not automatically mean that he or she can legally be forced to be subject to being seen by everyone.'"[25] Here, the court was able to distinguish between information that was public only as to several coworkers versus information publicized to the broadcast audience of *ABC News*.

A similar question was resolved in a similar way in *Y.G. v. Jewish Hospital* and *Multimedia WMAZ, Inc. v. Kubach.* In *Y.G.*, a young couple who underwent in vitro fertilization in violation of the doctrines of their conservative church found their images on the nightly news after attending a gathering at their hospital. Prior to the segment, only hospital employees and a parent knew of their plans to have a family, and the party was only attended by hospital employees and other participants in the in vitro fertilization program. The court rejected the argument that the couple's attendance at the party waived their privacy rights, holding that the couple "clearly chose to disclose their participation to only the other in vitro couples. By attending this limited gathering, they did not waive their right to keep their condition and the process of in vitro private, with respect to the general public."[26] And in *Kubach*, another HIV disclosure case, a television station neglected to obscure Kubach's face during an interview despite his request. He had disclosed his status to friends, health-care personnel, and his HIV support group, but asked that any discussion of his status on air remain anonymous. After the interview aired, Kubach sued. The court concluded that he retained a privacy interest in his identity despite previous disclosures. The court reasoned that a television station could not renege on its promise to pixilate his face merely because Kubach had told some people he was HIV-positive because those disclosures were only to those "who cared about him ... or because they also had AIDS." Kubach, the court said, could expect that those in whom he confided would not further disclose his condition.[27]

The results of these cases vary. But most importantly, there seems to be no coherent and consistent way of determining when a previous disclosure extinguishes a right to privacy. Rights-based theories alone are of little help. Sharers freely and voluntarily disclose information to others, and privacy theories based on separation, secrecy, and exclusion cannot adequately extend beyond an initial disclosure. They justify the rigid bright-line rules that characterized *Sipple, Nader, Duran,* and *Doe.* In cases like *Y.G.* and *Kubach,* the holdings were motivated, at least in part, by the fact that the plaintiffs' were promised privacy. In *Y.G.*, the plaintiffs "were 'assured' that 'no publicity nor public exposure' would occur" and "they twice refused interviews or to be filmed, and made every reasonable effort to avoid being filmed."[28] And in *Kubach,* the television station "explicitly agreed to respect plaintiff's privacy in order to secure his participation in the show."[29] These assurances allowed the plaintiffs to make their disclosures. When Strahilevitz analyzed these cases, he saw haphazard results, sometimes protecting privacy rights and sometimes not. He was right. But beneath the surface, an important shift was taking place – from determining the difference between public and private based solely on the actions of the sharer to also considering the context of disclosure.

A TRUST-BASED APPROACH

As we discussed in Chapter 3, Strahilevitz tried to provide a coherent approach to analyzing previous disclosure cases. He argued that previously shared information would be considered public, and thus not protected against further sharing, when the information shared was likely to spread through and among networks on its own, making the publicity of any future dissemination redundant. When the information was not likely to spread, it would be considered private and still protected by tort law.

Strahilevitz came to this conclusion based on social network theory, the cross-disciplinary study of how the structure of networks affects behavior.[30] A network is just a set of objects – people, cells, power plants – with connections among them – social encounters, synapses, grids. They are all around us: a family is a (social) network, as is the (neural) network in a brain and the (distribution) network of trash pick-up routes in New York City. To see one visualization of diffusion through a network,[31] dab the nib of a marker into the middle of a piece of construction paper and you will see, in real time, the diffusion of ink from one origin point, or node, through the lattice-like network of fibers that make up the paper. Facebook is the paradigmatic modern social network: its overarching network has billions of nodes (members), but it also has billions of subnetworks, where nodes overlap, interact, and share information. It is a network's ability to invite, disseminate, and retain information that concerns us.

Strahilevitz showed the theory of information flow within and among networks can begin the discussion of when information disclosed to a small group is still private. It helps establish two important conclusions – namely, that both the structure of a network and the nature of information disclosed into it affect the flow of information through and beyond it.

Although networks are evolving ecosystems[32] – people constantly drop in and out – human social networks tend to be close knit and highly "clustered,"[33] with "strong ties" linking us to our friends. Family members are good examples of individuals with strong ties: everyone knows everyone else and each member engages in repeated social interactions with each other.

They spend a lot of time together, have deep emotional connections, and reciprocate the connection with each other.[34] Members of other tightly clustered networks – support groups, recreational sports teams, individuals with the same political beliefs – share with each other. Social network theory does not tell us precisely *why* these persons feel comfortable sharing personal information with each other, but it does explain one form of information diffusion: the stronger the tie between two individuals, the more likely their friends overlap, and the more likely information will stay within those close-knit overlapping networks. For example, Michelle tells her best friend Nicole about her idea for a new mobile app, hoping Nicole will give her some advice. Nicole may tell Opher, her husband and Michelle's childhood friend. In this network, Michelle's mobile app idea is unlikely to spread. If networks only had strong ties, we would see many groups of friends that recycle information among themselves.[35] Based on this research, we can conclude that disclosures among close-knit strong ties will rarely diffuse to the wider public.

Information is spread between different clusters through what Mark Granovetter has called "weak ties."[36] Some weak ties are "supernodes," or society's socialites:[37] they have friends in different groups and make connections among them. More often than not, though, people are linked by the acquaintances they share – two strangers on a train marveling that they have the same mutual friend.[38] These weak-tie bridges, Granovetter has shown, are the driving force behind information dissemination from one close-knit group to another.[39] They are acquaintances we don't know well, but with whom interactions are essential if we want to bring outside information into a close-knit group full of strong ties.[40] Consider another example: Jennifer is a doctor, a soccer mom, and a hiker; she is friends with her work colleagues, casually acquainted with her child's teammates' moms and dads, and close with her hiking buddies, with whom she goes on an annual trip to Machu Picchu. An occasionally random conversation at work or at a soccer game about hiking may introduce a love for the outdoors to a soccer dad who has lived all his life in Manhattan. Granovetter showed that these types of weak ties are essential to, among other things, getting jobs:[41] Weak ties bring in contacts and information you would not otherwise have received.[42] When there are no weak ties between individuals otherwise connected by only a few steps, or when those ties are inactive, those even nearby nodes are highly unlikely to ever encounter each other or the information they disseminate. They have what Ronald Burt has called a "structural hole" between them.[43] As the active bridges between close-knit groups, then, weak ties are essential for information diffusion.

But the structure of the network – clustering, distance between clusters, and types of connections, as well as any exogenous limitations to the network – is not its only important element. The nature of the information also matters. Weak ties are not adept at transmitting all types of information. Job openings or rumors are easy to pass along; they are simple pieces of information that do not degrade along the line and are, therefore, amenable to transmission during short chance encounters with acquaintances.[44] But studies have shown that networks of weak ties are ill equipped to transfer complex information or to aggregate pieces of information into a richer picture.[45] In other words, weak ties cannot put two and two together to make four; conversations with acquaintances rarely involve in-depth analysis. Put another way, anyone who has ever played the game Telephone as a child remembers that simple statements make it through, but complex ones get mangled.

Putting this together, Strahilevitz made several conclusions that would help judges apply social network theory to answer privacy problems: First, it is difficult for loose networks to spread complex information. Therefore, "instances in which scattered private information about an individual is pieced together, and the aggregated information is disclosed, can be expected to be rare." However, when information is shared among networks with strong ties (like friends or people with extensive contacts among them), "aggregation of that information is much more likely, and the plaintiff's expectation of privacy with respect to the aggregated information ought to be low." Second, the more interesting or shocking a piece of information, the more likely it will spread efficiently and effectively among all types of networks. So, "if private information involves a highly unusual or surprising event . . . it is more likely to be disseminated through a network." Therefore, if someone "discloses previously private information that is likely to be regarded as highly interesting, novel, revealing, or entertaining, that information is rather likely to be disseminated."[46]

Strahilevitz went on to apply these lessons to the cases we discussed above. In *Kubach*, the plaintiff had told medical professionals as well as friends and family about his HIV-positive status. Strahilevitz concludes that since norms prevent doctors from disclosing patient information, and since several studies suggest that HIV-status information is rarely divulged outside of certain tight networks, the information was unlikely to get out on its own. Therefore, Kubach had a privacy interest on which he could sue ABC for its wide dissemination of his private information.[47] Strahilevitz finds Y.G. harder to decide. He has no study on how knowledge of in-vitro fertilization travels in a network. Instead, he relies on the assumption that "there appears to be less stigma associated with in vitro fertilization" than, say, HIV status. The pertinent information – that the couple was using in vitro in contravention of their religious community's wishes – was hard to piece together, so not many people at the gathering would be privy to it. And many of the participants would have been either co-participants or health care providers and thus less likely to spread the news. Strahilevitz found the court's decision to recognize a privacy interest "defensible," though not a slam dunk under social network theory.[48]

Social network theory, however, would say *Duran* came out wrong. Strahilevitz notes that shopping and eating in restaurants are "weak-tie interactions," so using one's real name would only become interesting and likely to spread through a network if a waiter was able to piece together that the Duran was the Colombian judge who indicted Pablo Escobar. "Perhaps," Strahilevitz notes, "a Colombian waiter would have put two and two together," but the interactions were too fleeting and the information too complex to be likely to get out and reach a wide audience.[49]

These conclusions make a great deal of sense. Like Helen Nissenbaum's approach to privacy as contextual integrity, a social network theory elevates the social context of a given interaction over formal rules and the mere fact of disclosure. It also highlights the important role social science can play in adjudicating modern legal questions. But there remains a question of evidence. Strahilevitz never states how lawyers would go about proving complexity of information, how fast or slow a given piece of information would flow in a network, or how to identify important nodes in a network. Absent proof, we are left with assumptions and a judge's personal views, which would further marginalize populations whose networks look very different from those of mainstream members of the American judiciary. For example, that someone took and shared an intimate or naked photograph of himself might be a rather ordinary piece of information for a network of millennials, single men and women under 40, and sexually active gay men. The same could not always be said for radically different networks of radically different people.

A social network theory of privacy also has a problematic relationship with strangers. Although Strahilevitz makes clear that his definition of publicity is when private information reaches people "from whom the plaintiff would like to keep it,"[50] it is not entirely clear that one stranger knowing something about us is any different than many strangers knowing the same. In some cases, if even one stranger knows something about us, social network theory would extinguish our privacy rights. Strangers, by definition, are outside our social networks.[51] But we know that should not be the case: privacy based on trust can exist among strangers given social cues that invite revelation and a subsequent interaction. Privacy-as-trust would amend Strahilevitz's network theory to appreciate the context of information sharing with strangers and retain privacy interests in information shared with anyone in contexts that manifest trust, confidence, and discretion.

Finally, social network theory ignores what motivated us to share in the first place. As an approach to the flow of information, looking at the structure and functioning of social networks helps us see how information will spread. That's what makes Strahilevitz's approach so appealing. But our reasons for sharing and the context in which we shared it at the time are essential for understanding social actors' expectations of confidentiality and discretion. Drawing the line between public and private information requires us to also look at indicia of trust in the initial disclosure context. Where applicable, then, social network and trust can work together to answer limited disclosure cases involving individual persons.

As we discussed in Chapter 5, privacy-as-trust offers judges several principles for distinguishing private from public in previous disclosure cases. First, sharing is inevitable and often involuntary. Therefore, the mere fact of sharing does not make information public for the purposes of the privacy torts. Second, we often want law and policy to encourage people to share. Coming out as HIV-positive and seeking emotional, medical, and political support among the HIV-positive community has overwhelmingly positive effects. Information privacy law should neither actively coerce nor effectively discourage people from emotionally rewarding, let alone economically productive, sharing. Third, when determining whether individuals retain privacy interests in previously disclosed information, judges should look to the original disclosure context and look for cues of trust based on the parties' experience, explicit or implicit social cues, norms of reciprocity, or transference.

Sometimes, privacy-as-trust and the social networks approaches come to similar conclusions in previous disclosure cases. Consider *Duran*, for example. In that case, the judge responsible for bringing Pablo Escobar to justice disclosed her real identity while shopping, renting a home, and to several neighbors. Strahilevitz notes that Duran's contacts with others were fleeting. She may have interacted with salespersons at several stores, but there was no evidence that those contacts were sufficient for people to even remember her name. The information about her was complex; someone would have had to piece together her name and her notoriety in Colombia for her identity to become public, and that was unlikely to happen in suburban Detroit.[52] Privacy-as-trust would look at the original disclosure context. Duran told three neighbors that she had bodyguards because she had been threatened by drug dealers and used her name during commercial transactions and while eating at a restaurant.[53] Salespersons and waiters are strangers, but, per Goffman, we trust that they will not put themselves in a position where they overhear information about us that steps over a social boundary appropriate for strangers; this is the concept of "civil inattention," or a form of polite recognition of strangers, manifesting itself as a respectful modesty not to intrude where you do not belong.[54] We interact with them under the norm of discretion, or, as Helen Nissenbaum would say, under expectations of information flow appropriate to the context and relationship.[55] And Duran's neighbors, new friends of hers, were clued into her past because it affected them, too. The nature of the information, combined with the close relationship between Duran and her friends, manifested trust and expectations of confidentiality.

Sometimes, trust and social networks offer contradictory approaches. Consider the two HIV disclosure cases, *Doe* and *Kubach*. Recall that in *Doe*, the plaintiff had told only a small group of close friends and coworkers. *Kubach* was out to some of his friends and his support group. Medical professionals also knew about both of them. Privacy-as-trust starts with the disclosure context. Individuals share their HIV status in contexts that manifest trust – to medical professionals, whose ethical norms include confidentiality; to close friends and loved ones, who are also expected to be discrete with the information; to support groups, which are founded on strong confidentiality mandates. Therefore, because the information was originally shared in contexts of trust, evidenced by ethical and prevailing social norms built up over time by experience (among friends), reciprocity (among support group members),[56] and transference (from medical ethics generally to specific doctors), the plaintiffs' HIV status was still private.

But one's HIV status is neither mundane nor a complex aggregation of information. It's simple and rather "revealing," to use Strahilevitz's word. This may be why Strahilevitz's analysis of *Kubach* (he did not address *Doe*) focused almost entirely on the context of the original disclosure. He notes that medical ethics prevent doctors from disclosing patient confidences and that stigmatizing personal information tends to be shared in tight-knit networks – namely, close friends and confidants. These facts allude to the trust at the heart of the original disclosure contexts, motivating the sharing in the first place.

Y.G. offers another contrast between a social networks and trust approach. In that case, attendance at the hospital gathering among other in-vitro couples and hospital personnel suggests that any information was being disclosed in an environment of trust, based on expertise and reciprocity ("We're all in this together"). The couple in *Y.G.* shared with other attendees what they thought was stigmatizing social identity; they became a tight-knit, socially embedded group. What's more, the hospital staff could also be trusted as experts in their fields. *Y.G.*, therefore, is a straight forward case for privacy-as-trust. But it was a tough case for Strahilevitz. Many of the party attendees were strangers to the plaintiffs because they had never met before. It is difficult to imagine, as

Strahilevitz himself admits, that this piece of information about Y.G. was still private if strangers knew it. Only if just our friends know a fact, "but not any strangers," he argues, could we expect it to remain with its intended recipients.[57]

Despite these differences, the social networks and trust approaches are both far superior to often extreme, rights-based approaches and can complement each other in certain disclosure cases. Both are approaches to the flow of information; they just look at context at two different points in time: privacy-as-trust looks at the initial context of disclosure, whereas a social networks approach looks at what happens after. As we will see in Chapter 9, those two perspectives can work together to solve a variety of disclosure problems.

8

Trust and Cyberharassment

Last chapter's case study applied privacy-as-trust to tort law, the legal rules governing our social interactions with others. We saw that these torts require judges to determine the difference between public and private information given certain disclosures. And we saw how autonomy- and trust-based conceptions of privacy draw those distinctions differently. Rights-based theories can erode privacy rights upon disclosure; trust looks at privacy from a relational standpoint, approaching privacy on a contextual, case-by-case basis. This chapter looks at another case study that raises similar questions: cyberharassment.

Cyberharassment is repeated online expression that amounts to a "course of conduct" targeting a particular person and causing the targeted individual substantial emotional distress and/or fear of bodily harm.[1] Nonconsensual pornography, also known as "revenge porn,"[2] is a form of cyberharassment. It is the distribution of sexually graphic or intimate images of individuals without their consent. As the two leading cyberharassment scholars, Danielle Keats Citron and Mary Anne Franks, have argued, revenge porn is, and should be treated as, a crime.[3] And, as of this writing, 38 states and the District of Columbia have done just that, enacting criminal revenge porn statutes,[4] while several more are considering similar proposals.[5] Revenge porn is also an egregious breach of the privacy and trust that make intimate relationships so dynamic, enduring, and socially beneficial. And it has damaging effects. Victims experience severe anxiety and depression, and they are often placed in physical danger. They lose their jobs and have difficulty finding new ones. Many have to recede from online life, move far away, and even change their names to escape revenge porn's long shadow.[6] Often, revenge porn narratives start innocently enough: two persons share intimate photos as an expression of love or romance; but when the relationship goes sour, a jilted man – it is almost always a man – lashes out at his ex-girlfriend by posting those intimate photos of her online for everyone to see.

Revenge porn is another example of what can go wrong when we share information with others without strong trust norms and safeguards. It is an abuse of the power that comes from disclosure. Current law has both the direct and indirect effect of making it difficult for victims to obtain civil redress. First, privacy torts are usually unhelpful, especially because many victims either take the photos themselves or consent to share them with their partners. As we have seen, if privacy is understood as protecting autonomy, freedom, choice, or secrecy, even such limited sharing eviscerates privacy rights. Second, because privacy law today focuses primarily on harms to the individual, current approaches miss the broader social harm of revenge porn – namely, the breach of trust. This has the expressive effect of making revenge porn seem like an individual's problem and not a cancer on society. It is, of course, both.

We can fix both problems if we conceptualize privacy as based on relationships of trust. Individuals could share intimate information within the boundaries of a trusted relationship and use the law to protect and enforce that trust to keep their photos away from the rest of the world. One way to do this is through the tort of breach of confidentiality. Well-developed in British law but atrophied in the United States, the tort holds liable those who share information in breach of our trust. It both perfectly reflects the meaning of privacy-as-trust and may be one more weapon practitioners can use to fight revenge porn. What's more, elevating the breach of confidentiality tort to the same level as Prosser's other privacy torts would have the powerful effect of building strong social norms of trust, solidarity, and responsibility to each another.

THE REVENGE PORN NARRATIVE

Revenge porn devastates its victims. It also damages society. Individual psychological and physical injury may help us appreciate the extent of the problem and help practitioners prove particularized injury for certain civil claims, but the broader social harm is also relevant for determining an appropriate response. For a particular tort claim to make sense as a weapon against revenge porn, it has to both compensate the victim and deter the undesirable social behavior at the core of the wrong.[7] It should, as Durkheim argues, express society's social values.[8] Current privacy law does not do that because it focuses almost exclusively on the individual harm aspect to revenge porn.

In *Hate Crimes in Cyberspace*, Danielle Citron tells the story of Holly, whose ex-boyfriend posted online nude photographs of her and a sexually revealing webcam video featuring her. The posts also included her full name, email address, screen shots of her personal Facebook page, and links to her online biography; he even included her work address. She was hounded with sexual and harassing emails from strangers, especially after her profile appeared on a website that arranged sexual encounters. Someone sent her photos to her boss and colleagues. By 2012, nearly 90 percent of the first 10 pages of a Google search of her name included links to the images and videos.[9]

Holly reported feeling "terrorized," "afraid," and "helpless," common reactions for victims of cyberharassment. She worried constantly about being stalked and raped; she never walked alone at night and would "get the chills" every time she noticed someone looking at her. She was "anxious" about her personal safety and professional prospects, and she felt blamed for what happened.[10]

In my own research, I have spoken to nearly 60 LGBTQ targets of cyberharassment. According to the latest studies, 15 percent of lesbian, gay, and bisexual Internet users in the United States say someone has threatened to post an explicit image an image of them, and 7 percent say someone has actually posted such an image.[11] My ethnographic research suggests that revenge porn hits the LGBTQ community when women come out as lesbians after breaking up with men and when gay men participate in geolocation networking mobile apps. Kate M., for example, a victim of revenge porn, stalking, and almost a victim of rape, stated that she "was constantly looking over her shoulder," and that she was "crippled" by "fear and anxiety. [She] couldn't go out of the house for days and eventually started believing that [she] brought this on [her]self."[12] Steven, who found several nude images of himself on multiple amateur pornography sites, felt "sick every day. [He] was nervous, sometimes shaking, from the moment [he] woke up to the moment [he] fell asleep, if [he] ever slept."[13]

Holly, Kate, and Steven are just three examples of a larger problem. Victims of cyberharassment, generally, and revenge porn, in particular, experience "significant emotional distress." Some experience panic attacks and develop eating disorders. They withdraw from both face-to-face and online social activities. As Citron and Franks have noted, revenge porn also raises the risk of stalking and physical attack. Young victims experience negative educational outcomes and report higher rates of suicidal thoughts; adults find it impossible to be productive, lose their jobs, and cannot find new ones.[14] Many have had to move to escape physical harm; some have had to change their names to escape the otherwise permanent stain of online harassment. Almost all victims report feelings of hopelessness, as well.[15]

Current legal responses to revenge porn reflect this focus on individual harm. The tort of public disclosure of private facts, for example, attacks the harm of revelation or publicity of private matters, which, though important, is only one part of the panoply of revenge porn harms. By redressing the harm of theft of one's creative property, copyright law offers practitioners another tool for taking down some images of revenge porn. But it minimizes attendant individual and social harm by ignoring revenge porn's moral evil. It lacks the expressive effect of a societal condemnation: what is wrong about nonconsensual pornography is not simply the unauthorized taking of someone else's picture, but the transformation of an otherwise private person into a sexual object for others against her will.

As we saw in Chapter 7, the tort of public disclosure of private facts is chiefly concerned with the unauthorized publicity of private matters. It creates liability where an individual widely discloses "a matter concerning the private life of another" that is "highly offensive to a reasonable person" and "not of legitimate concern to the public."[16] As the South Carolina Court of Appeals stated in *McCormick v. England*, "the gravamen of the tort is publicity as opposed to mere publication."[17] The disclosure must be public and, therefore, "[c]ommunication to a single individual or to a small group of people... will not give rise to liability."[18] As we have seen, however, this rule is unevenly applied. As both Daniel Solove and Lior Strahilevitz have shown, many courts confuse privacy with secrecy, thereby preventing a plaintiff who had confided in one or several others to recover for public disclosure of private facts.[19] There may be no clear rule for determining when some private matter has been given sufficient publicity to rise to the level of tort liability, but requiring a publicity trigger at all implies that the harm the tort intends to address is contingent upon revelation.

This is evident in many public disclosure cases. For example, courts have found insufficient publicity, thus denying recovery, where information was disclosed to two people;[20] a "handful of people";[21] a few coworkers;[22] several law enforcement officers;[23] an employer and a limited number of relatives;[24] an aunt and uncle and a friend;[25] two fellow employees and the plaintiff's mother;[26] store employees and plaintiff's son and daughter-in-law;[27] or a spouse, friends, acquaintances, and coworkers.[28] According to the opinions in these cases, the group of information recipients was simply not large or diverse enough to result in any harm to the plaintiff.

And yet, the unauthorized dissemination of one's sexually graphic and intimate pictures to even a "handful of people," a "few coworkers," or "an employer" would strike many as harmful, horrifying, and in need of legal redress. Indeed, many victims of revenge porn speak of the fear that specific other people – employers, future employers, relatives, and love interests – will see or receive the pictures from the victim's harasser.[29] Distribution to them should be just as actionable as dissemination to a large group of strangers. But because the core wrong addressed by public disclosure of private facts is widespread revelation, it is not clear that the tort could capture more limited disclosures of graphic images that nevertheless objectify victims and result in significant individual and social harm. Nor can the tort help victims if courts conflate privacy with secrecy. As we have seen, if anything not secret is also considered not private, than graphic images, once shared, are fair game for wider disclosure.

Another tool practitioners currently use to combat revenge porn is copyright law. The purpose of the Copyright Act is, among other things, to protect authors' creative expression, incentivize the creation of new works, and serve the public interest by making those works available for use and enjoyment.[30] Therefore, the law is chiefly concerned with the flow of creative property.[31] It is also focused on redressing wrongs. Unlike the tort of public disclosure of private facts, publicity is not the *sine qua non* of copyright infringement. Rather, it is unconsented taking and use.

This is evident in the statute itself. Section 106 of the Copyright Act grants copyright holders six exclusive rights: reproduction, creation of derivative works, public distribution, public performance, public display, and public performance of a sound recording via digital transmission.[32] Copyright infringement, then, can occur with a copy, regardless of distribution. As many courts have similarly acknowledged, copying is the core of copyright infringement.[33]

Academic, practitioner, and popular rhetoric makes the relationship even clearer. Attempting to explain why personal privacy protection lags far behind intellectual property protection in the United States, Larry Lessig argued that it was because the language of property – an infringer "takes my property" – is employed to speak about infringement of intellectual property but not about private data.[34] Lawyers use the word "piracy" when referring to copyright infringement all the time.[35] And its use was prejudicial and persuasive enough that at least one court has banned the practice.[36] Senator Orrin Hatch used it three times in the first four sentences to start his introductory statement during copyright legislation hearings in 2004. He also implied that those who induce infringement are aiding and abetting theft.[37]

To be sure, victims of revenge porn object to their images being "taken" and "misused" in a harmful, unexpected way.[38] But that concern is, at best, secondary to the victim's and society's chief objections to revenge porn: it invades victims' privacy and transforms them into sexual objects for others.

To suggest that these harms are adequately addressed by treating revenge porn as theft of property gives copyright law too much credit.[39] Nor can property be taken if it is not owned, and when images of revenge porn are not snapped by the victim herself, the core wrong copyright law is meant to address does not even apply.

A SOCIAL NARRATIVE OF REVENGE PORN

Revenge porn's harmful effects do not stop at the victim's psychological, social, and professional health. In addition to causing devastating harm to individuals, revenge porn damages society, as well. Citron has argued that revenge porn, as a gendered and sexualized phenomenon, discriminates against women.[40] I would like to add a further point: revenge porn is antisocial behavior that breaches the trust inherent in intimate social relationships and necessary for social interaction. Any response to the problem must adequately address this core wrong – breach of trust – if it hopes to both help victims seek redress and change social norms.[41]

Victims of revenge porn who have spoken about their experiences had developed trust with their harassers and had those expectations destroyed when they were betrayed. Holly "trusted" her ex-boyfriend to keep her nude images secret.[42] Kate "trusted" that her ex-boyfriend "at least was reasonable. I mean, after all, we were in love and we'd been together for some time. Is that so ridiculous?"[43] Steven, who shared a graphic photo of himself on a mobile app on which such photo sharing is common and expected, stated that "we're all in this together. If you don't share photos, you can't really participate. I think we all do it expecting that the guy on the other end can be trusted to be discrete."[44] They trusted that their interaction partners would act in keeping with the expectations and norms of the social context. Some of them trusted based on implicit cues and experience; some trusted based on their social network. In each case, nonconsensual pornography destroyed that trust.

Experts, lawmakers, and the media also use the language of trust to capture the social harm of revenge porn. When they introduced legislation to make it easier for law enforcement to prosecute those who engage in nonconsensual pornography, California State Senator Anthony Cannella and Assemblyman Mike Gatto stated that perpetrators were "exploit[ing] intimacy and trust" for financial gain or petty revenge. Senator Cannella described the problem as "lives ... being destroyed because another person they trusted distributed compromising photos of them online."[45] In an opinion piece for *Al Jazeera America*, Citron states that "the nonconsensual posting of people's nude photos [is] in violation of their trust and confidence."[46] Woodrow Hartzog, in *The Atlantic*, and Neil Richards and Citron, in *Al Jazeera*, do the same. Hartzog proposes various legal remedies for victims "whose trust has been betrayed." Richards and Citron argue that "[t]he disclosure of a nude photo of a person in breach of trust and privacy is . . . beneath the attention of the First Amendment, and rightly so."[47]

Individuals share graphic or intimate images with others when the social context includes expectations of trust that recipients will behave with discretion and keep those images confidential. Transforming those images into pornography for strangers is an invasion of privacy precisely because it erodes both the trust that developed between the victim and her harasser and, as we have seen, the broader social trust that keeps social interaction humming along. Therefore, to address revenge porn's particularized and social harms, it makes sense to look to legal remedies that hold liable those who breach trust.

A TRUST-BASED APPROACH

Coupled with practical considerations – the cost of retaining counsel and litigating claims, the difficult processes for unmasking anonymous perpetrators, and the likelihood that many of them are judgment proof – the misalignment between the core wrong of nonconsensual pornography and the wrongs addressed by the tort of public disclosure of private facts and copyright law suggests that these weapons are, by themselves, inadequate paths to justice for victims. And although no single weapon could fill all the gaps left by existing remedies, practitioners need additional tools in a diverse arsenal.

An underappreciated claim that comes closest to capturing the breach of trust and privacy inherent in revenge porn is the tort of breach of confidentiality. Though historically marginalized,[48] this tort has nevertheless existed in American law for some time.[49] It has traditionally been restricted to a few formal relationships, but there is no doctrinal basis for such a limitation. In fact, a litany of decisions involving explicit references to the tort of breach of confidentiality and breaches of implied duties of confidentiality[50] gives every indication that courts are open to a robust tort that applies to informal relationships – lovers and close friends, for example – that nevertheless maintain strong expectations of confidentiality. Therefore, the tort may be an effective tool in certain revenge porn cases.

The tort of breach of confidentiality holds liable those who, without consent, divulge information disclosed to them in a context that they knew or should have known included an expectation of confidentiality with respect to that information, thereby causing harm to the victim.[51] Based on current American and British case law, that context arises when information has "the necessary quality of confidence about it" and is disclosed "in circumstances importing an obligation of confidence."[52] These are independent, but overlapping factors: disclosure in a context where the facts taken together suggest an expectation of confidentiality may also suggest that the information disclosed is of a confidential nature, and the nature of the information is taken into account to determine a confidential context.[53] This means that, as we learned from Helen Nissenbaum, context is key.[54] This also means that the duty to maintain confidentiality need not be chained to a select few formal relationships.

Information with a "quality of confidence about it" is a broad category reaching far beyond the narrow confines of intimate facts. As Neil Richards and Daniel Solove have found, information about health and medicine, sex and intimacy, and finance and money have all qualified. So have photographs taken at private events, private communications, personal diaries, and information about children. Indeed, because much information can take on a "quality of confidence" given the context in which it is disclosed, there are few formal limits on the types of information eligible for enforcement of confidentiality through tort law. It simply must not be trivial nor in the public domain.[55] Woodrow Hartzog has shown that courts have internalized these and other considerations and have tended to find obligations of confidentiality where the information, if widely disseminated, could harm the victim and where information is intrinsically sensitive.[56] Sexually graphic or intimates images would undoubtedly qualify under several of these theories.

When determining whether a context included an obligation to keep confidences, American and British courts have almost always started at the relationship between the parties. But contrary to conventional wisdom, the duty is not restricted to a select few formal relationships. In the United States, relationships giving rise to a tort-based duty of confidence used to be limited and narrow: doctors owed duties of confidentiality to their patients[57] and banks owed a similar duty to their customers.[58] But courts have found implied duties of confidentiality in other, more informal noncontractual relationships: schools owe duties of confidentiality to their students,[59] social workers owe duties of confidentiality to families with which they work,[60] employees owe a duty to their employers,[61] and car dealerships owe similar duties to their customers.[62] Media interviewees promised confidentiality can claim tortious breach of confidentiality if their identities are disclosed.[63] As can a party engaged in an ongoing, though undefined and noncontractual business relationship with another that included disclosure of confidential information.[64]

And one who shares an idea (for a television show, for example) with another in confidence can bring an action for breach of confidentiality against the recipient if he uses, shares, or implements the idea without the disclosee's consent.[65] None of these duties, the courts stated, are based in contract; they are all based on the social obligations individual owe others, generally. The very diversity of the relationships giving rise to a duty to maintain confidentiality belies the conventional wisdom of a limited, narrow tort.

As Richards and Solove note, British courts have found duties of confidentiality in informal relationships, as well. In addition to duties of confidence arising in lawyer–client, doctor–patient, employer–employee, banker–customer, and accountant–client relationships,[66] British courts have recognized duties of confidentiality when artists share concept ideas,[67] and even when lovers and friends share personal information with each other. In *Stephens v. Avery*, for example, an individual told a reporter confidential details about the plaintiff's sex life – particularly, that she had been involved in a same-sex affair with the victim of a brutal homicide.[68] In *Barrymore v. News Group Newspapers*, the man having a sexual affair with Michael Barrymore disclosed details of their relationship, including letters Barrymore wrote, to a newspaper.[69] The courts held that both could be liable for breach of a duty of confidence springing from the close social relationship in which the information was disclosed.[70] At this point, then, the formal relationship requirement of the duty of confidence appears to have been lost.[71]

This more flexible approach, unmoored to specific and defined formal relationships, retains fidelity to the contextual nature of confidentiality and trust. Confidential contexts are fact-specific; formal relationships are just easy shorthand heuristics that save judges or juries from doing the necessary work of contextual analysis. But the latter is neither difficult nor beyond the scope of a fact-finder's talents. In *Stephens*, there was evidence that the plaintiff's disclosures followed an explicit reminder that everything discussed is discussed in confidence, something to which the defendant, like many close friends, took indignant exception.[72] In *Barrymore*, the judge cited several factors that created a context giving rise to a duty of confidentiality. First, the relationship itself: "common sense dictates that, when people enter into a personal relationship of this nature, [i.e., a sexual affair,] they do not do so for the purpose of it subsequently being published in" a newspaper. Second, the nature of the information: "[t]o most people the details of their sexual lives are high on their list of those matters which they regard as confidential."[73] And third, the context of the particular information disclosed: the letters, like the affair itself, were kept secret from almost everyone.

Nor need we stop there. In arguing that a robust concept of implied confidentiality could protect individuals who share personal information with others, Andrew McClurg has noted that custom, common understanding, and objective factors like "closed doors and drawn curtains" can lead to the inference that information is imparted in confidence.[74] Practitioners can use these and other social cues of confidentiality to create a narrative of confidential disclosure at trial. Beyond physical separation, which is but one cue of confidentiality, any fact that creates a reliable expectation that others either will not or know that they should not intrude can be used to paint a picture of a confidential context.[75] This includes a range of behaviors, from communicating via whispers and hushed voices, ensuring that no one else is within earshot, creating distance with others, and turning away from crowds, to the intimate nature of the information itself. These social cues, described at length in the sociologist Erving Goffman's analyses of human interaction in private and public places,[76] are also easily admitted into evidence through affidavits and witness testimony, supported by expert testimony from a social anthropologist or sociologist.

These cues also exist online.[77] Privacy settings and passwords are just two of the most obvious cues of confidentiality expectations.[78] Practitioners can go further. Ephemeral messaging services like Snapchat and Instagram Stories allow images sent across the system to disappear.[79] Signal, a secure messaging service, also has a setting that sunsets old messages. Certain platforms neither gather nor aggregate and sell user data. So-called "just-in-time" privacy notifications allow individuals to opt-in to a certain amount of data sharing.[80] Together, these and similar tools help create expectations of privacy and confidentiality among users because they create social norms under which all users operate. Practitioners can use them to tell a persuasive narrative that images were exchanged in a context that one could reasonably trust was confidential.

Applying these principles to two revenge porn cases illustrates the powerful role the tort of breach of confidentiality can play. Recall Kate M., whose name has been changed to protect her privacy. Kate broke up with her then-boyfriend when she came out as bisexual in 2013. Kate described herself as "pretty private." Her Facebook profile never mentioned whether or with whom she was in a relationship and she declined to post pictures. During her relationship, she exchanged nude and semi-nude images for several months. Kate told me it was "fun, and to be honest, it got him off my back about sex." After the relationship ended, Kate's ex posted several of those intimate pictures on a meet-up website along with her name, address, and a request for a rough roleplay "rape" fantasy. Over a three-week period, several men tried breaking into her home. She approached lawyers, but none of them knew what to do.

Kate M.'s boyfriend breached a duty of confidentiality. Most of the time, the intimate images, which depicted Kate in various stages of undress, were shared over Snapchat, which deletes images shared and notifies users when a recipient takes a screenshot of something sent. Once, Kate shared a photo over iMessage, Apple's instant messaging tool, but said, "this is just for us[,] del from yur phone," immediately after sending the image.[81] Like in *Stephens*, where an individual shared personal information only after explicitly stating that it is being told in confidence, Kate shared an image with an explicit request for confidentiality. Otherwise, she used a platform with strong norms of discretion. Kate never consented for her ex-boyfriend to post the images online, and the nature of the information – nude images – was highly personal. The harm was all too real: as a result of Kate's emotional distress and the prospect of men trying to break into her home to rape her, she had to move thousands of miles away.

Steven's story is a little different. Steven P. is an openly gay 24-year-old professional living in Boston. He is single and is one of millions of users of Grindr, a mobile geolocation app that, like Tinder, allows individuals to meet others nearby. He has met several people through Grindr, some of whom, he says, "have become my closest friends in this town. I moved here not knowing anybody." One man "seemed nice enough" and "very friendly and cool, so I sent him a few pictures. I remember one was naked, the other, from the waist up, both included my face." In our discussion, he preempted any pushback that would blame him for what happened: "It's ridiculous to suggest that it was my fault . . . If you don't share photos, you can't really participate. I think we all do it expecting that the guy on the other end can be trusted to be discrete." Steven also noted that he only sent his pictures after the other man sent his, noting explicitly that "that was how it worked." He went on: "I think the tit-for-tat exchange makes people trust the other person: it's not one of you being vulnerable to the other; it's both." Steve never met the other man "for whatever reason."[82] The next day, the images were posted online.

The relationship between Steven and the man he texted on Grindr is different than the long-term relationship between Kate and her ex-boyfriend. But the context of Steven's disclosure is filled with indicia of expectations of confidentiality: the norms of the platform favor confidentiality and discretion, the images sent were highly personal and were only sent after a good faith gesture of trust, and the entire interaction happened on a platform that is sequestered from general online social interaction.

As the law and technology scholar James Grimmelmann explains, social network sites

> piggyback on the deeply wired human impulse to reciprocate. People reciprocate because … participation in a gift culture demands that gifts be returned or passed along, because it's disrespectful to spurn social advances, because there's a natural psychological instinct to mirror what one's conversational partner is doing, and because we learn how to conduct ourselves by imitating others.[83]

Geosocial apps like Grindr and Tinder are designed to encourage the reciprocal behavior of sharing photos. Users cannot be blamed or punished for participating according to those norms. Similar facts were important to the court in *Barrymore*. In that case, Michael Barrymore went out of his way to conduct a clandestine same-sex affair, and the court found that the nature of the relationship, coupled with the work the men had done to keep the affair secret, suggested that all information was disclosed with strong expectations of confidentiality. The same can be said of Steven's interaction on Grindr.

Notably, these stories would end differently under a public disclosure of private facts claim. Both Kate and Steven shared their images with others. As we saw in Chapter 7, that is often fatal to a traditional invasion of privacy lawsuit. But to accept that status quo reduces privacy to mere secrecy and makes it impossible for many victims of online harassment to obtain justice. The tort of breach of confidentiality not only opens a new path, but also reinforces the norm that privacy is really about trust.

BENEFITS AND LIMITATIONS OF THE APPROACH

Even under a trust-based approach, these cases are not automatically slam dunks. It is clear that the law has to evolve to respond to the epidemic of revenge porn and other forms of cyberharassment.[84] But this type of incremental modernization is precisely the type of evolution for which the common law of torts is perfectly suited. Given a modern problem that, to date, lacks a solution, the common law can, and should, adjust, just like it has in the past.[85] That, after all, was Warren's and Brandeis's point when they argued for a "right to be let alone" in response to overzealous journalists and photographers taking advantage of new technologies to harass private persons.[86] And doing so would not only continue to fulfill the goals of the common law, but offer several other advantages, as well.

A robust tort of breach of confidentiality would both encourage and regulate disclosure: it would foster candid disclosures to friends and loved ones who can provide support and help us realize the psychological and social benefits of sharing; it would also regulate wider dissemination of that information, which could cause particularized and social harm.[87] Protecting confidential contexts also recognizes that we all, to some extent, trust others and entrust information – from purchasing habits to our most intimate secrets – to many third parties. That kind of sharing is both necessary and beneficial to society: we want people to feel comfortable sharing with others so they can, among other things, create the strong, stable relationships that flow from information sharing.[88] Relationships with counselors, teachers, mentors, and friends, for example, would all strengthen in a world where confidential disclosures are protected against release.

Importantly, too, the breach of confidentiality tort addresses the core wrong of revenge porn and other invasions of privacy, many of which are breaches of trust. That may have little impact on a practitioner searching for additional weapons to attack revenge porn cases, but it should have powerful expressive effects.[89] If we start talking about revenge porn and other invasions of privacy as breaches of trust, we begin to realize that failure to protect privacy or do anything to stop cyberharassment results in far more damage than the already devastating personal, emotional, and professional repercussions of revenge porn. Social solidarity is the ultimate victim.

Doctrinally, the tort of breach of confidentiality seems like a more powerful tool than public disclosure of private facts to address incidents of invasions of privacy, generally, and revenge porn, in particular. As discussed above, the latter requires relatively wide dissemination, an element that should not be necessary, though is often present anyway, in revenge porn cases. It also requires that the information disseminated be "a private" matter, something courts often confuse with secrecy.[90] And the "highly offensive" requirement and newsworthiness exception further serve to narrow the public disclosure tort. The breach of confidentiality tort appears to have few such limitations: it presumes sharing and, as evident from *Avery*, *Barrymore*, and other cases, an individual is not released of his obligation of confidentiality even where the subject of the information is of public interest.

The lack of a newsworthiness exception has moved some commentators to suggest that the breach of confidentiality tort is inconsistent with the First Amendment's guarantee of free speech. For example, Susan Gilles has argued that the tort has a chilling effect on speech: because of its lack of clarity, potential speakers cannot know when, if at all, they are subject to its requirements, thus raising barriers to speech.[91] In the leading work on the tort, Alan Vickery went so far as to include a newsworthiness requirement in his formulation of the tort's elements.[92]

Admittedly, the law of confidentiality is, as the legal scholars Daniel Solove and Neil Richards state, "in First Amendment limbo."[93] But the tort is not inconsistent with free speech and First Amendment values. In fact, in social situations like those in which individuals share intimate photos with each other, the First Amendment should not even apply. Solove and Richards have argued that the way to determine which forms of civil liability are subject to First Amendment limitations is to look at the nature of government power. "When the government uses tort law to establish substantive rules of social conduct that all members of society must follow" – like negligence and defamation – and in doing so restricts speech, the First Amendment applies. But when the government merely stands behind obligations that individuals create for themselves – like confidentiality in social contexts – it is not government power restricting speech. Rather, individuals are deciding for themselves that the social benefits of easy interaction, exchange, intimacy, and love that emanate from confidentiality expectations are more important to them than their freedom to speak as they please.[94] Intimate photos are most likely to be shared within this organic, bottom-up development of an obligation of confidentiality. Only an exaggerated First Amendment would impede that everyday social interaction.

Another limitation to consider is the application of the tort itself. In the United States, the tort of breach of confidentiality has most commonly been applied to formal relationships. Indeed, to determine if information was disclosed in a confidential context, an element of the tort, courts will often just look to the relationship and stop there. This history may scare practitioners away.

It is true that the law must evolve. But it can only do so after we start thinking about privacy and cyberharassment in terms of confidentiality and trust and lawyers start bringing breach of confidentiality cases, allowing judges to take the incremental steps for which the common law of torts is both famous and uniquely suited. Indeed, as Warren and Brandeis argue, without the evolution of tort law, we would not even have a law of privacy.[95] Leading practitioners may find themselves at the forefront of a new, modern evolution of tort law, but only if they try.

9

Information Flow in Intellectual Property

So far, we have applied privacy-as-trust to several information privacy law problems, from the legal relationship between Internet platforms and their users to interactions among individuals, including social sharing and cyber-harassment. But questions of information flow and the difference between public and private information are not the exclusive realm of those writing about privacy. Intellectual property lawyers have an interest in this fight, as well. After all, as the law and technology scholar Jonathan Zittrain has argued, privacy and intellectual property address the same issue: control over information.[1] The only difference is that privacy concerns information about persons; intellectual property deals in information about art, brands, or useful devices. There are a number of examples of the overlap, but this chapter will focus on one of them – namely, patent law's public use bar.[2]

A patent is a limited monopoly over an invention. Patents are granted by an arm of the federal government known as the Patent and Trademark Office (PTO), and if inventors follow all of the PTO's requirements, their patents can last up to 20 years. During that time, patent owners can set prices for their products and restrict, if they so choose, who else can use them. Section 102 of the Patent Act states that an invention "in public use" or "disclosed" or "otherwise available to the public" for more than one year prior to filing an application for the patent will not be considered novel and, thus, not eligible for a patent.[3] Public use bar claims are intellectual property's version of the previous disclosure cases we discussed in Chapter 7: they require judges to look at what information inventors have shared and determine if that information is now public or still protectable under the law. How they go about doing that is based on their conception of privacy.

Implementation of the public use bar gives us another example of unjust and draconian results stemming from traditional, rights-based approaches to information flow. Specifically, by focusing on an inventor's control over her invention, public use cases make confidentiality agreements paramount. But the presence of these agreements is not really about exercising control over information or creating and maintaining expectations of privacy. Rather, confidentiality agreements are really about power: the power to insist upon them, leverage them, and rely on them when something goes wrong. Public use law's reliance on traditional privacy principles, therefore, ends up privileging wealthy corporate inventors over entrepreneurs and hobbyists. Privacy-as-trust can fix that. Rather than focusing exclusively on the one manifestation of expectations of confidentiality most likely to be deployed by the rich, privacy-as-trust would look to the confidentiality norms arising out of the relationship between the inventor and the audience of her disclosures. If pre-patenting disclosure happens in relationships characterized by trust and expectations of confidentiality, information disclosed should remain protected and, thus, patentable.

THE PUBLIC USE BAR AND PRIVACY-AS-CONTROL

To get a patent, your invention must be novel. To be novel, it cannot have been in public use, disclosed, or otherwise available to the public more than one year prior to patenting.[4] This rule is known as the "public use bar." The purposes of the public use bar are noble ones: to incentivize prompt disclosure, to discourage inventors from selling their products without sharing their technology with the public, and to protect the public domain.[5]

Currently, public use case law states that lack of control is the shibboleth of public use: a public use occurs when an inventor allows others to use her invention without retaining control over the device.[6] In this way, one of the dominant conventional theories of privacy that we discussed in Chapter 2 – privacy as the right to control what others know about us – is reflected in patent law's novelty jurisprudence. The Supreme Court made this clear in 1877. In *Elizabeth v. Pavement Co.*, the Court stated that as long as an inventor "does not voluntarily allow others to make [the invention] and use it, and so long as it is not on sale for general use, he keeps the invention under his own control, and does not lose his title to a patent."[7] In practice, courts are supposed to determine control by looking at how the inventor shared his device, the public's access to the invention, whether there was any confidentiality agreement in place,[8] and any evidence of experimentation.[9] The one factor ostensibly focused on the relationship between the inventor and the public – the presence of confidentiality or secrecy obligations – is supposed to be flexible: a formal nondisclosure agreement is not supposed to be required.[10] But that isn't how it works in practice.

In *Lough v. Brunswick Corp.*, for example, the Court of Appeals for the Federal Circuit, the appellate court with jurisdiction over patent matters, invalidated a patent for boat motor seals because the inventor gave away his invention, installed it on another's boat, failed to keep track of the test boat's operation with the installed prototype, and never asked for secrecy.[11] In *Beachcombers, International, Inc. v. WildeWood Creative Products*, a designer lost her patent for a new kaleidoscope because she chose to demonstrate the invention for party guests and allowed them to handle and use it without a confidentiality agreement.[12] And in *Baxter International, Inc. v. COBE Laboratories, Inc.*, an inventor lost control of his invention (and thus lost his patent) not only because he demonstrated his new centrifuge for others without requiring they keep it secret, but also because he allowed a free flow of bodies through the lab that housed the device.[13] In these and many other cases, the court took away patents because inventors had ostensibly given up control of their inventions to others.

In this way, patent law's public use bar reflects one of the dominant conceptualizations of privacy: privacy as choice and control. We discussed this approach to privacy in Chapter 2. Privacy-as-control is the theory that a right to privacy means having the right to control one's personal information and the freedom to decide to share it with some and not others. Jean Cohen, for example, has argued that privacy is the right "to choose whether, when, and with whom" to share intimate information.[14] Alan Westin suggests that privacy "is the claim of individuals, groups, or institutions to determine for themselves when, how, and to what extent information about them is communicated to others."[15] It is, to Julie Inness, the idea that an individual has "control over a realm of intimacy"[16] and, to Jonathan Zittrain, control over our information in general.[17] For the philosopher Steve Matthews, exercising privacy is making the choice to "control" and "manage" the boundary between ourselves and others.[18] The common denominator in all these descriptions is free choice and control, and it is the same dynamic at play in cases like *Elizabeth, Lough, Beachcombers*, and *Baxter*, just with different information. And, as we saw in Chapter 7, the paradigm is pervasive, evident in previous disclosure cases. Like Oliver Sipple, who could not prevent the media from disclosing his sexual orientation after he had already disclosed it to friends in San Francisco,[19] and like Ralph Nader, who could not prevent General Motors from gathering personal information already known to others as part of the company's plot to discredit him,[20] the inventors in *Lough, Beachcombers*, and *Baxter* could not put the cat back in the bag. Their inventions, either from voluntary disclosures (*Lough* and *Beachcombers*)[21] or public availability (*Baxter*),[22] were already out of their control and were known and used by others.

APPLYING THE PUBLIC USE BAR

It seems evident, then, that the law of public use reflects the dynamics of privacy-as-control. That itself is problematic because it creates the potential for what Daniel Solove has called a "secrecy paradigm" to govern what should be a more flexible, case-by-case standard.[23] The secrecy paradigm's harsh conflation of secrecy and privacy helps explain several public use cases. In *Lough*, the inventor showed his device to five friends, who used it on their boats.[24] That was enough to make the device public. And in the classic case of *Egbert v. Lippmann*, the Supreme Court stated that one "intimate friend" wearing a corset under her clothes constituted public use: "If an inventor ... gives or sells it to another, to be used by the donee or vendee, without limitation or restriction, or injunction of secrecy, and it is so used, such use is public, even though the use ... may be confined to one person."[25] The secrecy paradigm may have the benefit of clarity, but it imposes a harsh bright line rule where case-by-case precision may be more appropriate.

But the secrecy paradigm alone fails to explain the majority of public use cases. As applied, public use law is less an indiscriminate blunt axe than a discriminatory scalpel. One distinct pattern emerges. Wealthy corporate inventors tend to win their public use cases; entrepreneurs tend to lose. And that is in part because the Federal Circuit treats confidentiality agreements – legal manifestations of control – as essential to retaining expectations of privacy in disclosed information. Even when corporate inventors lose their public use cases because they failed to secure confidentiality agreements, the privileged position of the agreements is a boon to corporate inventors because they alone have they leverage and clout to insist on them. Seen another way, courts ignore the informal, yet no less strong confidentiality norms of entre-preneurs, hobbyists, and other social sharers even though those norms give rise to expectations of trust and confidentiality. This is the primary effect of using privacy-as-control in the public use context: by focusing on control exercised by the inventor, the approach requires judges to locate public use law in the inventor's actions, not in relational norms.[26]

THE PRIVILEGED POSITION OF THE CORPORATE INVENTOR

Of the 23 public use cases included in this analysis,[27] 9 feature corporate defendants that won findings of nonpublic use despite disclosures occurring without formal confidentiality agreements.[28] At the same time, 10 solo entre-preneur defendants faced the opposite result – no confidentiality agreement and a finding of public use.[29] But beyond just the results, courts' perspectives on the importance of formal confidentiality agreements also change based on the type of public use defendant. For corporate inventors, rules are flexible; for lone entrepreneurs, confidentiality agreements are constructively essential. In *Bernhardt, L.L.C. v. Collezione Europa USA, Inc.*, for example, where one of the largest family-owned furniture companies in the United States displayed patented material at an industry trade show that did not require signed confidentiality agreements, the court noted that a formal secrecy agreement "is one factor to be considered" and immediately reframed the analysis as a totality of the circumstances test for inventor control in context.[30] And in *Dey, L.P. v. Sunovion Pharmaceuticals, Inc.*, a case involving two large pharmaceutical companies, the Federal Circuit determined that use of COPD medication in clinical trials did not constitute public use even though the subjects involved never signed confidentiality agreements. The court recognized that clinical trial subjects customarily do not sign confidentiality agreements; to require one in this case would ignore the contextual factors that implied a baseline of confidentiality regardless of any agreement.[31]

But courts are rarely so charitable and flexible in cases involving solo entrepreneur defendants. In *Baxter International, Inc. v. COBE Laboratories, Inc.*, for example, the Federal Circuit found that the use of a centrifuge by a National Institutes of Health researcher in his personal laboratory constituted disqualifying public use because he maintained no control over the device. The most important factor leaning against control seemed to be the fact that the inventor demonstrated the technology to colleagues without a confidentiality agreement or any indication that it should be kept secret.[32] In *Lough v. Brunswick Corp.*, a corrosion-proof seal for stern drives was tested on boats belonging to several of the inventor's friends and colleagues. The court determined that the use was public because the inventor lacked any control over the seals: he asked for no follow up, did not supervise their use, and never asked his friends to sign confidentiality agreements.[33] And in *Massachusetts Institute of Technology (MIT) v. Harman International Industries, Inc.*, inventors used their friends to test a car navigation system, but never required confidentiality agreements from them or corporate sponsors.[34] In each of these cases, the lack of a confidentiality agreement between the parties, though ostensibly only one of many factors to consider, was always among the most important.

The narrative in *Beachcombers* makes the point even more clear. In that case, the designer and developer of an improved kaleidoscope wanted to solicit feedback on the design from her friends and colleagues. She invited 20 to 30 of them to a private party at her home for a demonstration and, without asking them to sign a confidentiality agreement, allowed her guests to handle the invention.[35] The situation had all the indicia of a controlled social event: an invite-only guest list consisting of friends and colleagues who were invited for the purposes of testing, experimentation, and feedback. The only thing missing was a formal secrecy agreement. Without it, though, the use was considered sufficiently public for two reasons: first, the kaleidoscope was out of the developer's control during the party; second, she placed no restrictions on guests sharing what they learned.

The correlation may not be perfect: there are several examples where corporate defendants lose their public use cases in part because they failed to secure confidentiality agreements. But, in this case, the exceptions help prove the rule. Like those involving solo entrepreneur defendants above, the opinions in these cases elevate formal secrecy agreements to almost determinative status. In *Pronova BioPharma Norge AS v. Teva Pharmaceuticals USA, Inc.*, for example, where a pharmaceutical company sent drug samples to an outside doctor for testing, the court's holding highlighted the central importance of a confidentiality agreement, concluding the public use happened when samples were sent "with no confidentiality restrictions."[36] *Pronova* and several other cases[37] may not rest exclusively on the lack of formal confidentiality agreements. But the pattern is unmistakable: a nondisclosure contract is, in practice, more important than the black letter law would suggest.

This is a boon to corporate inventors even when they lose. Although simple nondisclosure agreements are freely available online,[38] solo entrepreneurs, part-time developers, and hobbyists lack the power and leverage to insist on confidentiality agreements from their business partners. Nor do they have the money to pay attorneys to draft professional ones. As courts and scholars have noted in the corporate and labor contexts, small businesses lack the bargaining power of large, entrenched interests.[39] During its onboarding process for new hires, for example, Apple devotes an entire week to confidentiality and requires employees sign several long, overlapping nondisclosure agreements and agree to abide by the company's well-known lock-down and secrecy practices.[40] A start-up would have difficulty attracting necessary talent if it copied Apple's practice.

IMPLICATIONS AND CRITIQUES OF THE CURRENT APPROACH

There are three implications of public use law's privileged treatment of corporate inventors, two of which are practical and one is theoretical. First, the unequal treatment directly increases barriers to entry into the innovation economy for a wide swath of the inventing class by making patent defense harder and more expensive.[41] Obtaining a patent is already an expensive ordeal. The average patent costs approximately $22,000 to successfully prosecute, with some costs reaching $30,000.[42] Additional costs from the likelihood of future (unsuccessful) litigation further discourages entrepreneurs. After all, it costs, on average, anywhere between "$420,000 for small and medium-sized companies to $1.52 million for large companies" to defend a patent in court.[43]

Second, the pattern of favoring corporate inventors entrenches an already unequal and strikingly homogenous patent landscape. According to the PTO, nearly all of the top 100 patentees in 2014 were large corporations,[44] which, although not itself evidence of inequality – large corporations with many employees likely have more inventions – feeds a larger narrative of entrenched privilege. For example, women remain a distinct minority among science and technology graduates employed in inventor roles at large corporations.[45] According to the Department of Labor, women make up only 29.8 percent of chemists, 24.5 percent of environmental scientists, 13 percent of chemical engineers, 16.5 percent of civil engineers, 12.3 percent of electrical engineers, 16 percent of industrial engineers, and 8.8 percent of mechanical engineers.[46] If male-dominated corporations continue to control the patent world, the contributions of women and other minorities could still be minimized. A recent study of 4.6 million utility patents granted by the PTO between 1976 and 2013 found that "[w]omen contributed less than 8% of all inventorships for the entire period," maxing out at 10.8 percent in 2013, an increase from 2.7 percent in 1976.[47] Men dominate patenting in almost every country, with 42 countries listing no female inventors whatsoever.[48] Among academic life science patentees, women patent at about 40 percent the rate of men.[49]

Underlying these practical problems is a broader doctrinal failure. At its heart, the public use bar is about disclosure, a transfer of information from one person to another. As such, it is a distinctly social phenomenon that is fact specific and highly contextual. And yet the principles of privacy-as-control, which, as discussed in Chapter 2, locate analysis within the disclosing party rather than in the social context of disclosure, dominate the doctrine. Judges tend to focus on the inventor's volitional acts and secondarily, if at all, consider the context in which those acts occurred. Only rarely are social norms respected like they are in *Bernhardt*, and when they are, corporate inventors are usually the beneficiaries.

In cases like *Bernhardt*, the Federal Circuit acknowledged that the relationship between the inventor and those to whom she discloses her invention should matter because certain relationships could give rise to an expectation of confidentiality. In *Bernhardt*, the court accepted that participants in the premarket furniture show could have a custom of confidentiality based on their status as industry partners.[50] And in *Dey*, the court recognized that patients in clinical trials typically do not sign confidentiality agreements, so, given that custom, none should be required in this case.[51] But those relationships are ignored in solo entrepreneur cases. If anything, the relationships between the parties in *Beachcombers* (friends and colleagues), *Lough* (friends and colleagues), and *MIT* (friends) were closer than the relationships in *Bernhardt* (participants in the same business) and *Dey* (clinical trial designers and subjects), and yet all three of the former lost their public use cases.

A TRUST-BASED APPROACH

Armed with the lessons of privacy-as-trust from Chapter 5, we can return to the public use cases discussed above. So far, we have seen that the public use bar is applied either haphazardly, at best, or in a discriminatory way, at worst, with no clear tools in the current doctrine to resolve the problem. The dominant theory of adjudication – what privacy scholars would call privacy-as-control – lends itself to the harsh, bright line, and uneven application of the law.

Privacy-as-trust offers a model for adjudicating public use cases. Using a totality of the circumstances test that focuses on the audience for a disclosure and the relationship and indicia of trust between the inventor and the audience, the standard will comport with what we know about how and why individuals share information with others. In this section, I revisit some of the leading public use cases discussed above and show how some would turn out the same, others would end differently, and others require more information to resolve. Luckily, a network-specific trust-based approach lays out clear pathways for the admission of evidence, allowing appellate judges to remand cases with specific instructions for fact finding.

A case like *Xerox Corp. v. 3Com Corp.*,[52] a corporate defendant case, would come to the same result. The analysis would vary only slightly. In *Xerox*, a company employee invented a method that improved computer handwriting recognition.[53] Concluding that the inventor's submission of a videotape of himself demonstrating the invention to conference organizers as part of an application to present did not invalidate his patent, the court explained that the videotape was not a public *use*: no one, other than the inventor, had actually used anything.[54] That can hardly be the rule in public use cases; cases like *Baxter* and *Eolas Technologies v. Microsoft Corp.* both found invalidating public uses after mere demonstration by the inventor.[55] But the court did rely on the norms, customs, and practices of the context of the disclosure. Although the inventor in *Xerox* did not include a secrecy agreement along with his submission, the court recognized that conference organizers keep submissions confidential as a matter of "professional courtesy and practice" and that they were under "a professional ethical obligation" to maintain secrecy.[56]

This holding makes sense under a social network and trust model, as well. Given the relationship between the inventor and his audience, norms of trust can be implied: academic conference organizers generally do not reveal the details of submissions made to them. And even if the submission was sent to the two organizers who shared it with a selection committee, that audience operates under the same norms of confidentiality. As such, the information was shared with expectations of confidentiality and discretion. The law should respect that.

The results of many cases would change, however. This is best illustrated by a solo entrepreneur case, *Beachcombers*[57] and a corporate case, *Honeywell International Inc. v. Universal Avionics Systems Corp.*[58] In *Beachcombers*, the Federal Circuit found that demonstration of a new kaleidoscope at the designer's home constituted invalidating public use. The court was not clear about its reasoning; the lack of any analysis may suggest that the court was simply relying on the lack of any confidentiality agreement. At a minimum, it is clear that the court ignored the social context of disclosure. The invite-only party was at the designer's private home gathered 20 to 30 of her friends and for the express purpose of soliciting feedback.[59] Despite the lack of any formal secrecy agreement, norms of trust were strong among this group: the audience members were her close friends, and they operated under norms of confidentiality; additional evidence could be admitted to describe the audience in more detail. Lior Strahilevitz's social networks approach to information flow problems would work well here. That those in attendance were the designer's social friends suggests that the technology of the kaleidoscope was relatively complex to them, making it the type of information that does not travel well through weak ties. Therefore, even if the invitees included some acquaintances or weak ties, the details of the invention would be unlikely to travel well from network to network. Nor should we ignore the fact that the alleged public use took place at the designer's home, a paradigmatic private context,[60] which not only makes further information diffusion even less likely, but also contributes to the emergence of reliable norms of confidentiality.

The result in *Honeywell* would also change. That case involved Honeywell's terrain warning system, which helped prevent pilots from flying into mountains and which was demonstrated to potential customers and a reporter more than one year before patenting.[61] The Federal Circuit found no public use because all demonstrations could be considered experimental. That rationale rings hollow: the demonstrations were for customers – more than 150 of them – who, the court admitted, would be purchasing the technology in the future. It was more important to the court that Honeywell personnel conducted the demonstrations and "maintained control over them," even though it is hard to imagine who else would be conducting the test runs. To make these demonstrations seem relatively private, the district court emphasized that there was no indication that the general public ever became aware of the technology.[62] That a reporter was on board was irrelevant.

Privacy-as-trust would conclude, from the totality of the circumstances, that Honeywell engaged in public use. The audience for its disclosure included members of the aviation industry who were likely going to purchase the system and a former pilot and aviation reporter who subsequently wrote an article about the technology. Unless reporters specifically promise to keep anything they learn from a subject on background, norms of confidentiality do not normally exist between a reporter and her subject, especially in contexts where the reporter is present specifically to write about what she sees. Under Lior Strahilevitz's social network approach, this type of audience of experts is constituted by precisely the kind of weak ties that could both understand the technology and disseminate it; indeed, the writer's job is to disseminate the information. There is also no indication, unlike, say, in *Bernhardt*,[63] that the norms and customs of the aviation industry ensure that all parties share the burden of keeping information confidential. Additional evidence about industry norms and practice could be admitted to buttress or challenge that conclusion.

There are undoubtedly some closer calls, but additional evidence could help us apply the social network and trust model. In *Lough*, for example, where a boat repairman installed his new device on his friends' boats,[64] we would want to know more about these friends, their history with the inventor, and the context in which the device was disclosed in the first place. In *National Research Development Corp. v. Varian Associates*, where the inventor's academic adviser disclosed his student's invention to an acquaintance at an academic conference,[65] applying trust theory would require additional evidence about the relationship between the parties. But this type of evidence is easily admitted, and the detour into social science is well worth the added fairness benefits.

In the end, privacy-as-trust offers a fair and administrable approach to public use cases. The proposal treats corporate and solo inventors equally and gives everyone a chance to contribute to the innovation economy. In some situations, cases would have come to different results under privacy-as-trust. But for most cases, the doctrine provides a robust intellectual foundation for reasoning through public use questions and helps ensure honest application of what was always meant to be a flexible standard for patent validity.

RESPONSES TO OBJECTIONS

Some might object to the structure or mode of analysis of privacy as trust as too indeterminate and inappropriate for patent law. Others might focus on the results, suggesting that the proposal would encourage risky business behavior and cut off more knowledge from the public domain, thus running counter to the goals of patent law. I respond to these objections in turn.

A totality of the circumstances test, the argument goes, is too flexible and too indeterminate, providing too much discretion, too few guidelines, and no way to prevent a judge from imposing his personal preferences on a given case. This is a common refrain in diverse areas of law,[66] but it rings hollow in this case. Totality of the circumstances tests, in general, allow fair and individual determinations of fact-specific cases. They are in use across intellectual property regimes.[67] And even under the current standard, public use cases are supposed to be highly fact specific, depending on the inventor's actions, the details of the disclosure, and whether she had the foresight and leverage to mandate nondisclosure. What's more, the very deficiencies we've discussed – discriminatory application of public use law to privilege corporate inventors over solo entrepreneurs – stem not from a boundless totality of the circumstances test, but a misapplication of the law through a bright line privacy-as-control standard. Although bright line rules are undoubtedly more definite, a privacy-as-trust approach comes with clear guidelines that limit the analysis to only relevant factors: the social context of disclosure, the information disclosed, and the relationships between the audience and the inventor and the audience and the information.

A second structural objection to applying privacy-as-trust in this context is that it imports a doctrine from unrelated areas of law and social science that address problems and policies distinct from patent law. I disagree. Not only did Samuel Warren and Louis Brandeis refer to the doctrinal and theoretical relationships between intellectual property and privacy law more than 125 years ago,[68] distinguished scholars in both fields have been learning lessons from each other ever since.[69] Indeed, paraphrasing Jonathan Zittrain's powerful argument, the "problem" of privacy and intellectual property is the same: information flow.[70] In privacy, individuals seek to protect the dissemination of personal data; many privacy questions concern the wrongful disclosure of intimate information. The public use bar addresses a similar matter – namely, the diffusion of information about an invention via first-person disclosure. To answer these questions, both fields seek a way to determine the difference between public and private after an initial, limited disclosure. Considering similar approaches, therefore, makes sense.

The final two objections concern the practical implications of employing a social network and trust approach to public use. Some might argue that by recognizing the norms of confidentiality of informal relationships between friends and intimates, privacy-as-trust would result in more findings of non-public use. But allowing more inventors to use their devices without the voluminous disclosures required in a patent application would run counter to a central goal of patent law, i.e., the disclosure of knowledge to the public.[71] This argument misreads the data and misses the point of privacy-as-trust. As discussed above, some public and nonpublic use cases would come to same results under a social network and trust approach. The proposal is merely a mode of analysis that also addresses inequality in the application of current public use law. If it does result in more solo entrepreneurs being allowed to retain their patents, so be it: the PTO has already recognized the need to improve access by part-time inventors and hobbyists[72] and the progress of science and technology in society, the salient and overarching purpose of the patent system,[73] could only benefit.

Some may argue, too, that even if secrecy commitments are not always possible, codifying norms of confidentiality as adequate replacements encourages risky behavior. The law, the argument continues, should incentivize corporate and solo entrepreneurs alike to take every necessary precaution to secure their inventions, and downplaying confidentiality agreements does the opposite. I resist the temptation to use a discriminatory weapon as a paternalistic tool, especially one that has a disparate impact on entrepreneurs. Focusing on the context of disclosure encourages risky behavior no more than privacy law does when it allows individuals to rely on their legitimate expectations of privacy. And the elevation of confidentiality agreements to near determinative status is less a tool of social policy than a giveaway to corporate entities that have the leverage to employ them. A privacy-as-trust model for public use, therefore, does not so much encourage bad behavior as implement an egalitarian approach to patentability.

10

Trust and Robots

When we start thinking about our privacy in terms of trust and social relationships, we bring privacy law in line with our social behavior. We've explored this throughout much of this book. In Chapter 6, we detailed the inadequacy of a notice-and-choice approach to the relationship between users and technology companies. Privacy-as-trust instead suggests that a wide range of data collectors, from ISPs like AT&T, Verizon, and Comcast, to Internet companies like Google, Facebook, and Amazon, should be held to the higher legal standard of trusted fiduciaries. Chapter 7 looked at previous disclosure cases. There, we saw that much current privacy law embraces the notion that voluntary disclosure of information to anyone erodes privacy rights. This fails to appreciate that we share personal information in context, relying on expectations of confidentiality and discretion among specific other people and groups. In Chapter 8, I argued that rights-based approaches to privacy left wide gaps in online harassment law, preventing some victims of the nonconsensual use and dissemination of their intimate photographs from finding justice. And in Chapter 9, we applied the central lesson of privacy-as-trust – namely, that information disclosed in social relationships characterized by confidentiality and discretion can still be considered private and protected – to intellectual property, where traditional approaches to information flow threaten to erode the rights of inventors.

Privacy-as-trust has another effect: it shines a spotlight on how our trust can be manipulated to compromise our privacy. As we discussed in Chapter 6, Facebook integrates the connection between trust and sharing into the design of its News Feed, where cues of trust are deployed to encourage us to engage with or click on a post. When we know that Amanda, Steven, Lucy and 19 of our friends have "liked" or commented on something, we are more likely to engage, as well.[1] This may be an effective and welcome strategy to increase social connection. But those cues may raise deceptive practice concerns when they are used on native advertisements. Knowing we are more likely to click on something when we are reminded that our friends have also clicked,[2] Facebook uses the same trust cues on social and sponsored posts to make those advertisements more valuable. But those posts raise different privacy concerns, especially when clicking on an advertisement takes us to a third party website with dubious or unknown data use practices.[3]

And technology's ability to inspire potentially misplaced trust is only growing.

Robots are the next big thing, even though they have been around industry and the military for some time.[4] Social robots, physically embodied agents that interact with and learn from humans on a social level, are a special breed.[5] Social robots are our therapeutic baby seals, household assistants, and Sony AIBO devices. They are Uma Thurman in the movie *Her.* As a form of "technosocial" change, to use Katherine Strandburg's term, social robots are at the center of social as well as technological evolutions, changing our behavior in profound ways, from how we socialize to how we get a cup of morning coffee.[6] They are extraordinary additions to our social lives, taking us closer to *Star Trek*'s Data. But at the same time, they create distinct privacy dangers: they collect troves of information about us, may inhibit our behavior, erode our capacity to manage our personae, and lull us into false senses of security, safety, and trust.

Traditional understandings of privacy are ill equipped to adequately and comprehensively characterize the privacy pitfalls posed by social robots for two main reasons. First, the entire purpose of a social robot is to connect, communicate, and share. If we conceive of privacy along the Lockean and Kantian lines we discussed in Chapters 1 and 2 – namely, based on notions of separation, choice, and autonomy – privacy as a concept is incompatible with social robots. That is, much like there is no privacy, conventionally understood, in a world of online data tracking, there is no privacy around a social robot. Second, as one of the founders of the field of law and robotics, Ryan Calo, has noted, much privacy scholarship to date has been principally focused on responding to only one facet of technological innovation – namely, technology's ability to gather and process more information faster and more efficiently.[7] This should come as no surprise. That body of scholarship starts from the idea that privacy is about separation, autonomy, or choice. And, as such, the collection of data without our consent gives scholars pause. But social robots do more than gather information.[8] Among other things, as Calo describes, social robots trigger our innate, psychological needs to connect, emote, and love. This is Calo's concept of "social valence"[9] and it is this social experience with robots that makes us vulnerable.

A consistent, yet underappreciated theme in the literature on privacy, social behavior, and robotics is that the real danger posed by social robots is that they are designed to cue trust, making us vulnerable to manipulated disclosures. They lull us into false senses of trust by their very nature,[10] even though there is usually a data-hungry technology company pulling the strings behind the curtain.[11] Therefore, consumers of social robots must be warned. A privacy-as-trust approach to social robots not only helps build a comprehensive picture of the dangers we face as technology takes on increasingly human-like characteristics, but also clears a path toward framing a regulatory response from the Federal Trade Commission.[12]

WHAT IS A ROBOT?

Definitions of "robot" vary depending on your perspective. *Star Wars* fans think of R2-D2 or C-3PO; Pixar fans think of Wall-E. I think of a roving toy I had as a child. But those are not definitions. In fact, they are constraining prejudices. If we only think of C-3PO and his voice, emotional reactions, and physical embodiment when we think of robots, then we will miss many things that are, in fact, robotic. A roboticist with a background in mechanical engineering would probably use a technical definition: a robot is a mechanical object that takes in data from the world, processes it, and then physically acts according to preprogrammed commands.[13] Bill Smart, a computer scientist whose research and writing focus on robotics and artificial intelligence, and Neil Richards, a privacy law scholar, note that robots are constructed by humans to behave intelligently as they interact with the world.[14]

A social robot is a subset of the broader population of robots. Social robots "augment" robots' ability to behave somewhat autonomously, with social abilities like communication, cooperation, and learning.[15] According to Calo, robots, in general, and certainly social robots, in particular, have three essential qualities that are relevant for any legal discussion: social robots are embodied, emergent, and have a social valence. They are embodied in the sense that they occupy physical forms. They may be programmed to act based on a coded series of 1's and 0's and may even be connected to the Cloud, but social robots take physical action.[16] Robots are also emergent in that they (and their programming) can learn and adapt to new circumstances. Although technology with this ability is still improving,[17] there are plenty of examples of robots that learn. Calo tells us about a new robot butler that tries, and tries, and tries various different ways to split an Oreo, learning from its mistakes. Learning robots are deployed in military settings, as well.[18] It is only a matter of time before robotic household assistants turn on our coffeemakers at 5:45 AM after noticing that we have, over the last several weeks, regularly done the same. Finally, Calo argues that robots have a social valence. They create emotional reactions in people and we use social models to understand them.[19] Why else, as various researchers have shown, would human subjects become uncomfortable with and resistant to behaviors that would "harm" robots?[20] Together, these studies show that we do not think of robots like we do machines, appliances, or mechanical tools. Nor do we think of them as human. From a phenomenological point of view,[21] we think of them as human*ish*, for lack of a better word, with some of the characteristics of humans and, therefore, with the related ability to inspire human emotions and reactions.[22]

In the end, then, what makes a robot "social," as Cynthia Breazeal, a professor and director of the Personal Robots Group at the MIT Media Laboratory, has noted, is the way we interact with it. Humans "apply a social model" to dealing with social robots in their physical world because these robots *feel* social to us. This isn't accidental: social robots are specifically designed to trigger our predisposition to anthropomorphize.[23] They are designed to induce the kind of trust that we usually reserve for other humans, lull us into false senses of security, and, as we have discussed throughout this book, increase our propensity to disclose. Woodrow Hartzog called this "the most fundamental reason we are vulnerable to robots."[24] And herein lies the risk to our privacy.

ROBOTS AND TRADITIONAL UNDERSTANDINGS OF PRIVACY

Unlike some of the other law and policy problems discussed in this book, robots are relatively new. There is, therefore, a considerable amount of educated guesswork involved in determining how current law applies. Several scholars pioneered this discussion, including, primarily, Calo and the law professors Ian Kerr and Michael Froomkin, among others.[25] Some have researched the law of driverless cars;[26] others work at the intersection of machines and criminal justice;[27] yet other scholars have considered how the First Amendment would apply to artificial intelligence.[28] My goal is less ambitious – namely, to consider the ways in which embodied social robots may invade our privacy and to critically examine the ability of traditional conceptions of privacy to recognize and respond to those dangers.

The rights-based visions of privacy we discussed in Chapters 1 and 2 can capture some of the ways social robots can invade our privacy; sometimes, they can't. A privacy-as-trust lens fills in the gaps, highlighting some of the most significant dangers. Even where traditional privacy recognizes a problem, it cannot always offer a solution. As such, as has been the argument throughout this book, the ways we are used to thinking through privacy are not wrong, but rather incomplete. The privacy dangers of social robots illustrate this point well.

First, social robots are designed to gather information about us and share it with others. Hartzog calls them "nothing short of . . . perfected surveillance machine[s]."[29] Information gathering and processing is essential to robots' daily functioning – Alexa can't know what we want to know unless we ask her – and necessary for robots to learn and adapt to new circumstances. Calo gives a particularly eye-opening example of how the information-gathering powers of a robot can challenge our privacy. Robotic shopping assistants, he notes, are used to approach customers and encourage purchases. But "[u]nlike ordinary store clerks . . . robots are capable of recording and processing every aspect of the transaction. Face-recognition technology permits easy re-identification. Such meticulous, point-blank customer data could be of extraordinary use in both loss prevention and marketing research."[30] This eventuality makes the Target predictive pregnancy incident pale in comparison. Target used disparate pieces of information scattered about the Internet to predict something about its customers;[31] social robots can examine our faces, body movements, gait, race, marital status, aural responses, and wrinkles, among other things, to predict everything we could possibly need. And they do so without context and usually without us evening knowing. Imagine a robot shopper examining a man's shopping behavior to predict his next purchase, only to confuse his purchasing habits for his mistress with his purchasing habits for his wife. Suddenly, a robot of convenience becomes a robot of marital discord. Another factor that make data gathering by robots more problematic than even Target's data gathering and analysis is that the information social robots learn is likely deeply personal: any robot that spends time with us in our homes is going to hear and see things many of us would prefer stay in the home.[32]

But to the extent that this type of collection and transfer of personal data strikes us as invasive, traditional approaches to privacy that focus on autonomy, choice, and control are ill equipped to respond. Consumers choose to have robots in their homes, consent to terms of use, and assume the risk that the information shared with their robot could be shared with others. If privacy is understood as the ability to choose to keep information hidden from some others, then these consumers chose to reveal intimate information to an information-gathering machine. And, as in cases like *Gill v. Hearst Publishing Company*, where a man and woman had no recourse against a company for publishing a candid photo of them kissing at a fair,[33] this type of assumption of risk is often fatal to a successful privacy claim. What's more, a privacy regime based on traditional forms of notice-and-choice is also inadequate to warn users of this problem. Robots engage in ongoing collection of data; consent at one point does not necessarily imply consent in perpetuity. Social robots also lack an available interface that allows users to input privacy and disclosure preferences, making it difficult for users to freely consent in the first place.[34] This is not to say that notice-and-choice cannot be adapted and changed to take advantage of robots' unique abilities.[35] But it does highlight the inadequacy of the current approach.

Another way robots can challenge our privacy is by eroding opportunities for solitude. Computers, generally, and robots, in particular, are stepping into places traditionally reserved for just us, like homes, cars, and even our pockets.[36] And yet solitude is an important value long coveted and recognized by privacy scholars. Warren and Brandeis wrote their famous article, *A Right to Privacy*, in reaction to a newly emboldened press trying to intrude on the privacy of their homes.[37] Other scholars have talked about privacy as an "existential condition" of being alone or as living a "secluded life" separated from the burdens of society.[38] And solitude's value is manifold, not the least of which are the chances for psychological respites from society and the ability, as legal theorists like Julie Cohen and Neil Richards have argued, to experiment, test out ideas, and act upon our curiosities outside the constraining pressure of social surveillance.[39] But although traditional conceptions of privacy have no problem recognizing robots' threat to solitude, it is not entirely clear what current law, based on this intellectual tradition, can do about it. There are two reasons why, both of which we've discussed in this book. First, user consent pursuant to notice is fatal to most privacy claims, and users consent to having these robots in their otherwise private places. Second, the harms wrought by constant surveillance and the lack of solitude are intangible and psychological. But as Daniel Solove and Danielle Citron point out, the law has been squeamish when it comes to recognizing these nonpecuniary privacy injuries, denying standing to anyone unless they can point to actual money lost.[40] Creepiness and no less serious psychological harms be damned.

But the most profound and problematic privacy harm posed by social robots is induced – and misplaced – trust. Social robots are not merely machines that gather data. Nor are they devices with eyes that watch us wherever we go. They are designed to engage with us on a social level, triggering deep, unconscious, and basic social needs. Nefarious technology companies can then take advantage of us.

SOCIAL REACTIONS TO SOCIAL ROBOTS

Humans are social animals. We have an innate, evolutionary need to connect with others.[41] And we apply social models to understand and interact with the world around us.[42] One of those social models is anthropomorphization, which is ascribing human characteristics to nonhuman things. In the movie *Cast Away*, for example, Tom Hanks created a relationship with a volleyball. The movie grossed nearly $430 million worldwide; clearly, many people could relate. Many children (and some adults) anthropomorphize their stuffed animals. We often attribute human-like qualities like sensation, intent, feelings, and autonomy, to name just a few, to otherwise inanimate objects. The desire is inborn, and the reaction is "hard wired" and subconscious.[43]

Research suggests that our social models grow stronger as objects take on more humanlike characteristics. Hanks painted a face on his volleyball, which only then could be perceived as a head. Many people put eyes on their Roombas,[44] and two-thirds of Roomba owners give them names.[45] Even disembodied computer platforms that take on human characteristics generate powerful reactions from their human users. Human subjects over-bonded with ELIZA, the computer psychoanalysis program that asked users questions like a therapist and filled in conversation with dummy placeholder comments, prompting the experiment's designer to issue a warning call about the manipulative potential of artificial intelligence.[46] And, as Calo describes, humans will engage politely and happily with computers that appear kind and polite.[47]

Human-robot social connection is even more powerful. The psychologist Sherry Turkle has shown that people of all ages establish tight bonds with social robots. After playing with a humanoid robot that could make eye contact, follow her around, and imitate her movements, 11-year-old Fara called her social robot "something that's a part of you, you know, something you love, kind of like another person, like a baby."[48] A 71-year-old interviewee said of a furry robot companion that looked like a koala bear: "[w]hen I looked into his large, brown eyes, I feel in love after years of being quite lonely ... I swore to protect and care for the little animal."[49] Others have powerful emotional reactions just being around a robot: "[w]hen I wake up in the morning and see [My Real Baby's] face over there, it makes me feel so nice, like somebody is watching over me."[50] Some people even report preferring social connection with robots. Referring to her AIBO, Sony's household entertainment robot, one interviewee said that "[i]t is better than a real dog ... It won't do dangerous things and it won't betray you ... Also, it won't die suddenly and make you feel very sad."[51]

Therefore, it stands to reason that as social robot technology improves, as they become even more human*ish*, our emotional responses to them will be even stronger. In one experiment, human subjects made better eye contact with human*ish* robots.[52] In another, people playing prisoner dilemma games with technological interfaces tended to keep their promises with more humanoid partners.[53] Calo has collected many other examples in his substantial work on the subject.[54] Suffice it to say, as Karl MacDorman and Hiroshi Ishiguro note, "[h]uman-like appearance and behavior are required to elicit the sorts of responses that people typically direct toward one another."[55] But the more human*ish* they get, "the more human-directed . . . expectations are elicited."[56] Among those expectations is trust.

SOCIAL ROBOTS AND PRIVACY

There are three related ways in which this strong human-robot connection is relevant for our discussion of privacy. First, social robots inspire trust, which, as we have discussed, is an important factor in our decision to share personal information with others. Second, those perceptions of trust, in addition to our other emotional responses to social robots, are entirely natural and often subconscious. This suggests that regardless of our rational ability to distinguish humans from that which is human*ish*, our responses to social robots are difficult, if not impossible, to stop. And, third, these natural, emotional responses are strongest when we are most vulnerable, suggesting that we are at risk of manipulation by design. That is, technology companies creating social robots are capable of leveraging for profit our "hardwired" need to connect when we need it most. Traditional understandings of privacy are ill equipped to handle this reality; but a trust-based approach can do better.

We trust social robots by design (theirs and ours), by the disclosures and representations of the companies that make them, and even by their participation in social interaction. Notably, these are some of the same ways we grow to trust humans.

As we discussed in Chapter 5, trust is a natural, designed-in response to uncertainty. It solves the problem posed by the need to act in a world of uncertainty over how others will behave and how things will turn out.[57] If we didn't trust, our social lives would be paralyzed. Similarly, trust is one of the designed-in, hardwired emotional reactions we have with human*ish* robots. When playing trust games, we are more likely to keep our promises when our partner has more human characteristics.[58] During an experiment in which subjects performed problem solving tasks on platforms that sometimes included an animated character that watched and followed their movements, subjects reported "trusting" the websites more when the character seemed interested in what they were doing.[59] This extends to more complicated machines, as well. Adam Waytz, Joey Heafner, and Nicholas Epley, experts in psychology and human behavior, conducted several experiments where human subjects used one of three different driving simulators: a normal car, a more autonomous car able to control steering and speed, or a more advanced self-driving vehicle augmented with additional anthropomorphic features – name, gender, and voice. The researchers found that, on various metrics, users trusted the vehicles more as they took on more human*ish* characteristics.[60] Subjects not only self-reported that they trusted the cars more as more human-like features were added; they also tended to like the anthropomorphic cars more and felt more relaxed during the simulation.[61]

Therefore, the capacity to trigger trust by design can be programmed. And technology companies have an interest in ensuring trust exists between con-sumers and their robots. Social robots cannot learn to anticipate our needs if we don't share with them; they cannot learn to perform tasks or give us the information we want unless we feed it opportunities (read: data) to process. Indeed, the trajectory of robot design is poised to take better advantage of this social effect as technology improves. Social robots are taking on more human characteristics; we have already come a long way from a smiling, leery-eyed paperclip assistant in Microsoft Office.[62] Therefore, companies will design robots to be increasingly social and human*ish* in order to generate the kind of data necessary for the robot's "emergent" properties.[63]

Another way we come to trust robots is through their designers. Much like we trust the security of an iPhone because we trust Apple's commitment to cybersecurity,[64] we may trust a robot because we trust its designer. This is not unique to robots, social or otherwise. Brand names, and the entire legal field of trademark law, are meant, at least in part, to help build, sustain, and protect consumer trust in certain products so consumers will remain loyal.[65] And, as Hartzog has noted, consumers also trust robots, like they do other products, based on the representations and promises of the companies that sell them.[66]

Finally, we may find social robots trustworthy through interaction. By virtue of the fact that social robots are embodied creatures, we interact with them in the real world. They use sounds, language, and movement in ways reminiscent of, if not identical to, humans. As such, social robots at least have the capacity to appear trustworthy if they seem to play along in the "social game," to use the philosopher Mark Coeckelbergh's phrase.[67] This idea evokes Erving Goffman's discussions of social relations in public. For Goffman, social interaction is an ongoing dance, with both leaders and followers sharing responsibility for continuing the dance. Individuals determine what they want to reveal and how they want to behave based on context. Their interaction partners (Goffman calls them the "audience") recognize this and play along.[68] Robots "play along." They generally behave in expected ways: Alexa answers questions; Roombas skate along the floor in seemingly random patterns; robot butlers get coffee. *Battlestar Galactica*-type concerns notwithstanding,[69] social robots will still generally behave in expected ways, giving them at least the appearance of conforming to behavioral norms.

This means that there are many reasons and mechanisms by which we may come to trust robots. Scholars who have studied and written about human interactions with social robots agree that this reaction is natural, unconscious, and biological. Kate Darling, a research specialist in MIT's Media Lab, notes that we have an "involuntary" tendency to over-ascribe autonomy and intelligence and project sentiments and feelings onto social robots because these robots "mimic lifelike behavior" by reacting to us, responding to our movements, speaking in sentences, and even using facial expressions to augment verbal communication just like humans.[70] Calo calls our anthropomorphic reactions to robots' physical activity in the world "hardwired" responses.[71] MacDorman and Ishiguro call it "largely subconscious."[72] As involuntary, hardwired, or predetermined by our biology, these responses are difficult, if not impossible to stop.

These responses are also particularly strong when we are at our most vulnerable. We know from an extensive literature on anthropomorphism that people who feel isolated or lonely attribute human-like qualities to inanimate objects at far higher rates that those who feel socially connected to others.[73] This translates into the marketplace, too, where isolated or disconnected consumers prefer goods, brands, and product designs with anthropomorphic qualities.[74] Lonely people also typically engage in what psychologists called "compensatory behaviors" to reestablish necessary social connection.[75] This scholarship inspired a group of researchers, led by the psychologist James Mourey, to test whether human*ish* robots can actually replace social connection with humans. Their results, published in a paper aptly titled, "Products as Pals," showed that social robots can indeed mitigate our need for social connection with real humans.

Mourey and his team conducted four experiments, leading them to conclude that while isolated or lonely individuals will generally seek to reach out and increase their social connections to compensate for their loss, introducing a social robot with human*ish* qualities actually reduces those compensatory social behaviors.[76] That is, people are *replacing* humans with human*ish* robots. The first experiment asked participants to write a short essay either about a time they were excluded from a social event or what they did the day before. Both groups were then asked questions about the functionality of their smartphones: some of those questions attributed agency to the phone, anthropomorphizing the device. Finally, the groups were asked, among other questions, to estimate the number of friends they had on Facebook.[77] This was a creative approach. Those disconnected socially in the physical world tend to estimate they have more Facebook friends than they actually do; it serves as a compensatory mechanism for social loss.[78] But Mourey found that those disconnected individuals primed to anthropomorphize their phones did not inflate their numbers of Facebook friends. In other words, they evidenced less of a need to compensate for loneliness.[79]

Mourey's second experiment went a few steps further. Subjects participated in an online ball tossing game with three other pre-programmed "players." In the control condition, participants were tossed the ball one-quarter of the time; in the social exclusion condition, participants got the ball three times at the beginning of the game, and never again. All participants were then shown pictures of Roombas, with varying degrees of anthropomorphic qualities. Among other things, the final survey asked participants to estimate how much time on the phone they anticipated spending with their friends or family, a social connection mechanism. Again, Mourey found that exposure to highly social robots mitigated respondents' need to socially connect with humans: Those who felt excluded from the ball tossing game and were shown a Roomba with human*ish* characteristics expected to spend far less time connecting with friends and family than those excluded from the game who saw a disinterested vacuuming machine.[80]

Next, Mourey tested social robots' effect on what psychologists call "social assurance." Social assurance is a reminder of our place in the social world. People with low levels of social assurance tend to agree with the statements, "My life is incomplete without a buddy beside me" or "I wish to find someone who can be with me all the time." And those with high social assurance exhibit greater independence and would disagree with both statements.[81] Mourey and his team found that people primed to feel socially disconnected or lonely who were then exposed to an anthropomorphized Roomba exhibited far lower need for social assurance. In other words, they felt better about their social lives, better about remaining independent, and less in need of social connection to be happy.[82]

This allowed Mourey to conduct one final experiment, which sought to determine whether reminding people that a Roomba was just a machine would affect their need for social assurance. And, indeed, it did. Socially excluded people who participated in the same experiment but were told that a Roomba is just vacuum reported lower levels of social assurance than those who completed the experiment without the reminder.[83]

This research has a number of implications, all of which confirm the existing literature discussed above. First, it shows that human*ish* machines can fulfill our social needs without us even knowing it; the process is entirely subconscious. The social assurance effect of machines only drops when we're reminded that anthropomorphism is different than human. Second, Mourey shows that human*ish* machines can partly replace real humans in the pursuit of social connection. The plotline of the movie *Her*, therefore, has a strong basis in research. Finally, these subconscious social effects are particularly notable among vulnerable people – namely, those socially disconnected or lonely, or those primed to think of themselves as such based on powerful memories.

What does all of this have to do with trust, sharing, and the privacy risks posed by social robots? In short, the literature teaches us that social robots can be deployed to induce trust. They are designed to trigger an innate, subconscious human need to connect. They can even sometimes replace social connection with humans, especially among those most vulnerable and isolated. But because they are still robots, programmed and designed to track and gather information about us, social robots are ripe to deceive us into disclosing information. Their design can lull us into false senses of trust because they seem human*ish*; they seem to exhibit some of the necessary cues upon which we base trust. We don't always realize that there is a data hungry technology company behind the curtain.

In highlighting some of the problems with these so-called Wizard-of-Oz setups, Jacqueline Kory Westlund and Cynthia Breazeal note that users "may disclose sensitive information to the robot that they would not tell a human, not realizing that a human is hearing everything they say."[84] Westlund and Breazeal continue, recognizing the implications: "[g]iven that social robots are designed to draw us in, often engaging us emotionally and building relationships with us, the robot itself could be deceptive in that it appears to have an emotional response to you but 'in reality' does not."[85] Kate Darling poses a series of questions:

> If people develop attachments to their robot companions, can the companies who control the hard- and software exploit this attachment? Should companies be allowed to make use of the fact that individuals might have a massively increased willingness to pay for technology upgrades or repairs? What about sneaking advertisements for products into children's dialogs with robotic toys?[86]

Woodrow Hartzog put the problem succinctly:

> Robots, particularly embodied ones, are uniquely situated to mentally manip-
> ulate people. Robots can mimic human socialization, yet they are without
> shame, fatigue, or internal inconsistency. Robots are also scalable, so the
> decision to design a robot to manipulate humans will impact hundreds, if not
> thousands or millions of people.[87]

The mechanism of manipulation that Westlund, Breazeal, Darling, and
Hartzog are talking about is inducing misplaced trust by design. Social robots
are designed to use their human*ish* qualities to inspire trust. But that trust may
be deceptively generated, manipulative, and unfair.

A TRUST-BASED APPROACH TO SOCIAL ROBOTS

If robots are designed to seem like our "pals" but really parasitically feed off of
us for our data, we are being used and manipulated. In this way, social robots
can be deceptive and manipulative. Through a veil of human*ish* qualities,
they can make people forget that a technology company is gathering data
behind a friendly exterior. Social robots are also tools of surveillance, tracking
us even without our knowledge. And they are programmed by algorithms that
are usually hidden from us.[88]

Traditional conceptions of privacy inadequately capture these problems.
So too do notice-and-choice and current approaches to standing in privacy
claims. An information fiduciary approach like the one advocated by Jack
Balkin, Jonathan Zittrain, and others, and discussed in Chapter 6, offers an
alternative. That would allow individuals to sue robot manufacturers when
they induce our trust and then betray us. It is a natural implication of privacy-
as-trust. But not all deceptions need to be actionable under a private lawsuit.
The Federal Trade Commission has a role to play.[89] Daniel Solove, Chris
Hoofnagle, and Woodrow Hartzog have done extensive work chronicling and
analyzing the FTC's privacy jurisprudence.[90] Hartzog in particular has argued
that the FTC is well situated to expand its current consumer protection work
to capture manipulation by robot. To do so, however, the FTC must recognize
that the core consumer privacy concern raised by manipulative social robots is
their capacity to breach trust. As such, privacy-as-trust can be a helpful intellectual umbrella for understanding and justifying FTC action to protect
consumers in this space.

The FTC has broad regulatory authority to police "unfair or deceptive trade
practices."[91] That charge includes holding companies' feet to the fire for any
representation, omission, or practice that is likely to mislead consumers, and

identifying unfair practices as they come up.[92] Under these doctrines, the FTC has challenged many deceptive practices, including misleading advertising and deceptive product demonstrations, both of which can come into play with social robots.[93] As noted earlier, social robots have the capacity to turn into Wizard-of-Oz setups, where users are confused about what is behind robots' social interfaces. When the data hungry technology company is revealed, users' trust is betrayed. As such, the deception lies in using the human*ish* qualities of social robots to manipulate people into thinking that the robot is something other than a voracious data gathering device. Companies that fail to adequately inform and remind users, whether through creative "visceral" notice or otherwise,[94] may be engaging in deception.

Social robots not only betray our trust when we discover the man behind the curtain, they betray our trust by hiding the extent of their surveillance. The FTC has already sued technology companies that have programmed their platforms to gather user data without notice on the theory that we "cannot reasonably avoid these injuries" when the surveillance "is invisible."[95] In *In re Frostwire, LLC*, for example, the company misled customers into thinking that certain files would not be publicly accessible on the peer-to-peer network.[96] And in *In re Sony BMG Music Entertainment*, the FTC alleged that software Sony installed on its CDs would transmit music-listening data back to Sony.[97] Although the word "trust" was missing from the complaints in *Frostwire* and *Sony*, broken trust played an important role: both companies gave "misleading impression[s]" by hiding surveillance behind an avalanche of interfaces that were meant to give users the impression of control. Social robots, with interfaces designed to induce trust, can make this deception even more effective.

Undoubtedly, determining when a social robot rises to the level of deception is a fact-based, contextual assessment. Not all human*ish* designs are actionable, even though they will all trigger trust. However, trust plays a role. The FTC can look to a company's disclosures, advertising campaign, product design, demonstrations, and other factors to determine if they are using the social characteristics of a social robot to deceive customers into misplaced trust. They can also gather evidence from consumers about how the trust was triggered by design. Doing so would protect the most vulnerable consumers from manipulation and provided a helpful intellectual foundation for FTC jurisprudence.

Conclusion
The Future of Privacy and Trust

Pundits have been writing privacy's obituary for years. In 2014, Thomas Friedman wrote in the *New York Times* that "privacy is over."[1] Facebook's Mark Zuckerberg said that "the age of privacy is over" in 2010.[2] And Sun Microsystem's former CEO Scott McNealy declared, back in 1999, that we "have zero privacy anyway. Get over it."[3] We have been told privacy is dying for so long that the average person on the street can be excused for thinking it died years ago, alone, gasping for breath.

Privacy is only dead if we think about it narrowly. We tend to confuse privacy with secrecy, or limit the private world to the constellation of intimate, sexual, or familial facets of our lives. Courts frequently (though not exclusively) do the same. We also tend to think about privacy spatially ("behind closed doors") or as the ability to exclude others from something by closing a window, locking a door, or stepping inside our homes.

In some ways, new technologies and the mandates of modern life have made this kind of privacy antiquated. It's hard to keep anything secret these days, especially since browsing the Internet is an information sharing event; our credit cards numbers, likes and dislikes, browsing histories, and purchasing patterns are collected, analyzed, and sold by websites, technology companies, and advertisers. This makes it difficult to control the flow of our information. What's more, disclosure is often a necessary prerequisite of modern social life and, for some, for access to legal rights and entitlements.

Even if we think that privacy ends at disclosure, the privacy-is-dead meme still doesn't make much sense. We still keep many things private. We wear clothes. We lock dairies. We warn others: "This stays between us." Social life functions with privacy. And yet, even these habits fail to tell the whole story. We do wear clothes, but not always in front of our romantic partners. We do write secrets down in diaries, but sometimes share them with our best friends, therapists, or relative strangers at support group meetings. We do make explicit requests for confidentiality, but often not when sharing with those with whom confidentiality is implied. In other words, we manage the flow of our information with selective disclosures based on contextual norms of trust.

So understood, privacy is very much alive. It is a fact of life so engrained in the social structure that we couldn't live without it. In this book, I try to show that privacy, at least in the information-sharing context, is not about separating from society, but rather about engaging with it on terms based on trust. We share when we trust, and we do so expecting that even though we shared information with others, it is not up for grabs for just anyone to hear, see, or use. We feel our privacy is violated when our trust is breached, like when we are induced to share or when our information is taken from one place and given to people or companies about which we know nothing. And we use trust to contextually manage our personae and the flow of our information in order to engage in social life. Information privacy, therefore, is really a trust-based social construct between social sharers, between individuals and Internet intermediaries, between groups of people interacting online and offline, broadly understood. As such, privacy law should be focused on protecting and repairing the relationships of trust that are necessary for disclosure.

In this way, privacy law can be put to work for us, not just for data collectors. Disclosing information creates vulnerability, creating an imbalance of power between social sharers and audiences. Privacy-as-trust is a counterweight to the risks of disclosure because it gives us the means to ensure that our information will be used only in accordance with the norms of trust under which it was shared in the first place.

The approach to privacy I propose in this book is just the first step in that journey. Information law for an information age begins with framing the debate, with understanding that privacy is so much more than we thought. Although privacy-as-trust is not without controversy, it reflects deeply rooted values and everyday social practice. Students and scholars can use this book to understand the multidimensional connections between social life, privacy, and the law. We can use what we've learned in this book to more wisely engage with others online. Judges and lawyers can use this book as a roadmap for leveraging privacy law to protect those interactions. And policymakers can adapt regulatory and legislative proposals to more effectively protect consumers. Together, we can reach a better world where privacy and trust are twin pillars of law and society.

But much work still needs to be done. With respect to privacy law, it is worth studying other implications of privacy-as-trust. For example, even though this book focused exclusively on information sharing between private parties – between individuals and between individuals and websites, e-commerce companies, and technology firms, among others – it is worth asking: what does privacy-as-trust mean for disclosures to governments, law enforcement searches, and the Fourth Amendment? It certainly would question the legitimacy of the Third Party Doctrine, which states that individuals have no Fourth Amendment expectation of privacy in information already in the hands of third parties.[4] Privacy-as-trust may also undermine the so-called doctrine of misplaced trust, which allows law enforcement agents and informants to gain access to information by deceit and then, for the most part, use that information against a suspect.[5] The Third Party Doctrine is the erosion of privacy interests upon disclosure; privacy-as-trust protects privacy even after some sharing. Furthermore, using deception to gain someone's trust in order to elicit disclosure is akin to a con job; privacy-as-trust suggests that such breaches of trust should be treated as invasions of privacy. If anything, by virtue of the Fourth Amendment's exclusive application to governments and their agents, government data gathering should be more restricted than private information collection, but that conclusion and related policy implications should be explored more comprehensively.

Social scientists must continue to study the connection between trust and sharing. For example, psychologists, economists, and sociologists have been exploring how trust facilitates sharing among individuals in face-to-face and arm's length interactions. More research is needed not only to confirm that trust operates in similar ways in online interactions, but also to further explore what trust between Internet users and websites looks like. Trust in e-commerce settings may be different than trust while using a social network. The work of scholars like Kirsten Martin, Lorie Cranor, James Mourey, and others, as well as some of my own scholarship, focus on these and related questions.

Privacy-as-trust aims to reorient the way we think and write about information privacy. One of its goals is to break convention and inspire further study. But its primary goal is the protection of privacy in a digital world where information flows are instantaneous, inexpensive, and constant. Situating privacy within its social role is a necessary step toward answering questions posed by Internet, mobile, and future, as yet unimagined technologies. Sometimes, protecting privacy in this world can feel like tilting at windmills. But I am hopeful that we can change that. We are savvier about our data than we have ever been before. We are more conscious of the implications of online disclosures. And because we are creeped out when data gathering goes too far, we are making those expectations known to technology companies. But at the same time, Internet and digital technologies have tapped into an innate human desire to share. We want to share, and we want a society that benefits from our connectedness. Building that society starts here.

Notes

Introduction

1. Woodrow Hartzog, *There Is No Such Thing as "Public" Data*, SLATE (May 19, 2016, 9:15 AM), www.slate.com/articles/technology/future_tense/2016/05/okcupid_s_data_leak_shows_there_s_no_such_thing_as_public_data.html.
2. Brian Resnick, *Researchers Just Released Profile Data on 70,000 OkCupid Users Without Permission*, VOX (May 12, 2016, 6:00 PM), www.vox.com/2016/5/12/11666116/70000-okcupid-users-data-release.
3. Taylor Hatmaker, *In 2006, Harvard Also Conducted a Facebook Study That Went Too Far*, THE DAILY DOT (July 12, 2014, 6:55 AM), www.dailydot.com/debug/facebook-t3-study-tastes-ties-time/. *See also* Michael Zimmer, *"But the Data is Already Public": On the Ethics of Research in Facebook*, 12 ETHICS INF. TECH. 313 (2010).
4. *See, e.g.*, Latanya Sweeney, *Discrimination in Online Ad Delivery*, COMM. ACM, May 2013, at 44.
5. Naomi Lachance, *Facebook's Facial Recognition Software Is Different from the FBI's. Here's Why*, NPR: ALL TECH CONSIDERED (May 18, 2016, 9:30 AM), www.npr.org/sections/alltechconsidered/2016/05/18/477819617/facebooks-facial-recognition-software-is-different-from-the-fbis-heres-why.
6. Charles Duhigg, *How Companies Learn Your Secrets*, N.Y. TIMES MAG. (Feb. 16, 2012), www.nytimes.com/2012/02/19/magazine/shopping-habits.html.
7. Chris Frey, *Revealed: How Facial Recognition Has Invaded Shops—and Your Privacy*, GUARDIAN (Mar. 3, 2016, 07.01 EST), www.theguardian.com/cities/2016/mar/03/revealed-facial-recognition-software-infiltrating-cities-saks-toronto.
8. The "it's already public" defense is remarkably common. For example, the FBI has argued that its agents do not need warrants to set up stingrays, or decoy cell towers, to capture our cellphone location because they are only

collecting public information in public places. *See* David Kravets, *FBI Says Warrants Not Needed to Use "Stingrays" in Public Places*, ARS TECHNICA (Jan. 5, 2015, 2:25 PM), http://arstechnica.com/tech-policy/2015/01/fbi-says-search-warrants-not-needed-to-use-stringrays-in-public-places; *see also* Smith v. Maryland, 442 U.S. 735 (1979). Perpetrators of so-called "revenge porn," or the publication of intimate or graphic photos of others without their consent, often justify their behavior by stating that the victim sent them the photos in the first place. *See* Danielle Keats Citron & Mary Anne Franks, *Criminalizing Revenge Porn*, 49 WAKE FOREST L. REV. 345, 346 (2014). Similar arguments are deployed in "up skirt" photo cases, too: snapping pictures of a woman's body underneath her skirt cannot be an invasion of privacy, the theory goes, because the pictures were taken in public places. *See* Justin Jouvenal & Miles Parks, *Voyeur Charges Dropped Against Photographer at Lincoln Memorial*, WASH. POST (Oct. 9, 2014), www.washingtonpost.com/local/crime/voyeur-charges-dropped-against-upskirt-photographer-at-lincoln-memorial/2014/10/09/7dc90eac-4ff5-11e4-aa5e-7153e466a02d_story.html.

9. *See* Thomas Friedman, *Four Words Going Bye-Bye*, NEW YORK TIMES (May 21, 2014), www.nytimes.com/2014/05/21/opinion/friedman-four-words-going-bye-bye.html; Marshall Kirkpatrick, *Facebook's Zuckerberg Says the Age of Privacy Is Over*, READWRITE (Jan. 9, 2010), https://readwrite.com/2010/01/09/facebooks_zuckerberg_says_the_age_of_privacy_is_ov/; Polly Sprenger, *Sun on Privacy: 'Get Over It'*, WIRED (Jan. 26, 1999 12:00 PM), www.wired.com/1999/01/sun-on-privacy-get-over-it/.

10. Dan Solove called this the "secrecy paradigm." DANIEL J. SOLOVE, THE DIGITAL PERSON 42 (2004).

11. Sandra Petronio, Boundaries of Privacy 3 (2002).

12. Robert C. Post, *The Social Foundations of Privacy: Community and Self in the Common Law Tort*, 77 CAL. L. REV. 957, 959 (1989).

13. Ferdinand David Schoeman, Privacy and Social Freedom 8 (1992) (Privacy is a social norm that gives people the confidence to share and the ability to develop relationships in the process.).

14. Helen Nissenbaum, *Privacy as Contextual Integrity*, 79 WASH. L. REV. 119 (2004).

15. Helen Nissenbaum, Privacy in Context (2010).

16. Andrew Abbott, *Things of Boundaries*, 62 SOC. RES. 857, 862 (1995).

17. Julie E. Cohen, CONFIGURING THE NETWORKED SELF 110–26 (2012).

18. Robert K. Merton, SOCIAL THEORY AND SOCIAL STRUCTURE (enlarged ed. 1968).

19. Michel Foucault, DISCIPLINE AND PUNISH (Alan Sheridan trans., 2d ed. 1995) (1977).

20. Nissenbaum, *supra* note 18; Nissenbaum, *supra* note 17.

21. There are three types of trust in the sociology literature. General social trust is the idea that most people can be trusted. Institutional trust refers to the trust we have in government, businesses, and other civic and corporate institutions. Particular social trust is the trust we have in each other. This study is about particular social trust.

22. Guido Möllering, *The Nature of Trust: From Georg Simmel to a Theory of Expectation, Interpretation and Suspension*, 35 SOCIOLOGY 403, 404 (2001); *see also* J. David Lewis & Andrew Weigert, *Trust as a Social Reality*, 63 SOC. FORCES 967, 968 (1985); Ken Newton & Sonja Zmerli, *Three Forms of Trust and Their Association*, 3 EUR. POL. SCI. REV. 169, 171 (2011).

23. J. David Lewis & Andrew J. Weigert, *Social Atomism, Holism, and Trust*, 26 SOC. Q. 455, 462 (1985); *see also* Patricia M. Doney et al., *Understanding the Influence of National Culture on the Development of Trust*, 23 ACAD. MGMT. REV. 601, 603 (1998).

24. Georg Simmel, The Philosophy of Money 379 (Tom Bottomore & David Frisby trans., 1978).

25. Niklas Luhmann, TRUST AND POWER 4 (1979).

26. Aaron T. Beck & Brad A. Alford, DEPRESSION: CAUSES AND TREATMENT 292–324 (2d ed. 2009); Talcott Parsons, ACTION THEORY AND THE HUMAN CONDITION 45–47 (1978).

27. The privacy law scholar Daniel Solove already warned us about those: they will inevitably fail because of hopeless generality and the contextual nature of privacy. Daniel J. Solove, UNDERSTANDING PRIVACY (2008).

28. Kenneth A. Bamberger & Deirdre K. Mulligan, PRIVACY ON THE GROUND (2015).

1 Privacy as Freedom *From*

1. Orin S. Kerr, *The Fourth Amendment and New Technologies: Constitutional Myths and the Case for Caution*, 102 MICH. L. REV. 801, 809–27 (2004) (reviewing Fourth Amendment jurisprudence and concluding that "both before and after Katz [v. United States, 389 U.S. 347 (1967),] Fourth Amendment protections have mostly matched the contours of real property law").

2. Robert S. Laufer & Maxine Wolfe, PRIVACY AS A CONCEPT AND A SOCIAL ISSUE: A MULTIDIMENSIONAL DEVELOPMENTAL THEORY, J. SOC. Issues, Summer 1977, at 22, 23.

3. *See, e.g.*, Julie E. Cohen, *Examined Lives: Informational Privacy and the Subject as Object*, 52 STAN. L. REV. 1373, 1380–81 (2000). In her discussion of how some have come to understand life online as somehow different and separate from social life offline, the legal scholar Mary Anne Franks also

invokes Locke. *See* Mary Anne Franks, *Unwilling Avatars: Idealism and Discrimination in Cyberspace*, 20 COLUM. J. GENDER & L. 224, 234–37 (2011).

4. John Locke, SECOND TREATISE OF GOVERNMENT ¶ 4 (C.B. Macpherson ed., 1980) (1960).

5. *Id.* ¶¶ 26–28.

6. *Id.* ¶ 28.

7. An in-depth discussion about the neo-Kantian foundation of modern liberalism is beyond the scope of this book. For that discussion, please see, e.g., John Rawls, A THEORY OF JUSTICE (1971); Michael J. Sandel, LIBERALISM AND THE LIMITS OF JUSTICE (2d ed. 1998).

8. Immanuel Kant, GROUNDWORK OF THE METAPHYSICS OF MORALS (Mary Gregor ed. & trans., 1998) (1785).

9. Christine M. Korsgaard, CREATING THE KINGDOM OF ENDS 124 (1996).

10. Sandel, *supra* note 7, at 22.

11. In defining these categories, I am consciously relying on Isaiah Berlin's famous distinction between positive and negative liberty. By negative liberty, Berlin was referring to the right to be free of government interference. By positive liberty, Berlin meant a government-backed affirmative right, like the right to vote, or the right to an education or healthcare. *See* Isaiah Berlin, Two CONCEPTS OF LIBERTY, in FOUR ESSAYS ON LIBERTY 118, 131 (1969). This discussion, however, does not rely on the fact that Berlin critiqued positive rights as "curbs to freedom." *Id.* at 169. It is merely a governing taxonomy to show that even seemingly disparate visions of privacy still fall under one of these two categories.

12. Samuel D. Warren & Louis D. Brandeis, *The Right to Privacy*, 4 HARV. L. REV. 193, 196 (1890).

13. Gini Graham Scott, MIND YOUR OWN BUSINESS: THE BATTLE FOR PERSONAL PRIVACY (1995).

14. Frank Luther Mott, AMERICAN JOURNALISM: A HISTORY OF NEWSPAPERS IN THE UNITED STATES THROUGH 260 YEARS: 1690 TO 1950 (rev. ed. 1950); Robert E. Mensel, *"Kodakers Lying in Wait": Amateur Photography and the Right of Privacy in New York, 1885–1915*, 43 AM. Q. 24 (1991).

15. Mason, *supra* note 13, at 46. *See also* Neil M. Richards & Daniel J. Solove, *Privacy's Other Path: Recovering the Law of Confidentiality*, 96 GEO. L. J. 123, 128 (2007) ("[T]he private papers of the two men suggest that perceived press invasions into the 'social privacy' of [Boston] Brahmin families like the Warrens prompted Warren to enlist his friend Brandeis in the project.").

16. Michael Schudson, DISCOVERING THE NEWS (1978); Eugene Volokh, *Unradical: "Freedom of the Press" as the Freedom of All to Use Mass Communication Technology*, 97 IOWA L. REV. 1275 (2012).

17. This possible origin story hints at an important, yet underappreciated aspect of traditional conceptions of privacy – namely, that the individualistic "right to be let alone" arose in elite Boston Brahmin society. It may have made sense to them, and still may make sense to members of the upper social classes today. But marginalized groups are not necessarily served by the same perspective. *See, e.g.*, Scott Skinner-Thompson, *Outing Privacy*, 110 NW. L. REV. 159 (2015).

18. Anita L. Allen, *Is Privacy Now Possible? A Brief History of an Obsession*, 68 SOC. RES. 301, 301 (2001).

19. David M. O'Brien, PRIVACY, LAW, AND PUBLIC POLICY 16 (1979).

20. Howard B. White, *The Right to Privacy*, 18 SOC. RES. 171, 172 (1951).

21. Sissela Bok, SECRETS: ON THE ETHICS OF CONCEALMENT AND REVELATION 10–11 (1983).

22. Edward Shils, *Privacy: Its Constitution and Vicissitudes*, 31 LAW & CONTEMP. PROBS. 281, 283 (1966).

23. Donald W. Ball, *Privacy, Publicity, Deviance and Control*, 18 PAC. SOC. REV. 259, 260 (1975).

24. Laufer & Wolfe, *supra* note 2, at 22, 26–27.

25. Raymond Williams, KEYWORDS: A VOCABULARY OF CULTURE AND SOCIETY 243 (rev. ed. 1983).

26. Julie E. Cohen, *Cyberspace as/and Space*, 107 COLUM. L. REV. 210, 213–26 (2007).

27. Joseph Rykwert, *Privacy in Antiquity*, 68 SOC. RES. 29, 33–34 (2001).

28. Georg Simmel, *The Sociology of Secrecy and of Secret Societies*, 11 AM. J. SOC. 441, 484 (1906).

29. Robert J. Maxwell, *Onstage and Offstage Sex: Exploring an Hypothesis*, 1 CORNELL J. SOC. REL. 75, 75–82 (1967) (arguing that stricter intimacy norms in societies were correlated with increased privacy, suggesting that individuals use self-help to find ways to hide their behaviors). Greater study is warranted here. Maxwell argued that certain behavior had to be hidden in societies that had strict rules about deviance and sex because publicity of those behaviors would weaken the norms against them. *Id.* at 75–76. However, he never considered the fact that societies with stronger norms against sexual practices may also have official and unofficial enforcement procedures for ferreting out deviant behavior.

30. Jeffrey Rosen, *Out of Context: The Purposes of Privacy*, 68 SOC. RES. 209, 217 (2001).

31. Milton R. Konvitz, *Privacy and the Law: A Philosophical Prelude*, 31 LAW & CONTEMP. PROBS. 272, 279–80 (1966).

32. Arnold Simmel, Privacy Is Not an Isolated Freedom, *in* Nomos XIII: Privacy 71, 72 (J. Roland Pennock & John W. Chapman eds., 1971), *quoted in* Daniel J. Solove, *Conceptualizing Privacy*, 90 Cal. L. Rev. D, 1131 (2002).

33. Erving Goffman, Behavior in Public Places 9 (1963).

34. Erving Goffman, Relations in Public 32–33, 38 (1971).

35. Erving Goffman, The Presentation of Self in Everyday Life 107–13 (1959).

36. Locke, *supra* note 4, ¶¶ 25–27.

37. Ruth Gavison, *Privacy and the Limits of Law*, 89 Yale L.J. 421, 446–47 (1980).

38. Alan P. Bates, *Privacy – A Useful Concept?*, 42 Soc. Forces 429, 429 (1964).

39. Lawrence Lessig, *Privacy as Property*, 69 Soc. Res. 247 (2002).

40. Jeffrey H. Reiman, Privacy, Intimacy and Personhood, *in* Philosophical Dimensions of Privacy 300, 309–14 (Ferdinand David Schoeman ed., 1984).

41. Warren & Brandeis, *supra* note 12, at 205.

42. Edward J. Bloustein, *Privacy as an Aspect of Human Dignity: An Answer to Dean Prosser*, 39 N.Y.U. L. Rev. 962, 970 (1964).

43. Warren & Brandeis, *supra* note 12, at 205.

44. Daniel J. Solove, The Digital Person 88–90 (2004).

45. In re Jet Blue Corp. Privacy Litig., 379 F. Supp. 2d 299, 327 (E.D.N.Y. 2005).

46. Olmstead v. United States, 277 U.S. 438, 464 (1928), *overruled in part by* Katz v. United States, 389 U.S. 507 (1967). Justice Brandeis, of course, famously dissented, arguing that the right to be let alone that he and Samuel Warren discussed decades earlier meant that a physical invasion was not required for an act of intrusion to constitute a privacy violation. "The protection guaranteed by the Amendments is much broader in scope. The makers of our Constitution undertook to secure conditions favorable to the pursuit of happiness. They recognized the significance of man's spiritual nature, of his feelings and of his intellect. They knew that only a part of the pain, pleasure and satisfactions of life are to be found in material things. They sought to protect Americans in their beliefs, their thoughts, their emotions and their sensations. They conferred, as against the Government, the right to be let alone – the most comprehensive of rights and the right most valued by civilized men." *Id.* at 478 (Brandeis, J., dissenting).

47. Orin S. Kerr, *The Fourth Amendment and New Technologies: Constitutional Myths and the Case for Caution*, 102 Mich. L. Rev. 801, 809–27 (2004). *See also, e.g.*, California v. Greenwood, 486 U.S. 35, 40–41 (1988) (finding no privacy interest in garbage when placed outside

a recognized private space: after all, if we "deposit[] ... garbage 'in an area particularly suited for public inspection and ... public consumption, for the express purpose of having strangers take it,'" we cannot reasonably expect to maintain privacy in that discarded trash).

48. Cohen, *supra* note 26, 213–26.
49. Franks, *supra* note 3, at 226.
50. Katrin Schatz Byford, *Privacy in Cyberspace: Constructing a Model of Privacy for the Electronic Communications Environment*, 24 Rutgers Computer & Tech. L.J. 1, 40 (1998), *quoted in* Solove, *supra* note 34, at 1131–32.
51. White, *supra* note 20, at 180–81.
52. Robert S. Gerstein, Intimacy and Privacy, *in* Philosophical Dimensions of Privacy, *supra* note 42, at 265; Jeffrey Rosen, The Unwanted Gaze: The Destruction of Privacy in America 8 (2000).
53. Jean L. Cohen, *The Necessity of Privacy*, 68 SOC. RES. 318, 319 (2001) (emphasis added).
54. Julie C. Inness, Privacy, Intimacy, and Isolation 56 (1992).
55. Solove, *supra* note 32, at 1121–22.
56. Tom Gerety, *Redefining Privacy*, 12 Harv. C.R.-C.L. L. Rev. 233, 263 (1977).
57. Scott Skinner-Thompson, *Outing Privacy*, 110 Nw. L. Rev. 159, 162 (2015) (arguing that in the constitutional informational privacy context intimate information should be given primacy).
58. *Id.* at 175–89.
59. 20 U.S.C. § 1232g(b)(1) (2012) ("No funds shall be made available under any applicable program to any educational agency or institution which has a policy or practice of permitting the release of education records or personally identifiable information contained therein.").
60. 12 U.S.C. §§ 3402–3403 (2012) ("No financial institution, or officer, employees, or agent of a financial institution, may provide to any Government authority access to or copies of, or the information contained in, the financial records of any customer except in accordance with the provisions of this chapter.").
61. 18 U.S.C. § 2710(b)(1) (2012) ("A video tape service provider who knowingly discloses, to any person, personally identifiable information concerning any consumer of such provider shall be liable to the aggrieved person ... "). This law was passed in reaction to the video rental history of Judge Robert Bork and his wife being publicized during his ultimately unsuccessful Supreme Court confirmation hearings. See Video Privacy Protection Act, Electronic Privacy Info. Center, https://epic.org/privacy/vppa/ (last visited Feb. 6, 2017).

62. 42 U.S.C. §§ 1320d-6, d-9 (2012) ("A person who knowingly ... (1) uses or causes to be used a unique health identifier; (2) obtains individually identifiable health information ...; or (3) discloses individually identifiable health information to another person, shall be punished ... ").

63. It goes back even further, to 1923. Though the Court never mentioned the word "privacy," its decisions in *Meyer v. Nebraska*, which struck down a law prohibiting the teaching of foreign languages in elementary schools, and *Pierce v. Society of Sisters*, which struck down a law requiring that all children attend public schools, suggest that there was something special, or intimate, about the parent-child relationship and the family unit. *See* Meyer v. Nebraska, 262 U.S. 390, 400–03 (1923); Pierce v. Soc'y of Sisters, 268 U.S. 510, 534–35 (1925). Both laws at issue in *Meyer* and *Pierce* intruded into the parents' process of raising their children as they saw fit. *See* Meyer, 262 U.S. at 400–01; Pierce, 268 U.S. at 534–35. The Court made the connection between these cases and privacy jurisprudence in *Lawrence v. Texas*, 539 U.S. 558, 564 (2003).

64. Griswold v. Connecticut, 381 U.S. 479, 484–85 (1965).

65. Roe v. Wade, 410 U.S. 113, 170 (1973) (Stewart, J., concurring).

66. Lawrence v. Texas, 539 U.S. at 567.

67. Obergefell v. Hodges, 135 S. Ct. 2584, 2599 (2015).

68. Inness, *supra* note 54, at 78–80.

69. Gerety, *supra* note 56, at 268.

70. Diane Vaughan, Uncoupling: Turning Points in Intimate Relationships 11–13 (1986).

71. Goffman, *supra* note 35, at 41, 48, 114, 116.

72. Kim Lane Scheppele, Legal Secrets: Equality and Efficiency in the Common Law 194 (1988).

73. Solove, *supra* note 44, at 42–43, 143.

74. Sipple v. Chronicle Publ'g Co., 201 Cal. Rptr. 665, 668–69 (Ct. App. 1984).

75. Nader v. Gen. Motors Corp., 255 N.E.2d 765, 770 (N.Y. 1970).

76. Doe v. Peterson, 784 F. Supp. 2d 831, 834–35 (E.D. Mich. 2011). The publication of intimate photographs or videos of another without her consent is known as nonconsensual pornography or, more commonly, "revenge porn." For a more in-depth discussion of revenge porn and the implications of privacy-as-trust on fighting it, please see Chapter 8 *infra*.

77. Lentz v. City of Cleveland, No. 1:04CV0669, 2006 WL 1489379, at *3–4 (N.D. Ohio May 22, 2006).

78. Diane Vaughan, The Challenger Launch Decision: Risky Technology, Culture, and Deviance at NASA 58 (1996); Ball, *supra* note 23, at 260.

79. Goffman, *supra* note 35, at 41, 44, 108, 132, 141, 174–75.

80. Goffman, *supra* note 35, at 65 (quoting Sam Bellow, DISTRACTIONS OF A FICTION WRITER, *in* NEW WORLD WRITING NO. 12, at 226, 231 (1957)).

81. For Durkheim, the profane was the opposite of the sacred; it was the everyday, the dirty and mundane activities of life that would destroy the sanctity of sacred things if they ever touched: "the only way to define the relation between the sacred and profane is their heterogeneity ... [which] is absolute." Emile Durkheim, THE ELEMENTARY FORMS OF RELIGIOUS LIFE 38 (Carol Cosman trans., 2001). Goffman may have been implying the same about private activities in the back stage because if any member of the audience saw what went on beyond the performance (the profane), the façade of the performance (the sacred) would be destroyed. For an in-depth discussion of Durkheim's sacred–profane distinction, please see the works of Mary Douglas, generally, and, in particular, Mary Douglas, PURITY AND DANGER: AN ANALYSIS OF CONCEPTS OF POLLUTION AND TABOO 2, 21 (1966).

82. Goffman, *supra* note 33, at 66, 130.

83. Erving Goffman, STIGMA 3, 31, 43, 78, 140 (1963).

84. Bates, *supra* note 38, at 433.

85. David A. Diekema, *Aloneness and Social Form*, 15 SYMBOLIC INTERACTION 481, 487 (1992).

86. Richard A. Posner, AN ECONOMIC THEORY OF PRIVACY, REGULATION, May/June 1978, at 19, 25.

87. Williams, *supra* note 25, at 242.

88. Cohen, *supra* note 3, at 1376.

2 Privacy as Freedom *For*

1. Stanley I. Benn, *Privacy, Freedom, and Respect for Persons, in* NOMOS XIII: PRIVACY 1, 6 (J. Roland Pennock & John W. Chapman eds., 1971); Daniel J. Solove, *Conceptualizing Privacy*, 90 CAL. L. REV. 1087, 1116–17 (2002).

2. Edward J. Bloustein, *Privacy as an Aspect of Human Dignity: An Answer to Dean Prosser*, 39 N.Y.U. L. REV. 962, 973–74 (1964).

3. Alan P. Bates, *Privacy—A Useful Concept?*, 42 SOC. FORCES 429, 432 (1964); Mark Alfino & G. Randolph Mayes, *Reconstructing the Right to Privacy*, 29 SOC. THEORY & PRAC. 1, 8 (2003).

4. Ruth Gavison, *Privacy and the Limits of Law*, 89 YALE L.J. 421, 450 (1980).

5. Neil Richards, *Intellectual Privacy*, 87 TEX. L. REV. 387, 387–93 (2008); Julie E. Cohen, *DRM and Privacy*, 18 BERKELEY TECH. L.J. 575, 576–79 (2003).

6. George Kateb, *On Being Watched and Known*, 68 SOC. RES. 269, 274–75 (2001).

7. Benn, *supra* note 1, at 7, 26.

8. Jeffrey Rosen, THE UNWANTED GAZE: THE DESTRUCTION OF PRIVACY IN AMERICA 7–9 (2000).

9. Frank Pasquale, THE BLACK BOX SOCIETY (2015).

10. Chad Terhune, *They Know What's in Your Medicine Cabinet*, BLOOMBERG (July 23, 2008), www.bloomberg.com/news/articles/2008-07-22/they-know-whats-in-your-medicine-cabinet.

11. Adam Datta et al., *Automated Experiments on Ad Privacy Settings*, PROC. ON PRIVACY ENHANCING TECHNOLOGIES, Apr. 2015, at 92.

12. Latanya Sweeney, *Discrimination in Online Ad Delivery*, COMM. ACM, May 2013, at 44.

13. Press Release, Jennifer Langston, U. Wash., Who's a CEO? Google Image Results Can Shift Gender Biases (Apr. 9, 2015), www.eurekalert.org/pub_releases/2015-04/uow-wac040915.php.

14. Quentin Hardy & Matt Richtel, *Don't Ask? Internet Still Tells*, N.Y. TIMES (Nov. 21, 2012), www.nytimes.com/2012/11/22/technology/in-search-engine-results-a-peek-at-what-we-wonder.html.

15. Solove, *supra* note 1, at 1117.

16. *Union Pac. Ry. Co. v. Botsford*, 141 U.S. 250, 251 (1891).

17. *Planned Parenthood of Se. Pa. v. Casey*, 505 U.S. 833, 851 (1992).

18. John Locke, SECOND TREATISE OF GOVERNMENT ¶ 123 (C.B. Macpherson ed., 1980) (1960).

19. Immanuel Kant, GROUNDWORK OF THE METAPHYSICS OF MORALS 71–72 (Mary Gregor ed. & trans., 1998) (1785).

20. John Rawls, A THEORY OF JUSTICE 561 (1971).

21. Jean L. Cohen, *The Necessity of Privacy*, 68 SOC. RES. 318, 319 (2001).

22. Charles Fried, *Privacy*, 77 YALE L.J. 475, 484 (1968).

23. Alan F. Westin, PRIVACY AND FREEDOM 7 (1967).

24. Julie C. Inness, PRIVACY, INTIMACY, AND ISOLATION 56 (1992); Jonathan Zittrain, *What the Publisher Can Teach the Patient: Intellectual Property and Privacy in an Era of Trusted Privication*, 52 STAN. L. REV. 1201, 1203 (2000).

25. Steve Matthews, *Anonymity and the Social Self*, 47 AM. PHIL. Q. 351, 351 (2010).

26. Daniel J. Solove, THE DIGITAL PERSON 90, 94, 102–04 (2004); Sec'y's Advisory Comm. on Automated Pers. Data Sys., U.S. Dep't of Health, Educ. & Welfare, Records, Computers, and the Rights of Citizens (1973) [hereinafter HEW Report], www.justice.gov/opcl/docs/rec-com-rights.pdf.

27. Daniel J. Solove & Woodrow Hartzog, *The FTC and the New Common Law of Privacy*, 114 COLUM. L. REV. 583, 592 (2014).

28. HEW REPORT, *supra* note 25, at 41–42.

29. Org. for Econ. Co-operation & Dev., OECD Guidelines on the Protection of Privacy and Transborder Flows of Personal Data (2001).

30. Privacy Online: Fair Information Practices in the Electronic Marketplace: Prepared Statement of the Fed. Trade Comm'n Before the S. Comm. on Commerce, Sci., & Transps. § III(1) (May 25, 2000).

31. Robert Ellis Smith, BEN FRANKLIN'S WEB SITE: PRIVACY AND CURIOSITY FROM PLYMOUTH ROCK TO THE INTERNET 327 (2004).

32. *See* Solove & Hartzog, *supra* note 27, at 592.

33. Joel R. Reidenberg et al., *Privacy Harms and the Effectiveness of the Notice and Choice Framework*, 11 I/S 485, 517 (2015).

34. HEW REPORT, *supra* note 25, at 41–42; *see also* William J. Clinton & Albert Gore, Jr., A FRAMEWORK FOR GLOBAL ELECTRONIC COMMERCE 17 (1997).

35. FED. TRADE COMM'N, PRIVACY ONLINE: A REPORT TO CONGRESS 7 (1998), www.ftc.gov/sites/default/files/documents/public_events/exploring-privacy-roundtable-series/priv-23a_0.pdf. Notably, these same Kantian principles animate the doctrine of informed consent in the medical and research contexts.

36. *See* M. Ryan Calo, *Against Notice Skepticism in Privacy (and Elsewhere)*, 87 NOTRE DAME L. REV. 1027, 1049 (2012).

37. *Smith v. Maryland*, 442 U.S. 735, 744 (1979).

38. *United States v. Miller*, 425 U.S. 435, 443 (1976).

39. *United States v. Kennedy*, 81 F. Supp. 2d 1103, 1110 (D. Kan. 2000); *United States v. Hambrick*, 55 F. Supp. 2d 504, 508–09 (W.D. Va. 1999).

40. Although this discussion focuses primarily on the lack of choice in disclosing information when engaging online, it is worth noting that there are numerous state laws targeting marginalized populations that force disclosure of personal information. For example, state laws requiring surgery as a prerequisite for changing genders on a birth certificate force transgender persons to "out" themselves as transgender, which can result in real harm. So-called bathroom laws or papers-to-pee laws that aim to restrict public bathroom usage based on the biological gender listed on one's original birth certificate also force transgender persons to out themselves. As Scott Skinner-Thompson argues, these laws not only force disclosure, they are direct violations of a right to information privacy. *See* Scott Skinner-Thompson, *Outing Privacy*, 110 NW. L. REV. 159, 191–94 (2015).

41. Tom Simonite, *What Facebook Knows*, MIT TECH. REV. (June 13, 2012), www.technologyreview.com/s/428150/what-facebook-knows.

42. *Id.*

43. Tom Simonite, *Facebook's Like Buttons Will Soon Track Your Web Browsing to Target Ads*, MIT TECH. REV. (Sept. 16, 2015), www.technologyreview.com/s/541351/facebookslike-buttons-will-soon-track-your-web-browsing-to-target-ads.

44. Solove, *supra* note 1, at 87.

45. *Id.* at 87–88 (citing Julie E. Cohen, *Examined Lives: Informational Privacy and the Subject as Object*, 52 STAN. L. REV. 1373, 1397 (2000)).
46. Alessandro Acquisti, Leslie K. John & George Loewenstein, *The Impact of Relative Standards on the Propensity to Disclose*, 49 J. MARKETING RES. 160, 160, 165, 172 (2012).
47. Han Li et al., *The Role of Affect and Cognition on Online Consumers' Decisions to Disclose Personal Information to Unfamiliar Online Vendors*, 51 DECISION SUPPORT SYSTEMS 434, 435 (2011).
48. Rosen, *supra* note 8, at 15–21.
49. Cohen, *supra* note 21, at 319.
50. Solove, *supra* note 1, at 1092.
51. *See* Woodrow Hartzog, *The Fight to Frame Privacy*, 111 MICH. L. REV. 1021, 1021–26 (2013) (the way privacy issues are framed influences our perception of whether some action is or is not an invasion).

3 Social Theories of Privacy

1. Georg Simmel, *The Sociology of Secrecy and of Secret Societies*, 11 AM. J. SOC. 441, 442–45, 463 (1906).
2. Erving Goffman, THE PRESENTATION OF SELF IN EVERYDAY LIFE 107, 112 (1959).
3. Emilé Durkheim, THE DIVISION OF LABOR IN SOCIETY (W.D. Halls trans., 1984) (1893).
4. Emilé Durkheim, THE ELEMENTARY FORMS OF RELIGIOUS LIFE 11 (Carol Cosman trans., 2001).
5. Daniel J. Solove, UNDERSTANDING PRIVACY 1 (2008).
6. Daniel J. Solove, THE DIGITAL PERSON (2004).
7. Solove, *supra* note 5, at 46.
8. *Id.* at ix, 1, 42–46
9. *Id.* at 50–65.
10. Danielle Keats Citron & Leslie Meltzer Henry, *Visionary Pragmatism and the Value of Privacy in the Twenty-First Century*, 108 MICH. L. REV. 1107, 1112–13 (2010).
11. Solove, *supra* note 5, at 84–88.
12. *Id.* at 93, 99.
13. *Id.* at 96–98, 178–79.
14. Michel Foucault, DISCIPLINE AND PUNISH (Alan Sheridan trans., 2d ed. 1995) (1977).
15. Robert K. Merton, SOCIAL THEORY AND SOCIAL STRUCTURE 423 (enlarged ed. 1968).
16. *Id.* at 429.
17. Goffman, *supra* note 2.

18. Erving Goffman, INTERACTION RITUAL: ESSAYS IN FACE-TO-FACE BEHAVIOR (1967).

19. Erving Goffman, STRATEGIC INTERACTION (1969).

20. Including the title, these 100 uses of "public" include "publicly." *See* Erving Goffman, BEHAVIOR IN PUBLIC PLACES (1963).

21. *Id.* at 4, 9, 10, 53, 66, 69, 86, 87, 113, 117, 128, 135, 155, 160, 165, 167, 173, Ch.11 n. 7, 200, 209. This includes "private," iterations thereof, "semiprivate" and "privacy."

22. Julie E. Cohen, *Examined Lives: Informational Privacy and the Subject as Object*, 52 STAN. L. REV. 1373, 1427 (2000).

23. Erving Goffman, STIGMA 72 (1963).

24. Goffman, *supra* note 2, at 75.

25. Cohen, *supra* note 22, at 1427.

26. Goffman, *supra* note 2, at 229.

27. Robert C. Post, *The Social Foundations of Privacy: Community and Self in the Common Law Tort*, 77 CAL. L. REV. 957, 959–68 (1989).

28. *Id.* at 959–60.

29. Hamberger v. Eastman, 206 A.2d 239, 239–42 (N.H. 1964).

30. RESTATEMENT (SECOND) OF TORTS § 652B (Am. Law Inst. 1977).

31. This is a particular problem for privacy tort plaintiffs whose injuries are often intangible and rarely pecuniary. *See* Spokeo, Inc. v. Robins, 136 S. Ct. 1540 (2016) (requiring privacy plaintiffs to show "concrete and particularized" and "actual or imminent, not conjectural or hypothetical" injury).

32. Post, *supra* note 27, at 964 ("[A] lawsuit against you for [a tort] can succeed only if it establishes that your [tortious] behavior has actually caused some demonstrable injury. The basic idea is 'no harm, no foul.'").

33. *See id.* at 959, 965 ("[T]he tort does not simply uphold the interests of individuals against the demands of community, but instead safeguards rules of civility that in some significant measure constitute both individuals and community[,]" and "[t]he most plausible interpretation of this legal structure is that the Restatement has empowered plaintiffs to use the tort to uphold the interests of social personality . . . ").

34. *Id.* at 963–65.

35. James Rachels, *Why Privacy Is Important*, 4 PHIL. & PUB. AFF. 323, 326–29 (1975).

36. *Id.* at 328.

37. *Id.* at 331.

38. SOLOVE, *supra* note 6, at 8, 43.

39. Edward Tverdek, *What Makes Information "Public"?*, 22 PUB. AFF. Q. 63 (2008).

40. *Id.* at 73–75.

41. Frank Pasquale, THE BLACK BOX SOCIETY (2015).

42. Lior Jacob Strahilevitz, *A Social Networks Theory of Privacy*, 72 U. CHI. L. REV. 919, 970–75 (2005).

43. Helen Nissenbaum, PRIVACY IN CONTEXT 2 (2010).

44. *Id.* at 129, 3.

45. Helen Nissenbaum, *Privacy as Contextual Integrity*, 79 WASH. L. REV. 119, 155 (2004).

46. Solon Barocas & Helen Nissenbaum, *Big Data's End Run Around Anonymity and Consent*, in PRIVACY, BIG DATA, AND THE PUBLIC GOOD 44, 47 (Julia Lane et al. eds., 2014).

47. Samuel D. Warren & Louis D. Brandeis, *The Right to Privacy*, 4 HARV. L. REV. 193, 205 (1890).

4 Trust and Sharing

1. Kenneth A. Bamberger & Deirdre K. Mulligan, PRIVACY ON THE GROUND (2015).

2. Kenneth A. Bamberger & Deirdre K. Mulligan, *Privacy on the Books and on the Ground*, 63 STAN. L. REV. 247 (2011).

3. Timothy Morey et al., *Customer Data: Designing for Transparency and Trust*, HARV. BUS. REV., May 2015, at 96.

4. Brian Fung, *Facebook Wants to Know If You Trust It. But It's Keeping All the Answers to Itself*, WASH. POST: THE SWITCH (Dec. 31, 2013), www .washingtonpost.com/blogs/the-switch/wp/2013/12/31/facebook-wants-to-know-if-you-trust-it-but-its-keeping-all-the-answers-to-itself.

5. James Grimmelmann, *Saving Facebook*, 94 IOWA L. REV. 1137, 1151 (2009).

6. *The Trust Engineers*, RADIOLAB (Feb. 9, 2015, 8:01 PM), www.radiolab .org/story/trust-engineers.

7. Kamala D. Harris, Cal. Dep't of Justice, MAKING YOUR PRIVACY PRACTICES PUBLIC: RECOMMENDATIONS ON DEVELOPING A MEANINGFUL PRIVACY POLICY 4 (2014); Fed. Trade Comm'n, Mobile Privacy Disclosures: Building Trust Through Transparency 3–4 (2013); *see also Protecting Mobile Privacy: Your Smartphones, Tablets, Cell Phones and Your Privacy: Hearing Before the Subcomm. for Privacy, Technology & the Law of the S. Comm. on the Judiciary*, 112th Cong. 90 (2011) (statement of Alan Davidson, Director of Public Policy, Google Inc.).

8. *See, e.g.*, Kirsten Martin, *Understanding Privacy Online: Development of a Social Contract Approach to Privacy*, 137 J. BUS. ETHICS 551 (2016); *see also* Roger C. Mayer et al., *An Integrative Model of Organizational Trust*, 20 ACAD. MGMT. REV. 709 (1995); Michael Pirson et al., *Public Trust in Business and Its Determinants*, in PUBLIC TRUST IN BUSINESS 116 (Jared D. Harris et al. eds., 2014).

9. Bénédicte Dambrine et al., Future of Privacy Forum, User Reputation: Building Trust and Addressing Privavy Issues in the Sharing Economy (2015), https://fpf.org/wp-content/uploads/FPF_SharingEconomySurvey_06_08_15.pdf.

10. Kirsten Martin, FORMAL VERSUS INFORMAL PRIVACY CONTRACTS: COMPARING THE IMPACT OF PRIVACY NOTICES AND NORMS ON CONSUMER TRUST ONLINE 1 (Oct. 5, 2015) (unpublished manuscript), www.law.uchicago.edu/files/file/martin_formal_versus_informal_privacy_contracts.pdf.

11. Ken Newton & Sonja Zmerli, *Three Forms of Trust and Their Association*, 3 EUR. POL. SCI. REV. 169, 177 (2011).

12. *See* Robert R. Hoffman et al., *Trust in Automation*, 28 IEEE INTELLIGENT SYS. 84, 84–5 (2013).

13. *Id.* at 170–72.

14. Alejandro Portes & Julia Sensenbrenner, *Embeddedness and Immigration: Notes on the Social Determinants of Economic Action*, 98 AM. J. SOC. 1320, 1332 (1993).

15. Robert D. Putnam, *Democracy in America at Century's End*, *in* DEMOCRACY'S VICTORY AND CRISIS 27, 31 (Axel Hadenius ed., 1997).

16. Michael Useem & Jerome Karabel, *Pathways to Top Corporate Management*, 51 AM. SOC. REV. 184 (1986).

17. Ronald S. Burt, *The Contingent Value of Social Capital*, 42 ADMIN. SCI. Q. 339 (1997).

18. Robert D. Putnam, BOWLING ALONE (2000); Francis Fukuyama, TRUST: THE SOCIAL VIRTUES AND THE CREATION OF PROSPERITY (1995).

19. Guido Möllering, *The Nature of Trust: From Georg Simmel to a Theory of Expectation, Interpretation and Suspension*, 35 SOCIOLOGY 403, 404 (2001); *see also* J. David Lewis & Andrew Weigert, *Trust as a Social Reality*, 63 SOC. FORCES 967, 968 (1985); Newton & Zmerli, *supra* note 11, at 171.

20. Niklas Luhmann, TRUST AND POWER 4 (1979).

21. *Id.* at 33–34; see also Patricia M. Doney et al., *Understanding the Influence of National Culture on the Development of Trust*, 23 ACAD. MGMT. REV. 601, 603 (1998).

22. *See* Piotr Sztrompka, TRUST: A SOCIOLOGICAL THEORY 18–27 (1999).

23. John K. Rempel et al., *Trust in Close Relationships*, 49 J. PERSONALITY & SOC. PSYCHOL. 95, 96 (1985).

24. Doney et al., *supra* note 21, at 605.

25. These implicit cues of confidentiality are discussed at length in ERVING GOFFMAN, THE PRESENTATION OF SELF IN EVERYDAY LIFE 112–32 (1959). *See also* Erving Goffman, STRATEGIC INTERACTION (1969).

26. Alberts v. Devine, 479 N.E.2d 113, 120 (Mass. 1985); Peterson v. Idaho First Nat'l Bank, 367 P.2d 284, 290 (Idaho 1961).

27. Joyce Berg, John Dickhaut & Kevin McCabe, *Trust, Reciprocity, and Social History*, 10 GAMES & ECON. BEHAV. 122 (1995).

28. Jerzy Surma, *Social Exchange in Online Social Networks. The Reciprocity Phenomenon on Facebook*, 73 COMPUTER COMM. 342 (2016).

29. Telephone Interview with "Steven P." (Aug. 11, 2015) (notes on file with author).

30. Doney et al., *supra* note 20, at 606.

31. Mark A. Hall et al., *Trust in Physicians and Medical Institutions: What Is It, Can It Be Measured, and Does It Matter?*, 79 MILBANK Q. 613, 619–20 (2001).

32. Shawn G. Kennedy, *About Real Estate; Law Firms Actively Leasing Office Space in Midtown*, N.Y. TIMES (Feb. 18, 1987), www.nytimes.com/1987/02/18/business/about-real-estate-law-firms-actively-leasing-office-space-in-midtown.html.

33. *The Best Law Firm Offices in America: The Finalists!*, ABOVE L. (Aug. 30, 2012, 6:19 PM), http://abovethelaw.com/2012/08/the-best-law-firm-offices-in-america-the-finalists/2.

34. Roni Caryn Rabin, *You Can Find Dr. Right, with Some Effort*, N.Y. TIMES (Sept. 29, 2008), www.nytimes.com/2008/09/30/health/30find.html.

35. Mark Granovetter, *Economic Action and Social Structure: The Problem of Embeddedness*, 91 AM. J. SOC. 481, 490 (1985).

36. Michele Williams, *In Whom We Trust: Group Membership as an Affective Context for Trust Development*, 26 ACAD. MGMT. REV. 377, 381, 385 (2001).

37. Trust is not a culturally static concept. And it doesn't have to be. Granted, white Americans tend to trust their neighbors (and their government) more than persons of color. The wealthy trust others more than the poor. George Gao, *Americans Divided on How Much They Trust Their Neighbors*, PEW RESEARCH CENTER (Apr. 13, 2016), www.pewresearch.org/fact-tank/2016/04/13/americans-divided-on-how-much-they-trust-their-neighbors/ (Trust in neighbors: White, 62 percent; Black, 31 percent; Hispanic, 27 percent; Income >$75,000, 67 percent; <$30,000, 37 percent). There are many factors that can contribute to those differences, but one is actually related to privacy. Several scholars, including Khiara Bridges and John Gilliom, have shown that some marginalized groups are subjected to such complex and all-encompassing surveillance that they develop deep mistrust of government and other institutions. Bridges spent 18 months studying poor, pregnant women who were receiving prenatal care provided by Medicaid's Prenatal Care Assistance Program (PCAP) at a large public hospital in New York City. *See* Khiara M. Bridges, *Privacy*

Rights and Public Families, 34 HARV. J. L. & GENDER 113 (2011). And Gilliom interviewed low-income mothers in southeastern Ohio. *See* John Gilliom, OVERSEERS OF THE POOR: SURVEILLANCE, RESISTANCE, AND THE LIMITS OF PRIVACY (2001). Both scholars found that the forced disclosures and ongoing monitoring that came with their participation in the social safety net made them distrust the government, institutions, and others. But although these differences in levels of trust are important as a matter of social policy, they do not change the basic relationship between trust and sharing: forced disclosures aside, we still tend to share in contexts that manifest trust. Information privacy law should reflect that.

38. Based on a series of formal and informal conversations with a non-random sample of Internet users conducted over a period of seven months, between May and December 2016. These discussions were not intended to provide an accurate assessment of the views of all Internet users.

39. Alessandro Acquisti, Leslie K. John & George Loewenstein, *What Is Privacy Worth?*, 42 J. LEGAL STUD. 249 (2013).

40. Amanda Lenhart & Marry Madden, Pew Internet & Am. Life Project, Teens, Privacy & Online Social Networks: How Teens Manage Their Online Identities and Personal Information in the Age of Myspace (2007), www.pewinternet.org/files/old-media//Files/Reports/2007/PIP_Teens_Privacy_SNS_Report_Final.pdf.pdf.

41. There are many reasons why. First, we don't have enough information: we rarely know what websites will do with our data and figuring it out is a complex, if not impossible, process. Second, even if we had access to all the information we need, we could not possibly process it all. Our decision-making processes are what scholars call "bounded," or limited, which is why we rely on heuristics (like brand loyalty) to make decisions. And third, even if we unbounded our decision-making and had all the information we could possibly need, there is no reason believe that the decisions we would make would be perfectly rational reflections of a balance of costs and benefits. Alessandro Acquisti & Jens Grossklags, *Privacy and Rationality in Individual Decision Making*, 3 IEEE SECURITY & PRIVACY 26 (2005).

42. Cass R. Sunstein, LAWS OF FEAR 35–63, 89–106 (2005); Mary Douglas & Aaron Wildavsky, RISK AND CULTURE (1982).

43. Alessandro Acquisti, Leslie K. John & George Loewenstein, *The Impact of Relative Standards on the Propensity to Disclose*, 49 J. MARKETING RES. 160, 160, 165, 171–73 (2012).

44. Lorrie Faith Cranor, WEB PRIVACY WITH P3P (2002); Lorrie Faith Cranor et al., *P3P Deployment on Websites*, 7 ELECTRONIC COM. RES. & APPLICATIONS 274, 274 (2008); Eric C. Turner & Subhasish Dasgupta, *Privacy on the Web: An Examination of User Concerns, Technology, and*

Implications for Business Organizations and Individuals, 20 INFO. SYSTEMS MGMT. 8, 16–17 (2003).

45. Acquisti, John & Loewenstein, *supra* note 42, at 164.

46. Han Li et al., *The Role of Affect and Cognition on Online Consumers' Decision to Disclose Personal Information to Unfamiliar Online Vendors*, 51 DECISION SUPPORT SYSTEMS 434, 441–43 (2011).

47. Pedro Giovanni Leon et al., *What Matters to Users? Factors that Affect Users' Willingness to Share Information with Online Advertisers*, SOUPS, July 24–26, 2013, at 1, 7.

48. Acquisti, John & Loewenstein, *supra* note 43, at 162.

49. Grimmelmann, *supra* note 5, at 1160–64. Grimmelmann also noted that these heuristics do not always effectively or accurately assess privacy risks on Facebook. *Id.*

50. Although Grimmelmann used the word "trust" several times in *Saving Facebook*, he stops short of grouping these tools as proxies for understanding privacy and sharing decisions as based on particular social trust. *Id.*

51. *Id.* at 1161–62.

52. And size matters when it comes to ad revenue on the web. *See, e.g.,* Jim Edwards, *In Just 2 Years, Google and Facebook Have Come to Control 75% of All Mobile Advertising*, BUS. INSIDER (Mar. 20, 2014, 5:29 PM), www .businessinsider.com/google-and-facebook-dominate-mobile-advertising-2014-3.

53. Danielle Keats Citron, HATE CRIMES IN CYBERSPACE 239–41 (2014).

54. Cass R. Sunstein, REPUBLIC.COM 2.0, at 53–54 (2007).

55. Max Weber, *The Protestant Sects and the Spirit of Capitalism, in* FROM MAX WEBER: ESSAYS IN SOCIOLOGY 302, 312 (H.H. Gerth & C. Wright Mills eds. & trans., 1946); Talcott Parsons, ACTION THEORY AND THE HUMAN CONDITION 47 (1978).

56. Grimmelmann, *supra* note 5, at 1162–63.

57. Sidney M. Jourard, THE TRANSPARENT SELF 5 (1971).

58. Mary J. Culnan & Pamela K. Armstrong, *Information Privacy Concerns, Procedural Fairness, and Impersonal Trust: An Empirical Investigation*, 10 ORG. SCI. 104 (1999).

59. The results of this survey are discussed in more detail at Ari Ezra Waldman, *Privacy, Sharing, and Trust: The Facebook Study*, 67 CASE W. RES. L. REV. 193 (2016).

60. Respondents were recruited through Amazon Mechanical Turk, an online marketplace that pays individuals to crowdsource the completion of various tasks, including research surveys. Responses were collected at several points during 2015. Workers were not permitted to complete the survey more than once. Turkers were paid for their time: on average, the survey took 19 minutes and 28 seconds to complete, resulting in a $4.62

hourly rate. To be eligible to participate, Turkers were required to have at least a 95 percent approval rating for 1,000 completed tasks on the platforms. This relatively high pay and high approval rating and experience, plus screening checks that determined, as best as possible, whether workers had made a good faith effort to complete the survey, were meant to ensure honest and accurate responses. Several studies have shown that Amazon Turk offers researchers a random sample of respondents with a demographic distribution roughly comparable to the United States population. *See, e.g.,* Tara S. Behrend et al., *The Viability of Crowdsourcing for Survey Research,* 43 Behav. Res. Methods 800, 800–13 (2011); Gabriele Paolacci et al., *Running Experiments on Amazon Mechanical Turk,* 5 Judgment & Decision Making 411, 416 (2010).

61. I first used bivariate correlation to test relationships and then partial correlation to determine if the relationship stood while controlling for other variables. Correlation generally refers to the degree and direction of association of variable phenomena: how well one can be predicted from the other. Bivariate correlations analyze the relationship between two variables and mainly serve to test hypotheses for further research. Partial correlations analyze the relationship between two or more variables while controlling, or removing, one or more variables from the relationship. For example, a data set may include information such as gender, highest degree level obtained, and annual income. A partial correlation could test the relationship between degree obtained and income, controlling for gender, or the relationship between annual income and gender, controlling for degree.

62. For total sharing, $r^2 = .197$, Sig. = .000; for total intimate sharing, $r^2 = .200$, Sig. =.000. Spearman's rho (r) correlation – a correlation for variables that are at least ordinal – was used because almost all variables in the data set were ordinal, i.e., ranked categories: age was reported in categories, as was education level, number of Facebook friends, and number of close friends on Facebook. All r coefficients were significant at the 0.01 level (2-tailed), indicating statistical significance.

63. For total sharing, $r^2 = .235$, Sig. = .000; for total intimate sharing, $r^2 = .201$, Sig. = .000.

64. For total sharing, $r^2 = .311$, Sig. = .000; for total intimate sharing, $r^2 = .301$, Sig. = .000.

65. Regression is a form of predictive analysis that tries to explain the relationship, if any exists, between one dependent variable and one or more independent variables. We use regression techniques to answer questions like the following: Are people who are left-hand dominant (independent variable) more or less likely than the general population to have high SAT scores (dependent variable)? Are red heads more or less

likely to be architects? Are those who identify as religious more or less likely to vote Republican? We want to know if any of a series of independent variables – age, gender, education level, and proxies for trust, for example – have an impact on a single dependent variable: the willingness to share more information, and more personal information, on Facebook.

66. Using all the independent variables in the survey, the model would have violated the multicollinearity assumption of multiple regression. Multicollinearity happens when two or more independent variables are highly correlated with each other, which makes it difficult to decipher which variable is actually causing the dependent variable to differ from the mean. As an example, when one football player sacks the quarterback, we have a good idea who did what. But when three football players tackle him at the same time, it is hard to identify which man made the biggest contribution to the sack. In the model, age and education are highly correlated with each other: older people tend to be more educated. To fix this problem, I eliminated age and education level from the regression analysis.

5 What Does Trust Mean for Privacy?

1. Cal. Bus. & Prof. Code §§ 22575–22579 (West 2017).
2. Fed. Trade Comm'n, Mobile Privacy Disclosures: Building Trust Through Transparency 3–4 (2013). www.ftc.gov/sites/default/files/documents/reports/mobile-privacy-disclosures-building-trust-through-transparency-federal-trade-commission-staff-report/130201mobileprivacyreport.pdf.
3. Neil Richards & Woodrow Hartzog, *Taking Trust Seriously in Privacy Law*, 19 Stan. Tech. L. Rev. 431, 464 (2016).
4. Jessica Litman, *Information Privacy/Information Property*, 52 Stan. L. Rev. 1283, 1308 (2000).
5. Mary J. Culnan & Pamela K. Armstrong, *Information Privacy Concerns, Procedural Fairness, and Impersonal Trust: An Empirical Investigation*, 10 Org. Sci. 104 (1999).
6. "Big data" is a buzzword, but not always understood. It refers, generally, to the use of enormous data sets in the science of predictive analytics. *See* Kate Crawford & Jason Schultz, *Big Data and Due Process: Toward a Framework to Redress Predictive Privacy Harms*, 55 B.C. L. Rev. 93, 98 (2014). Predictive analysis is exactly what Target used to identify pregnant potential customers. As the legal and information scholar Katherine Strandburg has noted, big data sets are acquired by "monitoring, acquisition as a byproduct of another activity, and transfer of pre-existing

information." Katherine J. Strandburg, *Monitoring, Datafication, and Consent: Legal Approaches to Privacy in the Big Data Context, in* PRIVACY, BIG DATA, AND THE PUBLIC GOOD: FRAMEWORKS FOR ENGAGEMENT 5 (Julia Lane et al. eds., 2014). For example, platforms like Google and Facebook take what they know about us from our "likes," friends, careers, locations, and other data, aggregate it with web browsing history, online purchasing behavior, and other metadata, and process it through complex algorithms that help them predict the kind of information we want to see in search results or on our News Feeds.

7. *See* Daniel J. Solove, THE DIGITAL PERSON 1–7 (2004); Howard Beales, THE VALUE OF BEHAVIORAL TARGETING (2010), www.networkadvertis ing.org/pdfs/Beales_NAI_Study.pdf.

8. Charles Duhigg, *How Companies Learn Your Secrets*, N.Y. TIMES MAG. (Feb. 16, 2012), www.nytimes.com/2012/02/19/magazine/shopping-habits .html.

9. Kate Crawford, *Think Again: Big Data*, FOREIGN POL'Y (May 10, 2013), http://foreignpolicy.com/2013/05/10/think-again-big-data.

10. Michal Kosinski et al., *Private Traits and Attributes Are Predictable from Digital Records of Human Behavior*, 110 PNAS 5802 (2013).

11. Solon Barocas & Andrew D. Selbst, *Big Data's Disparate Impact*, 104 CAL. L. REV. 671 (2016).

12. Latanya Sweeney, *Discrimination in Online Ad Delivery*, COMM. ACM, May 2013, at 44, 47.

13. Andrew D. Selbst, *Disparate Impact in Big Data Policing*, 51 GA. L. REV. (forthcoming 2017), https://ssrn.com/abstract=2819182.

14. When posed with a similar scenario by Pew Research Center interviewers, more than half (51 percent) of respondents found this an unacceptable invasion of privacy. Lee Raine & Maeve Duggan, Pew Research Ctr., PRIVACY AND INFORMATION SHARING 31 (2016), www.pewinternet.org/ files/2016/01/PI_2016.01.14_Privacy-and-Info-Sharing_FINAL.pdf.

15. Blase Ur et al., *Smart, Useful, Scary, Creepy: Perceptions of Online Behavioral Advertising*, SOUPS, July 11–13, 2012, at 1, 6–7.

16. This is the consumer–website relationship posited by social exchange theory. *See* Kelly D. Martin & Patrick E. Murphy, *The Role of Data Privacy in Marketing*, 45 J. ACAD. OF MARKETING SCI. 135 (2016).

17. *See* Mary J. Culnan & Robert J. Bies, *Consumer Privacy: Balancing Economic and Justice Considerations*, 59 J. SOC. ISSUES 323 (2003); Zhan Liu et al., *Privacy as a Tradeoff: Introducing the Notion of Privacy Calculus for Context-Aware Mobile Applications*, IEEE (2014), *available at* www.researchgate.net/publication/262251023_Privacy_as_ a_Tradeoff_Introducing_the_Notion_of_Privacy_Calculus_for_Context- Aware_Mobile_Applications.

18. Smith v. Maryland, 442 U.S. 735, 748 (1979) (Stewart, J., dissenting).

19. United States v. Jones, 565 U.S. 400, 413–18 (Sotomayor, J., concurring); *id.* at 418–31 (Alito, J., concurring in the judgment).
20. *Id.* at 956 (Sotomayor, J., concurring).
21. Chris Jay Hoofnagle, Federal Trade Commission Privacy Law and Policy (2016); Daniel J. Solove & Woodrow Hartzog, *The FTC and the New Common Law of Privacy*, 114 Colum. L. Rev. 583 (2014).
22. *See, e.g.*, Smith v. Maryland, 442 U.S. 735, 749 (Marshall, J., dissenting) (1979).
23. Ari Ezra Waldman, *Privacy, Notice, and Design*, 20 Stan. Tech. L. Rev. (forthcoming 2018).
24. The FTC's privacy work began and still centers around broken promises litigation, keeping companies honest about the data use practices and promises they disclose in their privacy policies. *See* Solove & Hartzog, *supra* note 21, at 628–30.
25. *See, e.g.*, Vindu Goel, *Flipping the Switches on Facebook's Privacy Controls*, New York Times (Jan. 29, 2014), www.nytimes.com/2014/01/ 30/technology/personaltech/on-facebook-deciding-who-knows-youre-a-dog.html?_r=0.
26. Keeping client confidences is deeply embedded in legal education and practice. Am. B. Ass'n, A.B.A. Canons of Professional Ethics (1937), *available at* www.americanbar.org/content/dam/aba/migrated/ cpr/mrpc/Canons_Ethics.authcheckdam.pdf ("Canon 37. Confidences of a Client. It is the duty of a lawyer to preserve his client's confidences. This duty outlasts the lawyer's employment, and extends as well to his employees; and neither of them should accept employment which involves or may involve the disclosure or use of these confidences, either for the private advantage of the lawyer or his employees or to the disadvantage of the client, without his knowledge and consent, and even tough [sic] there are other available sources of such information. A lawyer should not continue employment when he discovers that this obligation prevents the performance of his full duty to his former or to his new client."). The modern version of the Hippocratic Oath, written by Dr. Louis Lasgana, states, in part, "I will respect the privacy of my patients, for their problems are not disclosed to me that the world may know." Peter Tyson, *The Hippocratic Oath Today*, NOVA (Mar. 27, 2001), www.pbs.org/wgbh/nova/body/hippocratic-oath-today.html.
27. Bernard E. Harcourt, Exposed: Desire and Disobedience in the Digital Age (2015).
28. John Locke, An Essay Concerning Human Understanding, Bk. II, ch. XXI, § 8 (Peter H. Nidditch ed., 1975) (1690).
29. Gill v. Hearst Pub., Co., 253 P. 2d 441 (Cal. 1953).
30. Smith v. Maryland, 442 U.S. 735, 744 (1979).
31. Dwyer v. American Express Co., 652 NE.2d 1351 (Ill. App. Ct. 1995).

32. *In re* Nw. Airlines Privacy Litig., No. Civ. 04-126, 2004 WL 1278459 (D. Minn. June 6, 2004).

33. Émile Durkheim, The Rules of Sociological Method (Steven Lukes ed. & W.D. Halls trans., 1982) (1938) (discussing social facts); Pierre Bourdieu, The Logic of Practice 52–65 (Richard Nice trans., 1990) (1980) (on habitus); Julie E. Cohen, *Cyberspace as/and Space*, 107 Colum. L. Rev. 210 (2007).

34. *Smith*, 442 U.S. at 749 (Marshall, J., dissenting) (citations omitted).

35. *See, e.g.*, Scott Skinner-Thompson, *Performative Privacy*, 50 U.C. Davis L. Rev. 1673, 1734–37 (2015) (challenging current attempts to justify the existence of privacy rights in public and arguing that many efforts to maintain privacy while in "public" are properly conceptualized as forms of performance, or expressive resistance against an ever-pervasive surveillance society).

36. *Id.* at 1697–1705.

37. Richards & Hartzog, *supra* note 3, at 447–51.

38. Samuel D. Warren & Louis D. Brandeis, *The Right to Privacy*, 4 Harv. L. Rev. 193 (1890); Neil Richards, *Intellectual Privacy*, 87 Tex. L. Rev. 387, 387–93 (2008).

39. 15 U.S.C. § 45(n) (2012).

40. Richards & Hartzog, *supra* note 3, at 431–37, 451.

41. Cass R. Sunstein, *On the Expressive Function of Law*, 144 U. Pa. L. Rev. 2021, 2022 (1996).

42. 136 S. Ct. 1540 (2016).

43. *Id.* at 1544.

44. *Id.* at 1549–50.

45. Daniel J. Solove & Danielle Keats Citron, *Risk and Anxiety: A Theory of Data Breach Harms*, 96 Tex. L. Rev. (forthcoming 2017) (arguing that even though data privacy harms tend to be intangible, risk-oriented, and diffuse, courts should still recognize them).

46. Polly Sprenger, *Sun on Privacy: "Get Over It,"* Wired (Jan. 26, 1999), http://archive.wired.com/politics/law/news/1999/01/17538.

47. Amitai Etzioni, The Limits of Privacy 4, 43–44 (1999).

48. Richard A. Posner, *The Right of Privacy*, 12 Ga. L. Rev. 393, 399 (1978).

49. *Id.* at 398.

50. *Id.* at 399.

51. 1868 WL 1278 (N.C. 1868).

52. Catharine A. MacKinnon, Toward a Feminist Theory of the State (1989).

53. Catharine A. MacKinnon, *Privacy v. Equality: Beyond* Roe v. Wade, in Feminism Unmodified 102 (1987).

54. Daniel J. Solove, The Digital Person (2004).

55. *Cf.* Orin S. Kerr, *The Fourth Amendment and New Technologies: Constitutional Myths and the Case for Caution*, 102 MICH. L. REV. 801 (2004).

56. *See, e.g.*, Acquisti, John & Loewenstein, *supra* note 40.

57. Scott Skinner-Thompson, *Outing Privacy*, 110 NW. L. REV. 159, 161–62, 175–76 (2015) (arguing in part that understanding privacy as protecting against discrimination caused by the dissemination of intimate information has the benefit of being simple, categorical, and easy to administer).

58. *See, e.g.*, Gill v. Hearst Pub. Co., 253 P.2d 441, 444 (Cal. 1953) ("The photograph of plaintiffs merely permitted other members of the public . . . to see them as they had voluntarily exhibited themselves. Consistent which their own voluntary assumption of this particular pose in a public place, plaintiffs' right to privacy as to this photographed incident ceased and it in effect became a part of the public domain . . . In short, the photograph did not disclose anything which until then had been private, but rather only extended knowledge of the particular incident to a somewhat larger public then had actually witnessed it at the time of occurrence."); Moreno v. Hanford Sentinel, Inc., 91 Cal. Rptr. 3d 858, 862 (2009), as modified (Apr. 30, 2009) (The plaintiff's "affirmative act [of posting her comments to MySpace] made her article available to any person with a computer and thus opened it to the public eye. Under these circumstances, no reasonable person would have had an expectation of privacy regarding the published material."); Cox Broadcasting Corp. v. Cohn, 420 U.S. 469, 472-73 (1975) (allowing publication of rape victim's name because it was already available in a criminal indictment); Florida Star v. B.J.F., 491 U.S. 524, 527 (1989) (refusing to stop disclosure of rape victim's name because it was available in a pressroom report). *But see, e.g.*, Daily Times Democrat v. Graham, 162 So. 2d 474, 478 (Ala. 1964) (candid photo of a woman whose dress had been blown up by the wind was still considered private despite public locale).

59. Durkheim argued that law is most effective when it reflects deep structural social values built over time. Émile Durkheim, THE DIVISION OF LABOR IN SOCIETY 24 (W.D. Halls trans., 1984) (1893).

60. *See* Talcott Parsons, ACTION THEORY AND THE HUMAN CONDITION 45–47 (1978).

61. James S. Coleman, FOUNDATIONS OF SOCIAL THEORY 91 (1990).

62. Diego Gambetta, *Foreword* to TRUST: MAKING AND BREAKING COOPERATIVE RELATIONS, ix (Diego Gambetta ed., 1988).

63. Niklas Luhmann, TRUST AND POWER 4 (1979).

64. Barbara A. Misztal, TRUST IN MODERN SOCIETIES (1996).

65. *See, e.g.*, Aaron T. Beck & Brad A. Alford, DEPRESSION: CAUSES AND TREATMENT 292–324 (2d ed. 2009).

66. See S. V. Subramanian et al., *Social Trust and Self-Rated Health in U.S. Communities: A Multilevel Analysis*, 79 J. URBAN HEALTH S21, S21–22 (2002); Charles M. Tolbert et al., *Local Capitalism, Civic Engagement, and Socioeconomic Well-Being*, 77 Soc. FORCES 401, 405–06 (1998); Gerry Veenstra, *Social Capital, SES and Health: An Individual-Level Analysis*, 50 Soc. Sci. & MED. 619, 620 (2000).

67. See Jeffrey L. Bradach & Robert G. Eccles, *Price, Authority, and Trust: From Ideal Types to Plural Forms*, 15 ANN. REV. Soc. 97, 107 (1989).

68. Amy C. Edmondson, TEAMING TO INNOVATE 78 (2013). *See also* Amy C. Edmondson, *The Local and Variegated Nature of Learning in Organizations: A Group-Level Perspective*, in SOCIOLOGY OF ORGANIZATIONS: STRUCTURES AND RELATIONSHIPS (Mary Goodwyn & Jody Hoffer Gittel eds. 2012).

69. Ken Newton & Sonja Zmerli, *Three Forms of Trust and Their Association*, 3 EUR. POL. SCI. REV. 169, 176 (2011).

70. Peter Nannestad, *What Have We Learned About Generalized Trust, If Anything?*, 11 ANN. REV. POL. SCI. 413, 422 (2008); Newton & Zmerli, *supra* note 72, at 171.

71. Nannestad, *supra* note 69, at 422.

72. *Id.* at 428–30.

73. Eric M. Uslaner & Richard S. Conley, *Civic Engagement and Particularized Trust: The Ties That Bind People to Their Ethnic Communities*, 31 AM. POL. RES. 331, 332 (2003).

74. Richards & Hartzog, *supra* note 3, at 460.

75. 23 SAMUEL WILLISTON & RICHARD A. LORD, A TR CTS § 62:12 (4th ed. 2002).

76. Upjohn Co. v. United States, 449 U.S. 383, 389 (1981) (the attorney–client privilege "encourage[s] full and frank communication" and allows both parties to feel safe to share facts, details, and impressions without fear of disclosure).

77. Trammel v. United States, 445 U.S. 40, 44 (1980) (The modern justification for this privilege against adverse spousal testimony is its perceived role in fostering the harmony and sanctity of the marriage relationship.").

6 The Responsibilities of Data Collectors

1. The Health Insurance Portability and Accountability Act (HIPAA), for example, governs the collection, storage, and sharing of certain types of health and medical information. The Children's Online Privacy Protection Act (COPPA) applies to platforms that collect information about children 13-years-old or younger. And the Gramm-Leach-Bliley Act sets out rules for information management for some financial institutions.

These statutes have somewhat different rules, with each imposing additional restrictions on data sharing in certain contexts.

2. Jack M. Balkin, *Information Fiduciaries and the First Amendment*, 49 U. C. Davis L. Rev. 1183 (2016).

3. Daniel J. Solove & Woodrow Hartzog, *The FTC and the New Common Law of Privacy*, 114 Colum. L. Rev. 583, 592 (2014).

4. Sec'y's Advisory Comm. on Automated Pers. Data Sys., U.S. Dep't of Health, Educ. & Welfare, Records, Computers, and the Rights of Citizens (1973), www.justice.gov/opcl/docs/rec-com-rights.pdf.

5. *Id.* at 41–42.

6. Privacy Online: Fair Information Practices in the Electronic Marketplace:, Prepared Statement of the Fed. Trade Comm'n Before the S. Comm. on Commerce, Sci., & Transps. § III(1) (May 25, 2000).

7. Directive 95/46/EC of the European Parliament and of the Council of 24 October 1995 on the Protection of Individuals with Regard to the Processing of Personal Data and on the Free Movement of such Data, 1995 O.J. (L 281) 31, http://eur-lex.europa.eu/legal-content/en/TXT/?uri= CELEX:31995L0046. Notably, the directive is being replaced by the General Data Protection Regulation, with an effective date of the middle of 2018. *See Reform of EU Data Protection Rules*, Eur. Commission, http://ec.europa.eu/justice/data-protection/reform/index_ en.htm (last updated Jan. 18, 2016).

8. *See* Daniel J. Solove & Paul M. Schwartz, Information Privacy Law 37–39 (4th ed. 2011).

9. 42 U.S.C. §§ 300gg, 1320d (2012); 29 U.S.C. § 1181 (2012).

10. 15 U.S.C. §§ 6801–6809 (2012).

11. 15 U.S.C. §§ 6501–6506 (2012).

12. See Marc Rotenberg, *Fair Information Practices and the Architecture of Privacy (What Larry Doesn't Get)*, 2001 Stan. Tech. L. Rev. 1, 44.

13. Ari Ezra Waldman, *Privacy, Notice, and Design*, 20 Stan. Tech. L. Rev. (forthcoming 2017) (canvassing various state and federal statutes showing that the primary focus of law in this area is the implementation of notice-and-choice by mandating inclusion of certain substantive disclosures in privacy policies).

14. 15 U.S.C. §§ 6502(b)(1)(A)(i)-(ii).

15. *Id.* § 6502(b)(1)(A)(i).

16. 15 U.S.C. §§ 6803(a)(1)-(2); 16 C.F.R. §§ 313.6(a)(3), (6).

17. 45 C.F.R. § 1640.520(b)(1) (2016).

18. *See* Danielle Keats Citron, *The Privacy Policymaking of State Attorneys General*, 92 Notre Dame L. Rev. 746 (2016).

19. *See* Cal. Bus. & Prof. Code §§ 22575–22579 (West 2017).

20. *Id.* § 22575(b)(1), (3).

21. Cal. Civ. Code § 1789.83 (West 2017).

22. N.Y. State Tech. Law § 203 (McKinney 2017).
23. *Id.* § 203(1)(a)-(g).
24. CONN. GEN. STAT. § 42–471(b) (2015); MICH. COMP. LAWS § 445.841(1) (2016).
25. UTAH CODE ANN. § 63D-2–103(2) (LexisNexis 2016).
26. DEL. CODE ANN. tit. 6, § 1201 (2017).
27. *See* Paul M. Schwartz, *Property, Privacy, and Personal Data*, 117 HARV. L. REV. 2056, 2114 (2004) ("the agency is powerless – absent a specific statutory grant of authority – to regulate the collection of personal data by companies that either make no promises about their privacy practices or tell individuals that they will engage in unrestricted use and transfer of their personal data.").
28. Solove & Hartzog, *supra* note 3, at 589. As the authors point out, the FTC has developed a broader view of unfair or deceptive practices, including, for example, "deception by omission," *id.* at 631, "inducement" to share personal information, *id.* at 632–33, and "pretexting," *id.* at 633, to name just a few. Their persuasive argument is that "through a common law–like process, the FTC's actions have developed into a rich jurisprudence that is effectively the law of the land for businesses that deal in personal information." *Id.* at 589.
29. First Amended Complaint for Permanent Injunction and Other Equitable Relief, FTC v. Toysmart.com, LLC, No. 00-11341-RGS (D. Mass. July 21, 2000) [hereinafter Toysmart.com Complaint], www.ftc.gov/sites/default/files/documents/cases/toysmartcomplaint.htm.
30. *In re* Eli Lilly & Co., 133 F.T.C. 763, 767 (2002) (complaint).
31. *Id.* at 765-66.
32. *In re* Eli Lilly & Co., 133 F.T.C. 763.
33. *In re* Microsoft Corp., 134 F.T.C. 709, 715 (2002) (complaint).
34. *See, e.g., id.* at 712; Complaint for Permanent Injunction and Other Equitable Relief ¶ 43, FTC v. Rennert, No. CV-S-00-0861-JBR (D. Nev. July 12, 2000), www.ftc.gov/sites/default/files/documents/cases/2000/07/ftc.gov-iogcomp.htm.
35. Complaint, *In re* Compete, Inc., FTC File No. 102 3155, No. C-4384 (F.T.C. Feb. 20, 2013), www.ftc.gov/sites/default/files/documents/cases/2013/02/130222competecmpt.pdf.
36. Chris Jay Hoofnagle, FEDERAL TRADE COMMISSION PRIVACY LAW AND POLICY 159–166 (2016). Solove & Hartzog, *supra* note 3, at 628–38.
37. Complaint ¶¶ 13–14, *In re* GeoCities, FTC File No. 982 3015, No. C-3850 (F.T.C. Aug. 13, 1998), www.ftc.gov/sites/default/files/documents/cases/1998/08/geo-cmpl.htm.

38. Decision and Order, *In re* GeoCities, FTC File No. 982 3015, No. C-3850 (F.T.C. Feb. 12, 1999), www.ftc.gov/sites/default/files/documents/cases/1999/02/9823015.do_.htm.
39. Complaint for Permanent Injunction and Other Equitable Relief at 19, FTC v. Frostwire, LLC, No. 1:11-cv-23643 (S.D. Fla. Oct. 12, 2011) [hereinafter Frostwire Complaint], www.ftc.gov/sites/default/files/documents/cases/2011/10/111011frostwirecmpt.pdf.
40. Complaint at 4, *In re* Sony BMG Music Entm't, FTC File No. 062 3019, No. C-4195 (F.T.C. June 29, 2007) [hereinafter Sony BMG Complaint], www.ftc.gov/sites/default/files/documents/cases/2007/01/070130cmp0623019.pdf.
41. *See* Frostwire Complaint, at *supra* note 39, at 6; Sony Complaint, *supra* note 40, at 4.
42. Solove & Hartzog, *supra* note 3, at 610–11, 614–19.
43. *See* Ryan Calo, *Against Notice Skepticism in Privacy (and Elsewhere)*, 87 NOTRE DAME L. REV. 1027, 1049 (2012).
44. *See, e.g.*, Julie E. Cohen, CONFIGURING THE NETWORKED SELF 16–21 (2012); Michael J. Sandel, DEMOCRACY'S DISCONTENT 3–28 (1996); Julie E. Cohen, *Cyberspace as/and Space*, 107 COLUM. L. REV. 210, 225–27 (2007).
45. *See* Mary Anne Franks, *Unwilling Avatars: Idealism and Discrimination in Cyberspace*, 20 COLUM. J. GENDER & L. 224, 234–37 (2011); Jack Goldsmith & Tim Wu, WHO CONTROLS THE INTERNET?: ILLUSIONS OF A BORDERLESS WORLD 17 (2006).
46. John Perry Barlow, *A Declaration of the Independence of Cyberspace*, ELECTRONIC FRONTIER FOUND. (Feb. 8, 1996), https://projects.eff.org/~barlow/Declaration-Final.html. Barlow was one of the founders of the Electronic Frontier Foundation, a libertarian privacy advocacy group.
47. Peter Steiner, *Cartoon: On the Internet, Nobody Knows You're a Dog*, NEW YORKER, July 5, 1993, at 61.
48. *See* Alessandro Acquisti & Jens Grossklags, *What Can Behavioral Economics Teach Us About Privacy?*, in DIGITAL PRIVACY 363, 363–64 (Alessandro Acquisti et al. eds., 2008); Alessandro Acquisti & Jens Grossklags, *Privacy and Rationality in Individual Decision Making*, 3 IEEE SECURITY & PRIVACY 26 (2005).
49. "Embodied" experience refers to the phenomenological and pragmatic idea that things like comprehension, understanding, and truth are only possible through lived experience as mediated by the social structures around us. *See, e.g.*, Maurice Merleau-Ponty, PHENOMENOLOGY OF PERCEPTION xi (Ted Honderich ed., Colin Smith trans. 1962). It was applied to the context of cyberspace by Julie Cohen. *See, e.g.*, Julie E. Cohen, CONFIGURING THE NETWORKED SELF: LAW, CODE, AND

THE PLAY OF EVERYDAY PRACTICE 34–31 (2012); Julie E. Cohen, *Cyberspace As/And Space*, 107 COLUMB. L. REV. 210, 226–35 (2007).

50. Kenneth A. Bamberger & Deirdre K. Mulligan, *Privacy on the Books and on the Ground*, 63 STAN. L. REV. 247, 266–67 (2011).

51. Org. for Econ. Co-operation & Dev., OECD Guidelines on the Protection of Privacy and Transborder Flows of Personal Data 14–16 (2001).

52. Joel R. Reidenberg et al., *Disagreeable Privacy Policies: Mismatches Between Meaning and Users' Understanding*, 30 BERKELEY TECH. L. J. 39, 40, 87–88 (2015).

53. Janice Y. Tsai et al., *The Effect of Online Privacy Information on Purchasing Behavior: An Experimental Study*, 22 INFO. SYSTEMS RES. 254, 266–67 (2011).

54. Mark S. Ackerman et al., *Privacy in E-Commerce: Examining User Scenarios and Privacy Preferences*, 1 PROC. ACM CONF. ON ELECTRONIC COM. 1 (1999); Lorrie Faith Cranor & Joseph Reagle, Jr., *Designing a Social Protocol: Lessons Learned From the Platform for Privacy Preferences Project*, in TELEPHONY, THE INTERNET, AND THE MEDIA 215 (Jeffrey K. MacKie-Mason & David Waterman eds., 1998).

55. *See, e.g.*, George R. Milne & Mary J. Culnan, *Strategies For Reducing Online Privacy Risks: Why Consumers Read (or Don't Read) Online Privacy Notices*, 18 J. INTERACTIVE MARKETING 15 (2004); Jonathan A. Obar & Anne Oeldorf-Hirsch, *The Biggest Lie on the Internet: Ignoring the Privacy Policies and Terms of Service Policies of Social Networking Services* (Aug. 24, 2016) (unpublished manuscript), http://papers.ssrn .com/sol3/papers.cfm?abstract_id=2757465.

56. George R. Milne et al., *A Longitudinal Assessment of Online Privacy Notice Readability*, 25 J. PUB. POL'Y & MARKETING 238, 243 (2006).

57. *See* Mark A. Graber et al., *Reading Level of Privacy Policies on Internet Health Web Sites*, 51 J. FAM. PRAC. 642, 642 (2002).

58. Reidenberg et al., *supra* note 52, at 87–88.

59. Waldman, supra note 13 (arguing that privacy policies are aesthetically designed and presented to users in ways that make them impossible to comprehend, at best, and manipulative, at worst). *See also* Sheila F. Anthony, *The Case for Standardization of Privacy Policy Formats* (July 1, 2001), www.ftc.gov/public-statements/2001/07/case-standardization-priv acy-policy-formats ("If the goal of the industry's self-regulatory efforts is to provide informed consent for consumers, it has failed ... As a general rule, privacy policies are confusing, perhaps deliberately so, and industry has no incentive to make information sharing practices transparent.").

60. See Lorrie Faith Cranor, *Necessary But Not Sufficient: Standardized Mechanisms for Privacy Notice and Choice*, 10 J. TELECOMM. & HIGH TECH. L. 273, 274 (2012).

61. *See* Aleecia M. McDonald & Lorrie Faith Cranor, *The Cost of Reading Privacy Policies*, 4 I/S 543, 563 (2008).

62. Calo, *supra* note 43, at 1027, 1034–44.

63. Woodrow Hartzog, *Promises and Privacy: Promissory Estoppel and Confidential Disclosure in Online Communities*, 82 Temp. L. Rev. 891, 893–96 (2009).

64. Kate Crawford & Jason Schultz, *Big Data and Due Process: Toward a Framework to Redress Predictive Privacy Harms*, 55 B.C. L. Rev. 93, 94 (2014).

65. *Target Privacy Policy*, Target, www.target.com/c/target-privacy-policy/-/N-4sr7p (last updated Nov. 1, 2016).

66. Danielle Keats Citron & Frank Pasquale, *The Scored Society: Due Process for Automated Predictions*, 89 Wash. L. Rev. 1, 10–11 (2014).

67. Tal Z. Zarsky, *Transparent Predictions*, 2013 U. Ill. L. Rev. 1503, 1512.

68. *See* Van Lindberg, Intellectual Property and Open Source 130–31 (2008); Urs Gasser, *Regulating Search Engines: Taking Stock and Looking Ahead*, 8 Yale J.L. & Tech. 201, 232–33 (2006).

69. Deborah A. DeMott, *Beyond Metaphor: An Analysis of Fiduciary Obligation*, 1988 Duke L.J. 879, 882.

70. Balkin, *supra* note 2, at 1207–08.

71. *Id.*

72. *Id.* at 1208–09.

73. Daniel J. Solove, The Digital Person 102–03 (2004).

74. Danielle Keats Citron, *Big Data Brokers as Fiduciaries*, Concurring Opinions (June 19, 2012), www.concurringopinions.com/archives/2012/06/big-data-brokers-as-fiduciaries.html.

75. Balkin, *supra* note 2, at 1216–17.

76. *Id.* at 1222.

77. *Id.*

78. Mark Zuckerberg, Facebook (Aug. 20, 2013), www.facebook.com/zuck/posts/10100933624710391.

79. Match, www.match.com/cpx/en-us/match/IndexPage (last visited Mar. 29, 2017).

80. Dan Frommer, *Google Has Run Away with the Web Search Market and Almost No One Is Chasing*, Quartz (July 25, 2014), http://qz.com/239332/google-has-run-away-with-the-web-search-market-and-almost-no-one-is-chasing.

81. Kenneth A. Bamberger & Deirdre K. Mulligan, Privacy on the Ground 59, 65, 67 (2015); *see also* Bamberger & Mulligan, *supra* note 50, at 280.

82. Bamberger & Mulligan, *supra* note 81, at 67, 68.

83. *Id.* at 66.

84. *Id.* at 67.

85. Jack M. Balkin & Jonathan Zittrain, *A Grand Bargain to Make Tech Companies Trustworthy*, ATLANTIC (Oct. 3, 2016), www.theatlantic.co m/technology/archive/2016/10/information-fiduciary/502346.
86. *Id.*
87. Alejandro Portes & Julia Sensenbrenner, *Embeddedness and Immigration: Notes on the Social Determinants of Economic Action*, 98 AM. J. SOC. 1320, 1332 (1993).
88. Balkin & Zittrain, *supra* note 85.
89. Complaint, *In re* Snapchat, Inc., FTC File No. 132 3078, No. C-4501 (F.T. C. May 8, 2014), www.ftc.gov/system/files/documents/cases/140508snap chatcmpt.pdf.
90. *Id.* ¶¶ 6–17.
91. Solove & Hartzog, *supra* note 3.
92. *See id.* at 630–33; *see also* Volvo N.A. Corp., 115 F.T.C. 87 (1992) (an advertisement that depicted a monster truck crushing all rival cars except a Volvo was deceptive because the Volvo in the ad had been reinforced while the other cars' rooves had been weakened).
93. *See* Solove & Hartzog, *supra* note 3, at 631–33; *see also* Complaint for Permanent Injunction and Other Equitable Relief at 5-6, FTC v. Sun Spectrum Commc'ns Org., Inc., No. 03-CV-8110 (S.D. Fla. Oct. 3, 2005), available at www.ftc.gov/sites/default/files/documents/cases/2004/01/0312 02cmp0323032.pdf (inducement by falsely suggesting that company representatives were calling on behalf of a credit card company).
94. *See* Solove & Hartzog, *supra* note 3, at 641; *see also* Complaint at 4, In re Aspen Way Enters., Inc., FTC File No. 112 3151, No. C-4392 (F.T.C. Apr. 11, 2013), available at www.ftc.gov/sites/default/files/documents/cases/ 2013/04/130415aspenwaycmpt.pdf (installing spyware to collect data without notice was unfair).
95. James Grimmelmann, *Saving Facebook*, 94 IOWA L. REV. 1137, 1151 (2009).
96. *How Tagging Works*, FACEBOOK, www.facebook.com/about/tagging (last visited Mar. 29, 2017).
97. Grimmelmann, *supra* note 95, at 1156–58.
98. Research from the Pew Research Center suggests that 31 percent of young people have reported accepting friend requests from strangers, i.e. persons they have never met offline. Amanda Lenhart & Mary Madden, PEW INTERNET & AM. LIFE PROJECT, TEENS, PRIVACY, AND ONLINE SOCIAL NETWORKS, at ii (2007), www.pewinternet.org/files/old-media// Files/Reports/2007/PIP_Teens_Privacy_SNS_Report_Final.pdf.pdf.
99. Max Eulenstein & Lauren Scissors, *News Feed FYI: Balancing Content from Friends and Pages*, FACEBOOK NEWSROOM (Apr. 21, 2015), http:// newsroom.fb.com/news/2015/04/news-feed-fyi-balancing-content-from-friends-and-pages.

100. Lars Backstrom, *News Feed FYI: Helping Make Sure You Don't Miss Stories from Friends*, FACEBOOK NEWSROOM (June 29, 2016), http://newsroom.fb.com/news/2016/06/news-feed-fyi-helping-make-sure-you-dont-miss-stories-from-friends.
101. Balkin, *supra* note 2, at 1227.
102. Bartosz W. Wojdynski & Nathaniel J. Evans, *Going Native: Effects of Disclosure Position and Language on the Recognition and Evaluation of Online Native Advertising*, 45 J. ADVERT. 157, 161–62, 164–65 (2016).
103. Solove & Hartzog, *supra* note 3, at 631–33.

7 Previously Disclosed Information

1. Lior Jacob Strahilevitz, *A Social Networks Theory of Privacy*, 72 U. CHI. L. REV. 919 (2005).
2. WestlawNext, http://next.westlaw.com (sign in; search for "privacy & da (bef 1890)" in "allfeds").
3. *Id.* (search for "privacy & da(bef 1890)" in "allstates"). There are, of course, more than 10,000 cases before 1890 that include the word "private." At some point, that research might be helpful as a way of understanding how the term was used before the Warren and Brandeis article, but it is beyond the scope of this book.
4. Samuel D. Warren & Louis D. Brandeis, *The Right to Privacy*, 4 HARV. L. REV. 193 (1890); Neil M. Richards & Daniel J. Solove, *Prosser's Privacy Law: A Mixed Legacy*, 98 CAL. L. REV. 1887, 1891–92 (2010).
5. Roberson v. Rochester Folding Box Co., 64 N.E. 442 (N.Y. 1902).
6. Denis O'Brien, *The Right of Privacy*, 2 COLUM. L. REV. 437 (1902).
7. N.Y. CIV. RIGHTS LAW § 51 (McKinney 2017).
8. Pavesich v. New England Life Ins. Co., 50 S.E. 68, 70–71 (Ga. 1905).
9. Richards & Solove, supra note 4, at 1895.
10. Neil M. Richards & Daniel J. Solove, *Privacy's Other Path: Recovering the Law of Confidentiality*, 96 GEO. L.J. 123, 147 (2007).
11. Richards & Solove, *supra* note 4, at 1899–1900.
12. Richards & Solove, *supra* note 10, at 151–52.
13. *Id.* at 148.
14. G. Edward White, TORT LAW IN AMERICA (expanded ed. 2003).
15. Craig Joyce, *Keepers of the Flame: Prosser and Keeton on the Law of Torts (Fifth Edition) and the Prosser Legacy*, 39 VAND. L. REV. 851, 858 (book review).
16. Sharon K. Sandeen, *Relative Privacy: What Privacy Advocates Can Learn from Trade Secret Law*, 2006 MICH. ST. L. REV. 667.
17. Strahilevitz, *supra* note 1, at 973.

18. Daniel J. Solove, THE DIGITAL PERSON (2004).
19. Sipple v. Chronicle Publ'g Co., 201 Cal. Rptr. 665, 666–67 (Ct. App. 1984).
20. *Id.* at 669.
21. Nader v. Gen. Motors Corp., 255 N.E.2d 765, 770 (N.Y. 1970).
22. Johnston v. Fuller, 706 So. 2d 700, 701–03 (Ala. 1997).
23. Duran v. Detroit News, Inc., 504 N.W.2d 715, 720 (Mich. Ct. App. 1993).
24. Doe v. Methodist Hosp., 690 N.E.2d 681, 683–84, 693 (1997).
25. Sanders v. ABC, Inc. 978 P.2d 67, 70–72 (Cal. 1999).
26. Y.G. v. Jewish Hosp. of St. Louis, 795 S.W.2d 488, 501–02 (Mo. Ct. App. 1990).
27. Multimedia WMAZ, Inc. v. Kubach, 443 S.E.2d 491, 494 (Ga. Ct. App. 1994).
28. Y.G., 795 S.W.2d at 501.
29. *Kubach*, 443 S.E.2d at 494.
30. Duncan J. Watts, SIX DEGREES: THE SCIENCE OF A CONNECTED AGE 28 (2003).
31. Network structure is diverse. A simple search of "network visualization" in Google Images shows the wide range of visual representations of networks. GOOGLE, www.google.com (search "network visualization," then click "Images").
32. Watts, *supra* note 30, at 28.
33. *Id.* at 40; Strahilevitz, *supra* note 1, at 951.
34. *See* Mark S. Granovetter, *The Strength of Weak Ties*, 78 AM. J. SOC. 1360, 1361 (1973).
35. *Id.* at 1366 ("If one tells a rumor to all his close friends, and they do likewise, many will hear the rumor a second and third time, since those linked by strong ties tend to share friends.... [B]ridges will not be crossed.").
36. *Id.* ("[W]hatever is to be diffused can reach a larger number of people, and traverse greater social distance (i.e., path length), when passed through weak ties rather than strong." (footnote omitted)).
37. Strahilevitz, *supra* note 1, at 951.
38. Watts, *supra* note 30, at 38, 41. Duncan Watts's project, the "small world problem," is so named after the reaction when two strangers realize they have a friend in common. They say, "what a small world[!]" *Id.* at 38.
39. Granovetter, *supra* note 34, at 1366.
40. Watts, *supra* note 30, at 49.
41. Granovetter, *supra* note 34, at 1371–73.
42. Weak ties are, therefore, essential to overcoming the problem Cass Sunstein described in *Republic.com 2.0*, where he argued that online social networks contribute to greater political polarization in society

because network algorithms reinforce individuals' choices to seek out information with which they already agree. Cass R. Sunstein, REPUBLIC. COM 2.0 46–73 (2007).

43. Strahilevitz, *supra* note 1, at 952 (quoting Ronald S. Burt, STRUCTURAL HOLES: THE SOCIAL STRUCTURE OF COMPETITION 18 [1992]).

44. Morten T. Hansen, *The Search-Transfer Problem: The Role of Weak Ties in Sharing Knowledge Across Organizational Subunits*, 44 ADMIN. SCI. Q. 82, 105 (1999) (*cited in* Strahilevitz, *supra* note 1, at 957); Gabriel Weimann, *The Strength of Weak Conversational Ties in the Flow of Information and Influence*, 5 SOC. NETWORKS 245, 254–55 (1983).

45. Strahilevitz, *supra* note 1, at 957–58.

46. *Id.* at 972–75.

47. *Id.* at 977.

48. *Id.* at 978.

49. *Id.* at 979.

50. *Id.* at 973–74.

51. *Id.* at 974.

52. *Id.* at 978.

53. Duran v. Detroit News, Inc., 504 N.W.2d 715, 718 (Mich. Ct. App. 1993).

54. Erving Goffman, BEHAVIOR IN PUBLIC PLACES 85–87 (1963).

55. HELEN NISSENBAUM, PRIVACY IN CONTEXT (2010).

56. Gene A. Shelley et al., *Who Knows Your HIV Status? What HIV+ Patients and Their Network Members Know About Each Other*, 17 SOC. NETWORKS 189 (1995).

57. Strahilevitz, *supra* note 1, at 974.

8 Trust and Cyberharassment

1. Danielle Keats Citron, *Defining Online Harasment*, FORBES (Oct. 23, 2014, 11:07 AM), www.forbes.com/sites/daniellecitron/2014/10/23/defining-online-harassment/#3969df334360.

2. The essential evil of revenge porn is not the motive animating the behavior, but the invasion of privacy and the transformation of victims into objects without their consent. *See* Mary Anne Franks, *How to Defeat 'Revenge Porn': First, Recognize It's about Privacy, Not Revenge*, HUFFINGTON POST: BLOG (June 22, 2015, 8:22 AM), www.huffingtonpost.com/mary-anne-franks/how-to-defeat-revenge-porn_b_7624900.html. For ease of comprehension, I will use "revenge porn," "nonconsensual pornography," and "cyberexploitation" interchangeably. The latter two are, however, far more appropriate terms.

3. Danielle Keats Citron & Mary Anne Franks, *Criminalizing Revenge Porn*, 49 WAKE FOREST L. REV. 345, 346 (2014).
4. Ala. Code § 13A-6-240 (West 2017); Alaska Stat. Ann. § 11.61.120 (West 2015); Ariz. Rev. Stat. Ann. § 13–1425 (Supp. 2015); Ark. Code. Ann. § 5–26-314 (Supp. 2015); Cal. Penal Code § 647 (West Supp. 2016); Colo. Rev. Stat. Ann. § 18–7-107 (West Supp. 2015); Conn. Genn. Stat. Ann. § 53a-189a (West 2012 & Supp. 2016); Del. Code Ann. tit. 11, § 1335 (2015); D.C. Code Ann. §§ 22–3051 to 22–3057 (West 2016); Fla. Stat. § 784.049 (2015); Ga. Code Ann. § 16–11-90 (West Supp. 2015); Haw. Rev. Stat. § 711–1110.9 (2014); Idaho Code Ann. § 18–6609 (West 2016); 720 Ill. Comp. Stat. Ann. § 5/11–23.5 (2014); Iowa Code Ann. § 708.7.1.a(5) (West 2017); Kan. Stat. Ann. § 21–6101(8) (West 2016); La. Rev. Stat. Ann. § 14:283.2 (2004 & Supp. 2016); Me. Rev. Stat. Ann. tit. 17-A, § 511-A (West Supp. 2015); Md. Code Ann., Crim. Law § 3–809 (West Supp. 2015); Mich. Comp. Laws Ann. §§ 750.145e, 750.145f (West 2016); Minn. Stat. Ann. § 617.261 (West 2016); Nev. Rev. Stat. Ann. § 200.780 (West 2015); N.H. Rev. Stat. Ann. § 644:9-a (2016); N.J. Stat. Ann. § 2C:14–9 (West 2015); N.M. Stat. Ann. § 30-37A-1 (West 2016); N.C. Gen. Stat. § 14–190.5A (2015); N.D. Cent. Code § 12.1–17-07.2 (Supp. 2015); Okla. Stat. Ann. tit. 21, § 1040.13b (West 2016); Or. Rev. Stat. § 163.472 (2015); 18 Pa. Cons. Stat. § 3131 (2015); S.D. Codified Laws § 22-21-4 (West 2017); Tenn. Code Ann. § 39–17-318 (West 2016); Tex. Penal Code Ann. § 21.16 (West Supp. 2015); Utah Code Ann. § 76-5b-203 (West 2016); Vt. Stat. Ann. tit. 13, § 2606 (Supp. 2015); Va. Code Ann. § 18.2–386.2 (2014); Wash. Rev. Code Ann. § 9A.86.010 (West 2016); W. Va. Code Ann. § 61-8-28a (West 2017); Wis. Stat. § 942.09 (2013–2014).
5. Legislation has been introduced in Kentucky, Massachusetts, Missouri, New York, and South Carolina. See, e.g., Lana Jones, *Bill Would Make 'Revenge Porn' a Crime in Massachusetts*, CBS BOS. (June 5, 2015, 1:52 PM), http://boston.cbslocal.com/2015/06/05/bill-would-maker-evenge-porn-a-crime-in-massachusetts; Tammy Mutasa, *'Revenge Porn' Bill Passes Unanimously in Kentucky House*, WLWT5 (Feb. 15, 2016, 11:48 PM), www.wlwt.com/news/-Revenge-porn-bill-passes-unanimously-in-Kentucky-House/38013094; Collin Reischman, *Engler Files 'Revenge Porn' Bill*, MO. TIMES (Jan. 28, 2014), http://themissouritimes.com/7918/engler-files-revenge-porn-bill. Notably, Rhode Island's Governor, Gina Raimondo, recently became the first governor to veto a revenge porn bill. *See* Katherine Gregg, *Raimondo Vetoes 'Revenge Porn' Bill*, PROVIDENCE J. (June 21, 2016, 7:43 PM), www.providencejournal.com/news/20160621/raimondo-vetoes-revenge-porn-bill.
6. *See* Danielle Keats Citron, HATE CRIMES IN CYBERSPACE 6–10 (2014).
7. Christopher H. Schroeder, *Corrective Justice and Liability for Increasing Risks*, 37 UCLA L. REV. 439 (1990); Kenneth W. Simons, *Corrective Justice*

and Liability for Risk-Creation: A Comment, 38 UCLA L. REV. 113, 113–14 (1990); *see also* William M. LANDES & Richard A. Posner, THE ECONOMIC STRUCTURE OF TORT LAW (1987); Richard A. Posner, *The Concept of Corrective Justice in Recent Theories of Tort Law*, 10 J. LEGAL STUD. 187 (1981); Gary T. Schwartz, *Mixed Theories of Tort Law: Affirming Both Deterrence and Corrective Justice*, 75 TEX. L. REV. 1801, 1831 (1997).

8. Émile Durkheim, THE DIVISION OF LABOR IN SOCIETY 24 (W.D. Halls trans., 1984) (1893).

9. Citron, *supra* note 6, at 45–47

10. *Id.* at 47–49.

11. Amanda Lenhart et al., Data & Soc'y Research Inst. & CiPHR, Nonconsensual Image Sharing: One in 25 Americans Has Been a Victim of "Revenge Porn" (2016), https://datasociety.net/pubs/oh/Nonco nsensual_Image_Sharing_2016.pdf.

12. Telephone interview with "Kate M." (July 14, 2015) (notes on file with author).

13. Telephone interview with "Steven P." (Aug. 11, 2015) (notes on file with author). Steven, an openly gay man, sent sexually graphic images to individuals he met on the mobile app Grindr.

14. Citron & Franks, *supra* note 3, at 350–53.

15. Citron, *supra* note 6, at 35–55.

16. Restatement (Second) of Torts § 652D (Am. Law Inst., 1977).

17. McCormick v. England, 494 S.E.2d 431, 437–38 (S.C. Ct. App. 1997).

18. Rycroft v. Gaddy, 314 S.E.2d 39, 43 (S.C. Ct. App. 1984).

19. Daniel J. Solove, THE DIGITAL PERSON 42–47, 143–49; Lior Jacob Strahilevitz, *A Social Networks Theory of Privacy*, 72 U. CHI. L. REV. 919, 939–43 (2005).

20. *E.g.*, Huse v. Auburn Assocs., Inc., No. C064136, 2011 WL 3425607, at *7 (Cal. Ct. App. Aug. 5, 2011).

21. *E.g.*, Blackthorne v. Posner, 883 F. Supp. 1443, 1456–57 (D. Or. 1995).

22. *E.g.*, Vinson v. Koch Foods of Ala., LLC, No. 2:12–cv–1088–MEF, 2013 WL 5441969, at *7 (M.D. Ala. Sept. 27, 2013); Dietz v. Finlay Fine Jewelry Corp., 754 N.E.2d 958, 966 (Ind. Ct. App. 2001).

23. Ali v. Douglas Cable Commc'ns, 929 F. Supp. 1362, 1383–84 (D. Kan. 1996).

24. *E.g.*, Vogel v. W.T. Grant Co., 327 A.2d 133, 137–38 (Pa. 1974).

25. *E.g.*, McNemar v. Disney Store, Inc., 91 F.3d 610, 622 (3d Cir. 1996), *abrogation recognized by* Montrose Med. Grp. Participating Sav. Plan. Bulger, 243 F.3d 773 (3d Cir. 2001).

26. *E.g.*, Yoder v. Ingersoll-Rand Co., 31 F. Supp. 2d 565, 570 (N.D. Ohio 1997), *aff'd per curiam*, 172 F.3d 51 (6th Cir. 1998) (unpublished table decision).

27. *E.g.*, French v. Safeway Stores, Inc., 430 P.2d 1021, 1023 (Or. 1967).

28. *E.g.*, Barr v. Arco Chem. Corp., 529 F. Supp. 1277, 1278, 1280 (S.D. Tex. 1982).

29. Citron, *supra* note 6, at 48; Telephone interview with "Kate M.," *supra* note 12.

30. Twentieth Century Music Corp. v. Aiken, 422 U.S. 151, 156 (1975).

31. Jonathan Zittrain, *What the Publisher Can Teach the Patient: Intellectual Property and Privacy in an Era of Trusted Privication*, 52 STAN. L. REV. 1201, 1203 (2000).

32. 17 U.S.C. § 106 (2012).

33. *See, e.g.*, Peter F. Gaito Architecture, LLC v. Simone Dev. Corp., 602 F.3d 57, 63 (2d Cir. 2010) (quoting Hamil Am. Inc. v. GFI, 193 F.3d 92, 99 (2d Cir. 1999)); *see also* Baxter v. MCA, Inc., 812 F.2d 421, 423 (9th Cir. 1987); 4 Melville B. Nimmer & David Nimmer, NIMMER ON COPYRIGHT § 13.01, at 13–15, LexisNexis (Matthew Bender rev. ed.) (last visited Mar. 30, 2017).

34. Lawrence Lessig, *Privacy as Property2*, 69 SOC. RES. 247, 248, 253 (2002).

35. The word, or some derivation thereof, is used numerous times in trial and appellate court filings associated with *A&M Records, Inc.*, for example. *See generally* A&M Records, Inc. v. Napster, Inc., 284 F.3d 1091 (9th Cir. 2002).

36. Omnibus Order, Disney Enters., Inc. v. Hotfile Corp., No. 1:11-cv-20427 (S.D. Fla. Nov. 26, 2013) (Doc. No. 650); Defendants' Motion in Limine to Preclude Use of the Pejorative Terms "Piracy," "Theft," and "Stealing" (and Their Derivatives), Disney Enters., Inc. v. Hotfile Corp., No. 1:11-cv-20427 (S.D. Fla. Oct. 28, 2013) (Doc. No. 574).

37. Protecting Innovation and Art While Preventing Piracy: Hearing Before the Comm. on the Judiciary U.S. S., 108th Cong. 1–2 (2004) (statement of Sen. Orrin G. Hatch, Chairman, Comm. on the Judiciary).

38. Telephone Interview with "Steven P.," *supra* note 13.

39. Mitchell J. Matorin, *In the Real World, Revenge Porn Is Far Worse Than Making It Illegal*, TALKING POINTS MEMO (Oct. 18, 2013, 6:00 AM), http://talkingpointsmemo.com/cafe/our-current-law-is-completely-inadequate-for-dealing-with-revenge-porn.

40. *See* Amanda Levendowski, Note, *Using Copyright to Combat Revenge Porn*, 3 N.Y.U. J. INTELL. PROP. & ENT. L. 422, 439–40 (2014).

41. *See* Durkheim, *supra* note 8, at 24; *see also* Alex Geisinger, *A Belief Change Theory of Expressive Law*, 88 IOWA L. REV. 35, 68 (2002) (noting that motorcycle helmet laws impact our belief that helmets make us safe); Richard H. McAdams, *The Origin, Development, and Regulation of Norms*, 96 MICH. L. REV. 338, 349 (1997) (noting that laws can both intentionally and unintentionally affect social norms). Arti Kaur Rai, *Regulating Scientific Research: Intellectual Property Rights and the Norms of Science*, 94 NW. U. L. REV. 77, 86–88 (1999) (noting that behavior and laws are related); Cass R. Sunstein, *On the Expressive*

Function of Law, 144 U. Pa. L. Rev. 2021, 2043 (1996) (noting that civil rights laws have had an effect on the meaning of nondiscrimination).

42. Citron, *supra* note 6, at 45.

43. Telephone Interview with "Kate M.," *supra* note 12.

44. Telephone Interview with "Steven P.," *supra* note 13.

45. *Sen. Cannella Introduces Additional Legislation to Combat Cyber Exploitation and Revenge Porn*, Senator Anthony Cannella (Mar. 2, 2015), http://district12.cssrc.us/content/sen-cannella-introduces-addi tional-legislation-combat-cyber-exploitation-and-revenge-porn.

46. Danielle Keats Citron, *Expand Harassment Laws to Protect Victims of Online Abuse*, Al Jazeera Am. (Mar. 21, 2015, 2:00 AM), http://america .aljazeera.com/opinions/2015/3/expand-harassment-laws-to-protect-vic tims-of-online-abuse.html.

47. Woodrow Hartzog, *How to Fight Revenge Porn*, Atlantic (May 10, 2013), www.theatlantic.com/technology/archive/2013/05/how-to-fight-revenge- porn/275759 (proposing legal remedies for victims of revenge porn, i.e., "those whose trust has been betrayed"). Neil M. Richards & Danielle Keats Citron, *Regulating Revenge Porn Isn't Censorship*, Al Jazeera Am. (Feb. 11, 2015, 2:00 AM), http://america.aljazeera.com/opinions/2015/2/ why-regulating-revenge-porn-isnt-censorship.html (arguing that "[t]he disclosure of a nude photo of a person in breach of trust and privacy is similarly beneath the attention of the First Amendment, and rightly so").

48. Neil M. Richards & Daniel J. Solove, *Privacy's Other Path: Recovering the Law of Confidentiality*, 96 Geo. L.J. 123, 156–58 (2007).

49. Alan B. Vickery, Note, *Breach of Confidence: An Emerging Tort*, 82 Colum. L. Rev. 1426, 1449–51 (1982).

50. Woodrow Hartzog, *Reviving Implied Confidentiality*, 89 Ind. L.J. 763, 775–76 (2014).

51. Vickery, *supra* note 49, at 1428.

52. Coco v. A.N. Clark (Eng'rs) Ltd., [1969] R.P.C. 41 (U.K.), *quoted in* Richards & Solove, *supra* note 48, at 161–64.

53. Hartzog, *supra* note 50, at 787–88.

54. In this respect, the law of confidentiality applies Helen Nissenbaum's theory of privacy as contextual integrity. *See generally* Helen Nissenbaum, Privacy in Context (2010).

55. Richards & Solove, *supra* note 48, at 162.

56. Hartzog, *supra* note 50, at 785–90.

57. Alberts v. Devine, 479 N.E.2d 113, 120 (Mass. 1985) ("We hold today that a duty of confidentiality arises from the physician-patient relationship."); Doe v. Roe, 400 N.Y.S.2d 668, 674–75 (Sup. Ct. 1977) (holding that a physician and her husband, who cowrote a book that included information a patient disclosed to the physician, had an implied duty to keep patient disclosures confidential); Vickery, *supra* note 49, at 1448–49.

58. Peterson v. Idaho First Nat'l Bank, 367 P.2d 284, 290 (Idaho 1961) (holding a bank manager liable for breach of bank's duty of confidence when he divulged details of the plaintiff's unsteady finances to the plaintiff's employer).

59. Blair v. Union Free Sch. Dist. No. 6, 324 N.Y.S.2d 222, 227–28 (Dist. Ct. 1971).

60. Harley v. Druzba, 565 N.Y.S.2d 278, 279–80 (App. Div. 1991).

61. Food Lion, Inc. v. Capital Cities/ABC, Inc., 194 F.3d 505, 516 (4th Cir. 1999).

62. King Motor Co. of Fort Lauderdale v. Jones, 901 So. 2d 1017, 1020 (Fla. Dist. Ct. App. 2005).

63. Virelli v. Goodson-Todman Enters., 536 N.Y.S.2d 571, 575–76 (App. Div. 1989).

64. Coll. Watercolor Grp., Inc. v. William H. Newbauer Inc., No. 72-5475, 1973 WL 19866, at *5 (Pa. Ct. C.P. May 16, 1973) ("[I]nformation given defendants by plaintiff was imparted in confidence, and its use constitutes an improper breach of that confidence." (citations omitted)).

65. Faris v. Enberg, 158 Cal. Rptr. 704, 712 (Ct. App. 1979) ("An actionable breach of confidence will arise when an idea, whether or not protectable, is offered to another in confidence, and is voluntarily received by the offeree in confidence with the understanding that it is not to be disclosed to others, and is not to be used by the offeree for purposes beyond the limits of the confidence without the offeror's permission.").

66. Richards & Solove, *supra* note 48, at 163–64.

67. Talbot v Gen. Television Corp., [1981] R.P.C. 1 (U.K.) (finding duty to keep idea for a television show confidential).

68. Stephens v. Avery, [1988] Ch. 449, 451 (U.K.).

69. Barrymore v. News Grp. Newspapers, [1997] F.S.R. 600 (Ch.) (U.K.).

70. *Id.* at 602; Stephens, [1988] Ch. at 454. Personal information, in addition to trade secrets, literary confidences, and other private information, has long been included in the type of information that can give rise to obligations of confidence. *See* Hartzog, *supra* note 50, at 787–88; Richards & Solove, *supra* note 48, at 162–63.

71. *See* Joshua Rozenberg, PRIVACY AND THE PRESS 15 (2004) ("The need for a formal relationship between two parties has become attenuated almost to the point of nonexistence.").

72. Stephens, [1988] Ch. at 451.

73. Barrymore, [1997] F.S.R. at 602 (quoting Stephens, [1988] Ch. at 454).

74. Hartzog, *supra* note 50, at 773 (quoting Andrew J. McClurg, *Kiss and Tell: Protecting Intimate Relationship Privacy Through Implied Contracts of Confidentiality*, 74 U. CIN. L. REV. 887, 917 (2006)).

75. Erving Goffman, The Presentation of Self in Everyday Life 113 (1959).
76. *Id.* at 112–32; *see also* Erving Goffman, Strategic Interaction (1969).
77. Admittedly, not always perfectly. James Grimmelmann, *Saving Facebook*, 94 Iowa L. Rev. 1137, 1160–64 (2009).
78. *See* Patricia Sánchez Abril, *Recasting Privacy Torts in a Spaceless World*, 21 Harv. J.L. & Tech. 1, 42–43 (2007).
79. *But see* Complaint, *In re* Snapchat, Inc., FTC File No. 132 3078, No. C-4501 (F.T.C. May 8, 2014), www.ftc.gov/system/files/documents/cases/14 0508snapchatcmpt.pdf (alleging that Snapchat did not fulfill many of its privacy promises, including image deletion).
80. Fed. Trade Comm'n, Mobile Privacy Disclosures: Building Trust Through Transparency 15 (2013), www.ftc.gov/sites/default/ files/documents/reports/mobile-privacy-disclosures-building-trust-through- transparency-federal-trade-commission-staff-report/130201mobileprivacyre port.pdf.
81. Telephone Interview with "Kate M.," *supra* note 12.
82. Telephone Interview with "Steven P.," *supra* note 13.
83. Grimmelmann, *supra* note 77, at 1156.
84. Hartzog, *supra* note 50, at 772–73 (calling for courts to recognize implied duties of confidentiality, especially given extensive online social sharing of personal information and data).
85. There are countless examples of the common law of torts adapting to the changing needs of society. The transition from not allowing recovery for emotional distress to permitting it even without a connected physical injury is a particularly noticeable evolution. *See* Robert C. Post, *The Constitutional Concept of Public Discourse: Outrageous Opinion, Democratic Deliberation, and Hustler Magazine v. Falwell*, 103 Harv. L. Rev. 601, 604 (1990) (discussing the evolution of the common law to protect norms of civility that have become important in modern society). *Compare* Mitchell v. Rochester Ry. Co., 45 N.E. 354, 354 (N.Y. 1896) (denying recovery for fright when no immediate personal injury resulted from a horse carriage stopping just short of the plaintiff), *with* Battalla v. State, 176 N.E.2d 729, 731-32 (N.Y. 1961) (allowing recovery for emotional distress even without attendant showing of physical injury).
86. Samuel D. Warren & Louis D. Brandeis, *The Right to Privacy*, 4 Harv. L. Rev. 193 (1890).
87. Strahilevitz, *supra* note 19, at 927 (making a similar argument about the tort of public disclosure of private facts).
88. *Id.* at 923–24 & nn. 7–8 (citing various studies indicating that the exchange of personal information promotes intimacy and friendship).

89. *See, e.g.,* Danielle Keats Citron, *Law's Expressive Value in Combating Cyber Gender Harassment,* 108 MICH. L. REV. 373, 407 (2009) ("Law has an important expressive character beyond its coercive one. Law creates a public set of meanings and shared understandings between the state and the public. It clarifies, and draws attention to, the behavior it prohibits. Law's expressed meaning serves mutually reinforcing purposes. Law educates the public about what is socially harmful. This legitimates harms, allowing the harmed party to see herself as harmed. It signals appropriate behavior. In drawing attention to socially appropriate behavior, law permits individuals to take these social meanings into account when deciding on their actions. Because law creates and shapes social mores, it has an important cultural impact that differs from its more direct coercive effects." [footnotes omitted]).
90. Solove, *supra* note 19, 42–47, 143–49.
91. Susan M. Gilles, *Promises Betrayed: Breach of Confidence as a Remedy for Invasions of Privacy,* 43 BUFF. L. REV. 1, 82 (1995).
92. Vickery, *supra* note 49, at 1466–67.
93. Daniel J. Solove & Neil M. Richards, *Rethinking Free Speech and Civil Liability,* 109 COLUM. L. REV. 1650, 1672 (2009).
94. *Id.* at 1686–90.
95. Brandeis & Warren, *supra* note 86.

9 Information Flow in Intellectual Property

1. Jonathan Zittrain, *What the Publisher Can Teach the Patient: Intellectual Property and Privacy in an Era of Trusted Privication,* 52 STAN. L. REV. 1201, 1203 (2000).
2. Scholars have proposed changes to the public use bar before. *See, e.g.,* Katherine E. White, *A General Rule of Law Is Needed to Define Public Use in Patent Cases,* 88 KY. L.J. 423 (1999–2000).
3. 35 U.S.C. § 102(a)–(b) (2012). Fortunately, the current § 102(a) closely tracks the language of the pre-AIA §102(b). Mark A. Lemley, *Does "Public Use" Mean the Same Thing It Did Last Year?,* 93 TEX. L. REV. 1119, 1123–35 (2015).
4. 35 U.S.C. § 102(a)–(b).
5. Tone Bros., Inc. v. Sysco Corp., 28 F.3d 1192, 1198 (Fed. Cir. 1994); Kimberly-Clark Corp. v. Johnson & Johnson, 745 F.2d 1437, 1453 (Fed. Cir. 1984); *see also, e.g.,* Nancy S. Paik, *Implied Professional Obligation of Confidentiality Sufficient to Overcome Public Use Defense to a Claim of Patent Infringement? Bernhardt v. Collezione – The Federal Circuit Court of Appeals' Surprising Recent Announcement on the Public Use Bar,* 4 CHI.-KENT J. INTELL. PROP. 332, 333–34 (2005).

6. Moleculon Research Corp. v. CBS, Inc., 793 F.2d 1261, 1266 (Fed. Cir. 1986), *abrogation recognized by* Tinnus Enters., LLC v. Telebrands Corp., 846 F.3d 1190 (Fed. Cir. 2017).

7. 97 U.S. 126, 135 (1877).

8. Bernhardt, L.L.C. v. Collezione Europa USA, Inc., 386 F.3d 1371, 1379 (Fed. Cir. 2004), *abrogated on other grounds by* Egyptian Goddess, Inc. v. Swisa, Inc., 543 F.3d 665 (Fed. Cir. 2008).

9. Atlanta Attachment Co. v. Leggett & Platt, Inc., 516 F.3d 1361, 1368–69 (Fed. Cir. 2008) (Prost, J., concurring).

10. Moleculon Research Corp., 793 F.2d at 1266.

11. 86 F.3d 1113, 1121 (Fed. Cir. 1996).

12. 31 F.3d 1154, 1159–60 (Fed. Cir. 1994).

13. 88 F.3d 1054, 1058–59 (Fed. Cir. 1996).

14. Jean L. Cohen, *The Necessity of Privacy*, 68 SOC. RES. 318, 319 (2001).

15. Alan F. Westin, PRIVACY AND FREEDOM 7 (1967).

16. Julie C. Inness, PRIVACY, INTIMACY, AND ISOLATION 56 (1992).

17. Zittrain, *supra* note 1, at 1203 ("In my view, there is a profound relationship between those who wish to protect intellectual property and those who wish to protect privacy.").

18. Steve Matthews, *Anonymity and the Social Self*, 47 AM. PHIL. Q. 351, 351 (2010).

19. Sipple v. Chronicle Publ'g, 210 Cal. Rptr. 665, 668–69 (Ct. App. 1984) (finding that disclosure of Sipple's sexual orientation to a group of people extinguished his privacy interests in the information upon subsequent disclosure to the broader public).

20. Nader v. Gen. Motors Corp., 255 N.E.2d 765, 770 (N.Y. 1970) (including information gleaned from interviews with friends and acquaintances).

21. Lough v. Brunswick Corp., 86 F.3d 1113, 1121 (Fed. Cir. 1996); Beachcombers, Int'l, Inc. v. WildeWood Creative Prods., 31 F.3d 1154, 1159 (Fed. Cir. 1994).

22. Baxter Int'l, Inc. v. COBE Labs., Inc., 88 F.3d 1054, 1056, 1058–59 (Fed. Cir. 1996) (finding that the inventor showed others how the centrifuge worked and permitted free flow through his lab, allowing all who passed to see the device).

23. Daniel J. Solove, THE DIGITAL PERSON 42–47, 143–149 (2004).

24. *Lough*, 86 F.3d at 1121.

25. 104 U.S. 333, 335–36 (1881).

26. The cases for this analysis were chosen from a Westlaw search for reported Federal Circuit and district court cases after January 1, 1985 with the following search terms: "public use" & patent. That search resulted in 304 cases. Because a relatively in-depth discussion of the public use bar was necessary for analyzing its application, cases where "public use" was merely mentioned and not discussed or discussed in passing were

eliminated, reducing the data set to 97. A series of cases that seemed to hinge on the public use bar were actually "on sale" bar cases. Those were also eliminated from the data set, reducing the number to 88. In the vast majority of these cases, signed confidentiality agreements translated directly into findings of non-public use. To determine what happens when there are no confidentiality agreements and where the parties to a dispute differ in size and power, I did further analysis of 23 relevant cases in the sample.

27. I used hierarchical clustering to distinguish between two types of inventors: (A) those that are supported by large corporate structures, and (B) those that invent in their spare time or without corporate resources. Cluster analysis is a method for grouping objects together in groups (clusters) based on their similarities across a series of variables. *See* Kenneth D. Bailey, *Cluster Analysis*, 6 Soc. METHODOLOGY 59, 61 (1975). It is a way of drawing boundaries around things that generally behave similarly and, as such, it is widely applied in the social sciences, data mining, and even biology. *See* Brian S. Everitt et al., Cluster Analysis 1–13 (5th ed. 2011); STATISTICAL ANALYSIS OF GENE EXPRESSION MICROARRAY DATA (Terry Speed ed., 2003); Andrew Webb, STATISTICAL PATTERN RECOGNITION 361–62 (2d ed. 2002). Hierarchical clustering is based on the idea that objects are more related to objects nearby than objects far away. It employs algorithmic and graphical analysis to determine clusters. B. S. Everitt, *Unresolved Problems in Cluster Analysis*, 35 BIOMETRICS 169, 170–77 (1979); Baibing Li, *A New Approach to Cluster Analysis: The Clustering-Function-Based Method*, 68 J. ROYAL STAT. SOC'Y 457, 457 (2006). For this analysis, I plotted, in two-dimensional space, the relationship between inventor identity – defined by connection to and invention support by an employer – and public use result. Relative size and strength of employer was based on available corporate revenue data from Bloomberg or Hoover.com. As a result, Cluster A consists of engineers, programmers, and other inventors employed by large corporations who invent devices in course of their employment and with the institutional support of their employers. Cluster A includes experts at Xerox, biochemists at large pharmaceutical companies, and mechanical engineers at Honeywell, for example. Cluster B consists of students, hobbyists, and experts inventing in their spare time. The members of these groups were similar to each other on the relevant variables.

28. Delano Farms Co. v. Cal. Table Grape Comm'n, 778 F.3d 1243, 1248 (Fed. Cir. 2015); Dey, L. P. v. Sunovion Pharm., Inc., 715 F.3d 1351, 1357–58 (Fed. Cir. 2013); Am. Seating Co. v. USSC Grp., Inc., 514 F.3d 1262, 1268 (Fed. Cir. 2008); Honeywell Int'l Inc. v. Universal Avionics Sys. Corp., 488 F.3d 982, 998 (Fed. Cir. 2007); Eli Lilly & Co. v. Zenith

Goldline Pharm., Inc., 471 F.3d 1369, 1381 (Fed. Cir. 2006); Invitrogen Corp. v. Biocrest Mfg., L.P., 424 F.3d 1374, 1381–82 (Fed. Cir. 2005); Bernhardt, L.L.C. v. Collezione Europa USA, Inc., 386 F.3d 1371, 1380–81 (Fed. Cir. 2004), *abrogated on other grounds by* Egyptian Goddess, Inc. v. Swisa, Inc., 543 F.3d 665 (Fed. Cir. 2008); Allied Colloids Inc. v. Am. Cyanamid Co., 64 F.3d 1570 (Fed. Cir. 1995); Moleculon Research Corp. v. CBS, Inc., 793 F.2d 1261 (Fed. Cir. 1986), *abrogation recognized by* Tinnus Enters., LLC v. Telebrands Corp., 846 F.3d 1190 (Fed. Cir. 2017); Xerox Corp. v. 3Com Corp., 26 F. Supp. 2d 492, 495 (W.D.N.Y. 1998).

29. Motionless Keyboard Co. v. Microsoft Corp., 486 F.3d 1376, 1384–85 (Fed. Cir. 2007); JumpSport, Inc. v. Jumpking, Inc., 191 F. App'x 926, 935 (Fed. Cir. 2006); Eolas Techs. Inc. v. Microsoft Corp., 399 F.3d 1325, 1334–35 (Fed. Cir. 2005); Netscape Commc'ns Corp. v. Konrad, 295 F.3d 1315, 1321 (Fed. Cir. 2002); Baxter Int'l, Inc. v. COBE Labs., Inc., 88 F.3d 1054, 1058, 1059 (Fed. Cir. 1996); Lough v. Brunswick Corp., 86 F.3d 1113, 1121–22 (Fed. Cir. 1996); Beachcombers, Int'l, Inc. v. WildeWood Creative Prods., Inc., 31 F.3d 1154, 1160 (Fed. Cir. 1994); Nat'l Research Dev. Corp. v. Varian Assocs., Inc., No. 93-1421, 17 F.3d 1444, 1994 WL 18963, *2–3 (Fed. Cir. Jan. 26, 1994) (unpublished table decision); *In re* Hamilton, 882 F.2d 1576, 1580–81 (Fed. Cir. 1989); Mass. Inst. of Tech. v. Harman Int'l Indus., Inc., 584 F. Supp. 2d 297, 313 (D. Mass. 2008).

30. 386 F.3d at 1374, 1379–80.

31. *Dey*, 715 F.3d at 1354, 1357–58.

32. *Baxter*, 88 F.3d at 1058–59 (reasoning that the inventor's "lack of effort to maintain the centrifuge as confidential coupled with the free flow into his laboratory of people, including visitors to the NIH, who observed the centrifuge in operation and who were under no duty of confidentiality" necessitated a finding of "public use.").

33. *Lough*, 86 F.3d at 1116, 1120–21.

34. 584 F. Supp. 2d at 303–04.

35. Beachcombers, Int'l, Inc. v. WildeWood Creative Prods., Inc., 31 F.3d 1154, 1156, 1159–60 (Fed. Cir. 1994).

36. 549 F. App'x 934, 939, 942 (Fed. Cir. 2013).

37. *See, e.g.*, Minn. Mining & Mfg., Co. v. Appleton Papers, Inc. 35 F. Supp. 2d 1138, 1149 (D. Minn. 1999) ("No 3M employee was asked to sign a secrecy agreement before using them. And 3M announced no special company-wide policy regarding [the invention's] use or circulation."); Petrolite Corp. v. Baker Hughes Inc., 96 F.3d 1423, 1428 (Fed. Cir. 1996) ("Moreover, there was no evidence that Quaker had entered into any secrecy agreement with Sohio. . . ."); New Railhead Mfg., L.L.C. v. Vermeer Mfg. Co., 298 F.3d 1290 (Fed. Cir. 2002) (no confidentiality agreement).

38. A Google search for "free nondisclosure agreement sample," retrieved 1.97 million hits (as of March 2017) in less than half a second. GOOGLE, www.google.com (search in search bar for "free nondisclosure agreement sample").

39. Postal Instant Press, Inc. v. Sealy, 51 Cal. Rptr. 2d 365, 373–74 (Ct. App. 1996); Kenneth M. Casebeer, *Supreme Court Without a Clue: 14 Penn Plaza LLC v. Pyett and the System of Collective Action and Collective Bargaining Established by the National Labor Relations Act*, 65 U. MIAMI L. REV. 1063, 1066–67, 1067 n.18 (2011).

40. Jay Yarow, *What It's Like on Day One as an Apple Employee*, BUS. INSIDER (Jan. 26, 2012, 11:39 AM), www.businessinsider.com/what-its-like-on-day-one-as-an-apple-employee-2012-1.

41. For a discussion of using evidence of patents as a measure of economic innovation, please see, e.g., Jacob Schmookler, INVENTION AND ECONOMIC GROWTH 18–56 (1966); Bjørn L. Basberg, *Patents and the Measurement of Technological Change: A Survey of the Literature*, 16 RES. POL'Y 131 (1987); Zvi Griliches, *Patent Statistics Indicators as Economic Indicators: A Survey*, 28 J. ECON. LITERATURE 1661 (1990); Zvi Griliches et al., *The Value of Patents as Indicators of Inventive Activity* (Nat'l Bureau of Econ. Research, Working Paper No. 2083).

42. David Fagundes & Jonathan S. Masur, *Costly Intellectual Property*, 65 VAND. L. REV. 677, 690 & n.39 (2012).

43. James Bessen & Michael J. Meurer, *The Direct Costs from NPE Disputes*, 99 CORNELL L. REV. 387, 400 (2014); *see Inventive Warfare*, ECONOMIST (Aug. 20, 2011), www.economist.com/node/21526385; David Schwartz, *Claim Construction Reversal Rates I – Overall Reversal Rates*, PATENTLY-O (Feb. 27, 2008), www.patentlyo.com/pate nt/2008/02/claim-construct.html.

44. See Patent Tech. MONITORING TEAM, U.S. PATENT & TRADEMARK OFFICE, PATENTING BY ORGANIZATIONS (UTILITY PATENTS) 2014 (2015), www.uspto.gov/web/offices/ac/ido/oeip/taf/data/topo_14.htm; *see also* Annette I. Kahler, *Examining Exclusion in Woman-Inventor Patenting: A Comparison of Educational Trends and Patent Data in the Era of Computer Engineer Barbie®*, 19 AM. U. J. GENDER SOC. POL'Y & L. 773, 785–89 (2011).

45. Nat'l Ctr. for Sci. & Eng'g Statistics, Nat'l Sci. Found., Women, Minorities, and Persons with Disabilities in Science and Engineering 6–7 (2017).

46. U.S. Bureau of Labor Statistics, WOMEN IN THE LABOR FORCE: A DATABOOK 36–37 (2015).

47. Cassidy R. Sugimoto et al., *The Academic Advantage: Gender Disparities in Patenting*, PLOS ONE, May 27, 2015, at 1, 5.

48. U.S. Patent & Trademark Office, U.S. Dep't of Commerce, Buttons to Biotech: 1996 Update Report with Supplemental Data Through 1998: U. S. Patenting by Women, 1977 to 1996 (1999), www.uspto.gov/web/offices/ac/ido/oeip/taf/wom_98.pdf.

49. Waverly W. Ding et al., *Gender Differences in Patenting in the Academic Life Sciences*, SCIENCE, Aug. 4, 2006, at 665, 666.

50. Bernhardt, L.L.C. v. Collezione Europa USA, Inc., 386 F.3d 1371, 1381 (Fed. Cir. 2004), *abrogated on other grounds by* Egyptian Goddess, Inc. v. Swisa, Inc., 543 F.3d 665 (Fed. Cir. 2008).

51. Dey, L.P. v. Sunovion Pharm., Inc., 715 F.3d 1351, 1357–58 (Fed. Cir. 2013).

52. 26 F. Supp. 2d 492 (W.D.N.Y. 1998).

53. *Id.* at 493.

54. *Id.* at 495–96.

55. Eolas Techs. Inc. v. Microsoft Corp., 399 F.3d 1325, 1334 (Fed. Cir. 2005) (involving demonstration to Sun Microsystems employees); Baxter Int'l, Inc. v. COBE Labs., Inc., 88 F.3d 1054, 1056, 1058 (Fed. Cir. 1996) (involving inventor who showed others how the centrifuge worked).

56. *Xerox*, 26 F. Supp. 2d at 496.

57. 31 F.3d 1154 (Fed. Cir. 1994).

58. 488 F.3d 982 (Fed. Cir. 2007).

59. *Beachcombers*, 31 F.3d at 1160.

60. *See* Kyllo v. United States, 533 U.S. 27, 34 (2001) ("[T]he interior of homes [is] the prototypical and hence most commonly litigated area of protected privacy . . .").

61. Honeywell, 488 F.3d at 987, 998.

62. Honeywell Int'l, Inc. v. Universal Avionics Sys. Corp., 343 F. Supp. 2d 272, 307–08 (D. Del. 2004), *aff'd*, 488 F.3d 982.

63. Bernhardt, L.L.C. v. Collezione Europa USA, Inc., 386 F.3d 1371, 1381 (Fed. Cir. 2004), *abrogated on other grounds by* Egyptian Goddess, Inc. v. Swisa, Inc., 543 F.3d 665 (Fed. Cir. 2008).

64. 86 F.3d 1113, 1121 (Fed. Cir. 1996).

65. No. 93-1421, 17 F.3d 1444, 1994 WL 18963, at *3 (Fed. Cir. Jan. 26, 1994) (unpublished table decision).

66. *See, e.g.*, Wayne R. LaFave & Jerold H. Israel, CRIMINAL PROCEDURE § 3.3, at 143–45 (2d ed. 1992) (probable cause determinations); Barry C. Feld, *Criminalizing Juvenile Justice: Rules of Procedure for the Juvenile Court*, 69 MINN. L. REV. 141, 173–77 (1984) (juvenile criminal justice); Samuel Issacharoff, *Polarized Voting and the Political Process: The Transformation of Voting Rights Jurisprudence*, 90 MICH. L. REV. 1833, 1845 (1992) (voting rights); B. J. Huey, Note, *Undue Hardhip or Undue Burden: Has the Time Finally Arrived for Congress to Discharge Section 523(A)(8) of the Bankruptcy Code?*, 34 TEX. TECH L. REV.

89, 108 (2002) (tax); *see also* Lough v. Brunswick Corp., 103 F.3d 1517, 1519 (Fed. Cir. 1997) (Lourie, J., concurring) ("With respect to . . . public use . . ., courts have been accustomed to referring to their determinations as involving 'the totality of the circumstances,' a phrase that some have objected to as being indefinite."); Seal-Flex, Inc. v. Athletic Track & Court Constr., 98 F.3d 1318, 1323 n.2 (Fed. Cir. 1996) (stating, in the on-sale bar context, that the totality of the circumstances test is often criticized as being unnecessarily vague).

67. *See, e.g.*, Chance v. Pac-Tel Teletrac Inc., 242 F.3d 1151, 58 U.S.P.Q.2d 1222 (9th Cir. 2001) (applying a totality of the circumstances test for determining priority in trademark law).

68. Samuel D. Warren & Louis D. Brandeis, *The Right to Privacy*, 4 HARV. L. REV. 193, 198–205 (1890).

69. *See, e.g.*, Zittrain, *supra* note 1.

70. *Id.* at 1203.

71. Sinclair & Carroll Co. v. Interchemical Corp., 325 U.S. 327, 330–31 (1945) ("[t]he primary purpose of our patent system is not reward of the individual but the advancement of the arts and sciences. Its inducement is directed to disclosure of advances in knowledge which will be beneficial to society; it is not a certificate of merit, but an incentive to disclosure.").

72. *See* Pro Se Assistance Program, at www.uspto.gov/patents-getting-started/using-legal-services/pro-se-assistance-program.

73. *Sinclair*, 325 U.S. at 330–31. *See also* U.S. Const., art. I, § 8, cl. 8.

10 Trust and Robots

1. Ari Ezra Waldman, *Privacy, Sharing, and Trust: The Facebook Study*, 67 CASE W. RES. L. REV. 193 (2016).

2. Alessandro Acquisti, Leslie K. John, & George Loewenstein, *The Impact of Relative Standards on the Propensity to Disclose*, 49 J. MARKETING RES. 160, 160 (2012).

3. Think Before You Click: How Facebook Clickbait Puts Users at Risk, WRAL.com (May 10, 2016), www.wral.com/think-before-you-click-how-facebook-clickbait-puts-users-at-risk-/15682285/; Claire Suddeth, *The Weather Channel's Secret: Less Weather, More Clickbait*, BLOOMBERG BUSINESSWEEK (Oct. 9, 2014), www.bloomberg.com/news/articles/2014–1 0-09/weather-channels-web-mobile-growth-leads-to-advertising-insights.

4. P.W. Singer, WIRED FOR WAR (2009).

5. Kate Darling, *Extending Legal Protection to Social Robots*, in ROBOT LAW 214 (Ryan Calo, A. Michael Froomkin & Ian Kerr eds., 2016).

6. Katherine J. Strandburg, *Home, Home on the Web and Other Fourth Amendment Implications of Technosocial Change*, 70 MD. L. REV. 614, 619 (2011).

7. M. Ryan Calo, *People Can Be So Fake: A New Dimension to Privacy and Technology Scholarship*, 114 PENN ST. L. REV. 809 (2010). It is hard to overstate Calo's contributions to this field. The citations to his work in this chapter offer just one indication of his thought leadership.

8. *Id.* at 812–13.

9. M. Ryan Calo, *Robotics and the Lessons of Cyberlaw*, 103 CAL. L. REV. 513, 532, 545–46 (2015).

10. Margot Kaminski touches on this concept in Margot E. Kaminski, *Robots in the Home: What Will We Have Agreed To?*, 51 IDAHO L. REV. 661, 664 (2015). This chapter teases out this concern in more detail.

11. For a discussion of the deceptive nature of "Wizard-of-Oz setups" in robotics and human-robot interaction, please *see, e.g.*, Laurel D. Riek, *Wizard of Oz Studies in HRI: A Systematic Review and New Reporting Guidelines*, 1 J. HUMAN-ROBOT INTERACTION 119, 119 (2012).

12. Woodrow Hartzog, *Unfair and Deceptive Robots*, 74 MD. L. REV. 785 (2015).

13. Calo, *Robotics, supra* note 9, at 529. There is a broad literature offering technical definitions of artificial intelligence along these same lines. *See, e.g.*, ROLF PFEIFER & CHRISTIAN SCHEIER, UNDERSTANDING INTELLIGENCE 37 (1999).

14. Neil M. Richards & William D. Smart, *How Should the Law Think About Robots?*, in ROBOT LAW 6 (Ryan Calo, A. Michael Froomkin & Ian Kerr eds., 2016). Richards and Smart phrase their definition this way: "A robot is a constructed system that displays both physical and mental agency but is not alive in the biological sense." *Id.*

15. Cynthia Breazeal, *Toward Sociable Robots*, 42 ROBOTICS & AUTONOMOUS SYS. 167, 168 (2003).

16. Calo, *Robotics, supra* note 9, at 532–37. The physical embodiment of robots raises the issue, beyond the scope of this book, of how the law should respond when embodied robots cause harm in the real world. This is an ongoing debate. For a scholarly discussion of the question, see David C. Vladeck, *Machines without Principals: Liability Rules and Artificial Intelligence*, 89 WASH. L. REV. 117, 121 (2014).

17. Calo calls it a researchers' "dream." Calo, *Robotics, supra* note 9, at 539.

18. *Id.*

19. *Id.* at 545–46.

20. *See, e.g.*, Peter H. Kahn, Jr., et al., *The New Ontological Category Hypothesis in Human-Robot Interaction*, 2001 PROC. 6TH INT'L CONF. ON HUMAN-ROBOT INTERACTION 159.

21. Mark Coeckelbergh has done significant work on the ethical implications of approaching robots from a social, experiential, or phenomenological perspective, concluding, among other things, that the only way to develop an ethics of how to treat robots is to start from the point of human perception of robots, not an ontological definition of robot. *See, e.g.,* Mark Coeckelbergh, *Robot Rights? Towards a Social-Relational Justification of Moral Consideration,* 12 ETHICS & INFO. TECH. 209 (2010); Mark Coeckelbergh, *Humans, Animals, and Robots: A Phenomenological Approach to Human-Robot Relations,* 3 INT'L J. OF SOC. ROBOTICS 197 (2010); Mark Coeckelbergh, *Personal Robots, Appearance, and Human Good: A Methodological Reflection on Roboethics,* 1 INT'L J. SOC. ROBOTICS 217 (2009); Mark Coeckelbergh, *Virtual Moral Agency, Virtual Moral Responsibility,* 24 AI & SOCIETY 181 (2009).

22. There is a growing field of technoethical scholarship on the conceptualization of robots and its impact on social interaction. *See, e.g.,* Patrick Lin et al. EDS., ROBOT ETHICS: THE ETHICAL AND SOCIAL IMPLICATIONS OF ROBOTICS (2012). Because robots can do more than just a precise set of functions, Don Idhe, the philosopher of science and technology, has argued that their meaning is "multistable": we may see robots as machines, but we also see them as more than machines. *See* Don Idhe, TECHNOLOGY AND THE LIFE WORLD (1990).

23. Darling, *supra* note 5, at 214.

24. Hartzog, *supra* note 12, at 791.

25. *See, e.g.,* Ryan Calo, A. Michael Froomkin & Ian Kerr eds., ROBOT LAW (2016).

26. *See, e.g.,* Vladeck, supra note 16, at 150; Kevin Funkhouser, *Paving the Road Ahead: Autonomous Vehicles, Products Liability, and the Need for A New Approach,* 2013 UTAH L. REV. 437, 462. Tracy Pearl, Fast and Furious: The Misregulation of Driverless Cars, We Robot Conference (2017), www.werobot2017.com/wp-content/uploads/2017/03/Pearl-AV-1.pdf.

27. *See, e.g.,* Andrew D. Selbst, *Disparate Impact in Big Data Policing,* 51 GA. L. REV. (forthcoming 2017), https://ssrn.com/abstract=2819182,

28. *See, e.g.,* Toni Massaro et al., *Siri-ously 2.0: What Artificial Intelligence Reveals About the First Amendment,* 102 MINN. L. REV. (forthcoming 2018), *available at* https://ssrn.com/abstract=2896174.

29. Hartzog, *supra* note 12, at 797.

30. M. Ryan Calo, *Robots and Privacy,* in ROBOT ETHICS, *supra* note 22, at 194.

31. *See* Charles Duhigg, *How Companies Learn Your Secrets,* N.Y. TIMES MAG. (Feb. 16, 2012), www.nytimes.com/2012/02/19/magazine/shopping-habits.html.

32. Kaminski, *supra* note 10, at 663–64.

33. Gill v. Hearst Pub. Co., 253 P.2d 441, 445 (Cal. 1953).

34. Hartzog, *supra* note 12, at 789–91.

35. *See* M. Ryan Calo, *Against Notice Skepticism in Privacy (And Elsewhere)*, 87 NOTRE DAME L. REV. 1027, 1030 (2012); *see also* Hartzog, *supra* note 12, at 818.

36. Calo, *People Can Be So Fake, supra* note 7, at 843–46.

37. Alpheus Thomas Mason, BRANDEIS: A FREE MAN'S LIFE 54–70 (1946).

38. David M. O'Brien, PRIVACY, LAW, AND PUBLIC POLICY 16 (1979); Edward Shils, *Privacy: Its Constitution and Vicissitudes*, 31 LAW & CONTEMP. PROBS. 281, 283 (1966).

39. *See* Neil Richards, *Intellectual Privacy*, 87 TEX. L. REV. 387 (2008) (arguing that the ability to test out inchoate or unpopular ideas in private is essential to First Amendment freedoms); Julie E. Cohen, *DRM and Privacy*, 18 BERKELEY TECH. L.J. 575, 576–79 (2003) (identifying intellectual privacy as an important value).

40. *See* Spokeo, Inc. v. Robins, 136 S. Ct. 1540 (2016) (holding that an individual could not sue a website for posting inaccurate information about the individual because Article III standing required a showing of injury that is "concrete and particularized" and "actual or imminent, not conjectural or hypothetical"); Daniel J. Solove & Danielle Keats Citron, *Risk and Anxiety: A Theory of Data Breach Harms*, 96 TEX. L. REV. (forthcoming 2017) (arguing that courts have been hesitant to recognize the diffuse, psychological harms usually associated with data privacy invasions).

41. There is a long literature on this point going back decades. *See, e.g.*, Roy F. Baumeister & Mark R. Leary, *The Need to Belong: Desire for Interpersonal Attachments as a Fundamental Human Motivation*, 117 PSYCH. BULLETIN 497 (1995); Abraham H. Maslow, *A Theory of Human Motivation*, 50 PSYCH. REV. 370 (1943).

42. This is what Daniel Dennett meant by our "intentional stance." We can anticipate and interact with others about whom we know little by adopting a stance of presumed rationality. *See* Daniel C. Dennett, THE INTENTIONAL STANCE (1987).

43. Calo, *People Can Be So Fake, supra* note 7, at 811, 826.

44. This practice has reached into popular culture. *See* May the Best Stan Win, AMERICAN DAD (Feb. 14, 2010).

45. Robert Boyd, *Robots Are Narrowing the Gap With Humans*, MCCLATCHY NEWSPAPERS, Apr. 27, 2009 (cited in Calo, *People Can Be So Fake, supra* note 7, at 838).

46. Calo, *People Can Be So Fake, supra* note 7, at 836.

47. *Id.* at 837.

48. Sherry Turkle, *In Good Company? On the Threshold of Robotic Companions*, in CLOSE ENGAGEMENTS WITH ARTIFICIAL COMPANIONS: KEY SOCIAL, PSYCHOLOGICAL, ETHICAL AND DESIGN ISSUES 4 (Yorick Wilks ed. 2010).

49. *Id.* at 5.

50. *Id.* at 6.

51. *Id.* at 7.

52. Karl MacDorman & Hiroshi Ishiguro, *The Uncanny Advantage of Using Androids in Cognitive and Social Science Research*, 7 INTERACTION STUD. 297, 316 (2006) (cited in Calo, *People Can Be So Fake, supra* note 7, at 838).

53. Salvatore Parise et al., *Cooperating with Life-Like Interface Agents*, 15 COMPUTERS IN HUM. BEHAVIOR 123, 124 (1999).

54. For an in depth discussion of many of the field experiments on human–computer and human–robot interaction, see Calo, *People Can Be So Fake, supra* note 7, at 840).

55. MacDorman & Ishiguro, *supra* note 52, at 309.

56. *Id.*

57. *See* PIOTR SZTROMPKA, TRUST: A SOCIOLOGICAL THEORY 18–27 (1999).

58. Parise et al., *supra* note 53, at 124, 128–135.

59. Roaul Richenberg & Byron Reeves, *The Effects of Animated Characters on Anxiety, Task Performance, and Evaluations of User Interfaces*, 2 CHI LETTERS 49, 52–55 (2000) (cited in Calo, *People Can Be So Fake, supra* note 7.

60. Adam Waytz, Joy Heafner, & Nicholas Epley, *The Mind in the Machine: Anthropomorphism Increases Trust in an Autonomous Vehicle*, 52 J. EXPERIMENTAL SOC. PSYCH. 113, 115 (2014).

61. *Id.* at 115–16.

62. His name was Clippy (more formally known as "Clippit"), but he was never popular. *See, e.g.,* Robinson Meyer, *Even Early Focus Groups Hated Clippy*, ATLANTIC (June 23, 2015), www.theatlantic.com/technol ogy/archive/2015/06/clippy-the-microsoft-office-assistant-is-the-patriar chys-fault/396653/.

63. Recall, this is Calo's name for the learning capacities of robots. *See* Calo, *Robotics, supra* note 9, at 539.

64. Apple has made security a central element of its business and marketing strategy. *See* Tim Cook, A Message to Our Customers, Feb 16, 2016, www .apple.com/customer-letter/ ("Customers expect Apple and other technology companies to do everything in our power to protect their personal information, and at Apple we are deeply committed to safeguarding their data. Compromising the security of our personal

information can ultimately put our personal safety at risk. That is why encryption has become so important to all of us. For many years, we have used encryption to protect our customers' personal data because we believe it's the only way to keep their information safe. We have even put that data out of our own reach, because we believe the contents of your iPhone are none of our business.").

65. One way to understand trademark law is through an economic lens: trademark protections help reduce consumer search costs. According to William Landes and Richard Posner, for example, trademarks allow buyers to choose among what could be a litany of options (think of a toothpaste aisle at the drug store) and allow sellers to capture all the information a buyer needs to make her choice in one logo, design, or slogan. *See* William M. Landes & Richard A. Posner, *Trademark Law: An Economic Perspective*, 30 J. L. & Econ. 265, 268–69 (1987). Another function of trademark law is to allow consumers to make quality comparisons. Consumers can rely on trademarks to help them determine which product is likely to be better made, more effective, or reliable. At least one scholar has called this trademark law's "trust" function. Ariel Katz, Beyond Search Costs: The Linguistic and Trust Functions of Trademarks, 2010 B.Y.U. L. Rev. 1555, 1563.

66. Hartzog, *supra* note 12, at 791–92.

67. Mark Coeckelbergh, *Can We Trust Robots?*, 14 Ethics and Info. Tech. 53, 57–58 (2012).

68. Erving Goffman, The Presentation of Self in Everyday Life (1959). This is the essential argument of *Presentation of Self*, which compares social interaction to a dramatic play. But Goffman wrote about this phenomenon elsewhere. *See, e.g.*, Erving Goffman, Relations in Public (1971) (detailing the nonverbal communications that help establish behavioral expectations among strangers coming into contact with one another in public places).

69. In the popular science fiction drama, human-created, emergent robots called Cylons evolve, rebel against their masters, and end up destroying most of humanity. *See Battlestar Galactica* (1978–1978, 2004–2009).

70. Darling, *supra* note 5, at 218.

71. Calo, *Robotics*, *supra* note 9, at 545.

72. MacDorman & Ishiguro, *supra* note 52, at 309.

73. *See, e.g.*, Nicholas Epley et al., *Creating Social Connection through Inferential Reproduction: Loneliness and Perceived Agency in Gadgets, Gods, and Greyhounds*, 19 Psych. Sci. 114 (2008); Nicholas Epley et al., *When We Need a Human: Motivational Determinants of Anthropomorphism*, 26 Soc. Cognition 143 (2008).

74. Rocky Peng Chang, Echo Wen Wan, & Eric Levy, *The Effect of Social Exclusion on Consumer Preference for Anthropomorphized Brands*, 27 J. CONSUMER PSYCH. 23 (2017).

75. *See* John C. Maner et al., *Does Social Exclusion Motivate Interpersonal Reconnection? Resolving the "Porcupine Problem"*, 92 J. PERSONALITY & SOC. PSYCH. 42 (2007).

76. James A. Mourey et al., *Products as Pals: Engaging with Anthropomorphic Products Mitigates the Effects of Social Exclusion*, 44 J. CONSUMER RES. 414 (2017).

77. *Id.*

78. *See* Keith Wilcox & Andrew T. Stephen, *Are Close Friends the Enemy? Online Social Networks, Self-Esteem, and Self-Control*, 40 J. CONSUMER RES. 90 (2013) (cited in Mourey et al., *supra* note 76).

79. *Id.*

80. *Id.*

81. *See* Richard M. Lee & Steven B. Robbins, *Measuring Belongingness: The Social Connectedness and the Social Assurance Scales*, 42 J. COUNSELING PSYCH. 232 (1995) (cited in Mourey et al., *supra* note 76).

82. Mourey et al., *supra* note 76.

83. *Id.*

84. Jacqueline Kory Westlund & Cynthia Breazeal, *Deception, Secrets, Children, and Robots: What's Acceptable?*, 10th ACM/IEEE Conference on Human-Robot Interaction (HRI), at 1 (2015), www.openroboethics.org/hri15/wp-content/uploads/2015/02/Mf-Westlund.pdf

85. *Id.*

86. Darling, *supra* note 5, at XX.

87. Hartzog, *supra* note 12, at 804.

88. *Id.* at 791–809.

89. Beyond law, which is discussed here, design guidelines can play a role in mitigating the privacy risks associated with social robots. *See* Margot E. Kaminski et al., *Averting Robot Eyes*, 76 MD. L. REV. 983, 1001–20 (2017).

90. Chris Jay Hoofnagle, FEDERAL TRADE COMMISSION PRIVACY LAW AND POLICY (2016); Daniel J. Solove & Woodrow Hartzog, *The FTC and the New Common Law of Privacy*, 114 COLUM. L. REV. 583 (2014).

91. Federal Trade Commission Act, Pub. L. No. 75-447, § 3, 52 Stat. 111 (1938).

92. Hartzog, *supra* note 12, at 812–13.

93. *Id.* at 792–95.

94. *See* Calo, *Notice Skepticism*, *supra* note 35.

95. Hartzog, *supra* note 12, at 798 (*citing* Aspen Way Enters. Inc., F.T.C. File No. 112 3151, No. C-4392 (F.T.C. Apr. 11, 2013).

96. Complaint for Permanent Injunction and Other Equitable Relief at 19, FTC v. Frostwire, LLC, No. 1:11-cv-23643 (S.D. Fla. Oct. 12, 2011)

[hereinafter, Frostwire Complaint], available at www.ftc.gov/sites/default/ files/documents/cases/2011/10/111011frostwirecmpt.pdf.

97. Complaint at 4, *In re* Sony BMG Music Entm't, FTC File No. 062 3019, No. C-4195 (F.T.C. June 29, 2007) [hereinafter, Sony Complaint], *available at* www.ftc.gov/sites/default/files/documents/cases/2007/01/0701 30cmp0623019.pdf.

Conclusion

1. Thomas Friedman, *Four Words Going Bye-Bye*, NEW YORK TIMES (May 21, 2014), www.nytimes.com/2014/05/21/opinion/friedman-four-words-going-bye-bye.html.

2. Marshall Kirkpatrick, *Facebook's Zuckerberg Says the Age of Privacy Is Over*, READWRITE (Jan. 9, 2010), https://readwrite.com/2010/01/09/face books_zuckerberg_says_the_age_of_privacy_is_ov/.

3. Polly Sprenger, *Sun on Privacy: "Get Over It"*, WIRED (Jan. 26, 1999 12:00 PM), www.wired.com/1999/01/sun-on-privacy-get-over-it/.

4. *See* Smith v. Maryland, 442 U.S. 735 (1979).

5. *See* Hoffa v. U.S., 385 U.S. 293 (1966). *See also* Katherine J. Strandburg, *Home, Home on the Web and Other Fourth Amendment Implications of Technosocial Change*, 70 MD. L. REV. 614, 652–53 (2011).

Index

Acquisti, Alessandro, 32, 55
Alfino, Mark, 27
Allen, Anita, 16
Armstrong, Pamela, 57
Assumption of risk, 68

Balkin, Jack, 8, 78, 79, 85, 86, 87, 88, 91, 146
Ball, Donald, 16
Bamberger, Kenneth, 86
Barrymore v. News Group Newspapers, 116, 119
Bates, Alan P., 18, 24, 27
Baxter v. COBE Laboratories, 124, 126, 129
Beachcombers v. WildeWood Creative Products,
    124, 126, 129, 130
Benn, Stanley, 27
Bernhardt v. Collezione Europa USA, 126, 128,
    129, 131
Bloustein, Edward, 26
Bok, Sissela, 16
Brandeis, Louis, 11, 15, 16, 18, 45, 69, 94, 95, 119,
    121, 132, 139
Breach of confidentiality, tort of, 114–19
    and the First Amendment, 121
Breazeal, Cynthia, 137, 145, 146

California Online Privacy Protection Act
    (CalOPPA), 81, 82, 61
Calo, Ryan, ix, 135, 136, 137, 138, 140, 141, 143
Children's Online Privacy Protection Act
    (COPPA), 80, 81
Citron, Danielle Keats, ix, 86, 108, 109, 110,
    113, 139
Coeckelbergh, Mark, 142
Cohen, Jean, 20, 29, 124
Cohen, Julie, 19, 25, 27, 32, 38, 139
Culnan, Mary, 57

Darling, Kate, 143, 145, 146
Dey v. Sunovision Pharmaceuticals, 126, 129
Diekema, David, 24
Doe v. Methodist Hospital, 98–99, 106
Duran v. Detroit News, 98, 104, 105
Durkheim, Emile, 23, 68, 109

Egbert v. Lippmann, 125
Eli Lilly & Co., 82
Elizabeth v. Pavement Company, 123
Eolas Technologies v. Microsoft, 129
Etzioni, Amitai, 70

Facebook
    and cues of trust, 56–57
    and data collection, 32
    study of user sharing behavior, 58–60
Fair Information Practices Principles (FIPPs),
    30, 80
Family Educational Rights and Privacy Act
    (FERPA), 20
Federal Trade Commission (FTC)
    and enforcement of notice-and-choice, 82–83
    and social robots, 147
    and trust, 92
Foucault, Michel, 6
Fourth Amendment
    and misplaced trust, 150
    and the spatial analogy of privacy, 18–19
    and the Third Party Doctrine, 150
Franks, Mary Anne, 19, 108, 110
Fried, Charles, 30
Future of Privacy Forum, 50

Gavison, Ruth, 18, 27
Gerety, Tom, 21

Gerstein, Robert, 20
Gill v. Hearst Publishing Company, 68, 138
Gilles, Susan, 120
Goffman, Erving, 17, 18, 22, 23, 24, 30, 34,
    35, 37, 38, 39, 40, 41, 43, 44, 105, 117,
    142, 143
    front stage/back stage, 17–18
    Presentation of Self in Everyday Life, 23–24
Gramm-Leach-Bliley Act, 80, 81
Granovetter, Mark, 54, 102
Grimmelmann, James, 56, 89, 119
Grindr, 53, 118
Griswold v. Connecticut, 21
Grossklags, Jens, 55

Harcourt, Bernard, 67
Hartzog, Woodrow, 61, 62, 69, 74, 75, 83, 89, 92,
    114, 115, 137, 138, 142, 146, 151
Health Insurance Portability and
    Accountability Act (HIPAA), 21, 80, 81
HIV, 3, 20, 24, 44, 53, 98, 100, 103, 105, 106
Honeywell v. Universal Avionics Systems, 130

In re Frostwire, 82, 83, 147
In re GeoCities, 82
In re JetBlue Privacy Litigation, 18
In re Northwest Airlines Privacy Litigation, 68
In re Snapchat, 88–89
In re Sony BMG Music Entertainment, 83, 147
Information fiduciaries, 85–88
Inness, Julie, 20, 21, 30, 124
Ishiguro, Hiroshi, 141, 143

John, Leslie, 32, 55
Johnston v. Fuller, 98
Jourard, Sidney Marshall, 57

Kant, Immanuel, 6, 14, 15, 25, 26, 27, 29, 135
Kateb, George, 27, 159
Kerr, Orin, 19
Konvitz, Milton, 17
Korsgaard, Christine, 15

Laufer, Robert, 16
Lawrence v. Texas, 21
Lessig, Larry, 18, 112
Litman, Jessica, 62,
Locke, John, 6, 14, 15, 18, 20, 25, 26, 27, 29, 135
Loewenstein, George, 32, 55, 57
Lough v. Brunswick Corporation, 124, 125, 126,
    129, 131, 192, 197

MacDorman, Karl, 141, 143
MacKinnon, Catherine, 71
Martin, Kirsten, 50, 150
Matthews, Steve, 30, 124
Maxwell, Robert, 17
Mayes, Randolph, 27
McClurg, Andrew, 117
McCormick v. England, 111
Merton, Robert, 6, 35, 37, 38, 40, 41, 43, 44
MIT v. Harman International Industries,
    126
Mourey, James A., x, 143, 144, 145, 150
Mulligan, Deirdre, 86
Multimedia WMAZ, Inc. v. Kubach, 100, 103

Nader v. General Motors, 98
Nader, Ralph, 22, 98, 99, 124
*National Research Development Corp.
    v. Varian Associates*, 131
Nissenbaum, Helen, 6
Notice-and-choice, 30–31, 62, 79, 80, 82, 83, 84,
    85, 88, 139, 146
    critiques of, 83–85

O'Brien, David, 16
Obergefell v. Hodges, 21
Olmstead v. United States, 18, 19

Pasquale, Frank, 28, 41
*Pavesich v. New England Life Insurance
    Company*, 95
Posner, Richard, 24, 71
Post, Robert, 3, 35, 39
Privacy
    and data analytics, behavioral targeting,
        62–64
    and social networks, 41–43, 101–5
    and social value, 35–37
    and trust, 61
    as a social form, 37–39
    as autonomy, 29–33
    as contextual integrity, 43–44
    as freedom *for*, 26
    as freedom *from*, 13
    as intimacy, deviance, 19–24
    as personhood, 26
    as separation, exclusion, 15–19
    critiques of, 70–71
    from a social perspective, 34
    rights-based definitions, 13–23
Privacy torts, 94–96

Pronova BioPharma Norge As v. Teva
    Pharmaceuticals, 127
Prosser, William, 95, 96, 109
Public use bar, 122

Rachels, James, 40, 41, 42
Rawls, John, 29
Reiman, Jeffrey, 18
Revenge porn
    and copyright law, 112–13
    and experiences of victims, 109–10
    and the LGBTQ community, 110, 118–19
    and the tort of breach of confidentiality, 114–19
    and trust, 113–14
    definitions, 108
Richards, Neil, 27, 61, 62, 69, 74, 75, 95, 114, 115, 116, 121
Right to Financial Privacy Act, 20
Roberson v. Rochester Folding Box
    Company, 94
Roe v. Wade, 21
Rosen, Jeffrey, 17, 20, 28
Rykwert, Joseph, 17

Sandeen, Sharon, 96
Sanders v. American Broadcasting
    Company, 99
Scheppele, Kim Lane, 22
Secrecy paradigm, 22, 40, 41, 72, 73, 93, 97, 125
Shils, Edward, 16
Simmel, Georg, 17, 34
Sipple v. Chronicle Publishing Company, 97
Sipple, Oliver, 22, 97, 99, 124
Skinner-Thompson, Scott, 20, 69
Smith v. Maryland, 65
Snapchat, 89
Social robots
    and rights-based definitions of privacy,
        137–39
    as information collectors, 138–39
    definitions, 136–37
Solove, Daniel J., 18, 20, 22, 28, 30, 32, 35–37,
    40, 43, 72, 83, 86, 89, 92, 95, 97, 111, 115, 116,
    121, 125, 139, 146
Spokeo v. Robins, 70

Stephens v. Avery, 116
Strahilevitz, Lior, 35, 42, 43, 93, 97, 98, 101, 103,
    104, 105, 106, 107, 111, 130
Strandburg, Katherine, 135
Sunstein, Cass, 70

Target, 63, 64, 84, 138
Trust, 164, 165, 168, 170, 175, 201, 202
    and Apple, 49
    and Facebook, 49, 56–57
    and information fiduciaries, 85–88
    and previously disclosed information, 107
    and privacy law, 75
    and reciprocity, 53–54
    and revenge porn, 108, 113–14
    and sharing, 58–60
    and sharing on Facebook, 58–60
    and social cues, 52–53
    and social robots, 147
    and the public use bar, 122
    and transference, 54
    and use by Facebook, 92
    definition of, 51–52
    development of, 52–54
Turkle, Sherry, 140
Tverdek, Edward, 41, 42

United States v. Jones, 65

Vaughan, Diane, 22, 158
Video Protection Privacy Act (VPPA), 20

Warren, Samuel, 11, 15, 16, 18, 45, 69, 94, 95,
    119, 121, 132, 139
Westin, Alan, 30, 87, 124
Westlund, Jacqueline Kory, 145, 146
White, Howard, 16, 20
Williams, Raymond, 17
Wolfe, Maxine, 17

Xerox v. 3Com, 129

Y.G. v. Jewish Hospital, 100, 103, 106, 107

Zittrain, Jonathan, 8, 30, 87, 88, 122, 124, 132